E.T.

THE EXTRA-TERRESTRIAL
FROM CONCEPT TO CLASSIC

The Illustrated Story of the
Film and the Filmmakers

Introduction by STEVEN SPIELBERG
Screenplay by MELISSA MATHISON
Interviews by LAURENT BOUZEREAU
Edited by LINDA SUNSHINE
Designed by TIMOTHY SHANER

POCKET BOOKS
PUBLISHED BY SIMON & SCHUSTER

LONDON · SYDNEY · NEW YORK · TOKYO · SINGAPORE · TORONTO

KNOWSLEY LIBRARY SERVICE
26688608

Design and compilation copyright © 2002 by Newmarket Press.

Copyright © 2002 Universal Studios Publishing Rights, a division of Universal Studios Licensing, Inc. E.T.: The Extra-Terrestrial is a trademark and copyright of Universal Studios. All rights reserved.

All rights reserved. This book may not be reproduced, in whole or in part, in any form, without written permission. Inquiries should be addressed to Permissions Department, Newmarket Press, 18 East 48th Street, New York, NY 10017.

Manufactured in the United States of America.

10 9 8 7 6 5 4 3 2 1

POCKET BOOKS
Simon & Schuster UK Ltd.
Africa House
64-78 Kingsway
London
WC2B 6AH

www.simonsays.co.uk

First Pocket Books edition 2002

A CIP catalogue record for this book is available from the British Library.

ISBN 0-7434-5024-8

Contents

Introduction 7
by Steven Spielberg

Part ONE 10
From Concept to Casting

Part TWO 42
A Boy's Life:
The Annotated, Illustrated Screenplay

Part THREE 150
Postproduction and Beyond

Credits 186

Introduction

Bringing Back the Magic

When production started on *E.T.* more than twenty years ago, none of us could have dreamed there would be a twentieth anniversary release and a book such as this. We had no illusions about the ultimate success of the film, but we knew it was a story we wanted to tell and we told it the way we wanted to tell it.

You will get a real sense of that as you go through this journey with me and those who joined in bringing E.T. and *E.T.* to life. We want to invite you into our filmmaking family and take you behind the scenes—behind the magic, surprises, and emotional experiences that meant so much in our own lives. This book is our *E.T.* family album filled with details from our personal memory banks and production archives.

For me, *E.T.* was—and still is—my most personal film.

The journey actually began when I was growing up in Scottsdale, California. Suburbia. They say write what you know, and it's the same with filmmaking.

In suburbia, you can look up at the clear night sky, and I've always been intrigued with outer space, starting as early as five years old. One night, my dad woke me up and took me out in a field, laid out a picnic blanket, and we stared at a fantastic meteor shower. I saw all those streaks of light moving across the sky, and it gave a jump-start to my fascination with the universe.

Science fiction was big then as it is now. Dad would read a lot of it—stories filled with scary aliens taking over the world—but he never imagined it that way. He would say he thought if other life forms had the technology to travel all those light years, they would never do it to spread hate and evil—they'd do it to satisfy their curiosity. They would want to share their knowledge with other planetary systems and other species. That's what I tried to show in both *Close Encounters of the Third Kind* and *E.T.*

ABOVE: Steven Spielberg poses for a publicity photo with his lead actor in E.T. LEFT: A still from the original 1982 release of the film.

There's a lot of my life in the film. All the kids are combinations of my family and me. I intended the film to reflect the feelings I had as a kid, although I wasn't very articulate about that when I talked to reporters at press junkets in 1982. I never once mentioned that the movie also grew out of the divorce of my parents, although it was always there subconsciously. Then it finally hit me and I felt comfortable including it.

The *E.T.* concept bounced around in my head for years. I came up with the original story and Melissa Mathison wrote a genius screenplay, which for the first time, is included here as the centerpiece for the book. You'll see how the ideas and words became dialogue and images that have become part of our collective culture.

The positive impact that *E.T.* had on audiences throughout the world was perhaps the most rewarding result of what became a phenomenon. Two examples drove that home. The first was a letter from Eunice Shriver of the Special Olympics. She recognized that our extraterrestrial, a creature who was different, represented the same spirit of overcoming challenges as demonstrated by the athletes of Special Olympics. The other was a note from a mother who said that her autistic child, who had not spoken, spoke his first words after seeing *E.T.* Something in that heart light reached out.

Would there ever be a sequel to *E.T.*? That's been the most-asked question, and I've had the same response for twenty years: "I'm not going to do it." A sequel would diffuse the memory of the first one. Instead, I thought it would be great to reissue the movie and the twentieth anniversary seemed the perfect opportunity to put it back in theaters where I most want people to see it. A generation has grown up since the film was last in theatres. Some of you reading this now may have seen it as a child and now have your own children—mothers and dads now have grandkids.

Everyone involved in making *E.T.* is thrilled to have this opportunity for a re-release. The film has always been a celebration of friendship and love and promoting understanding between races and cultures. As I said, I never imagined it could become such a phenomenon. I simply wanted to tell this story, which was so close to my heart.

I hope you will agree that E.T.'s heart light glows as well as ever.

—Steven Spielberg
January 2002

ABOVE: The moon, used in the scene of Elliott and E.T. flying, was shot in Nicasio, California, near the ILM studios. The image became the logo for Amblin Entertainment.

9

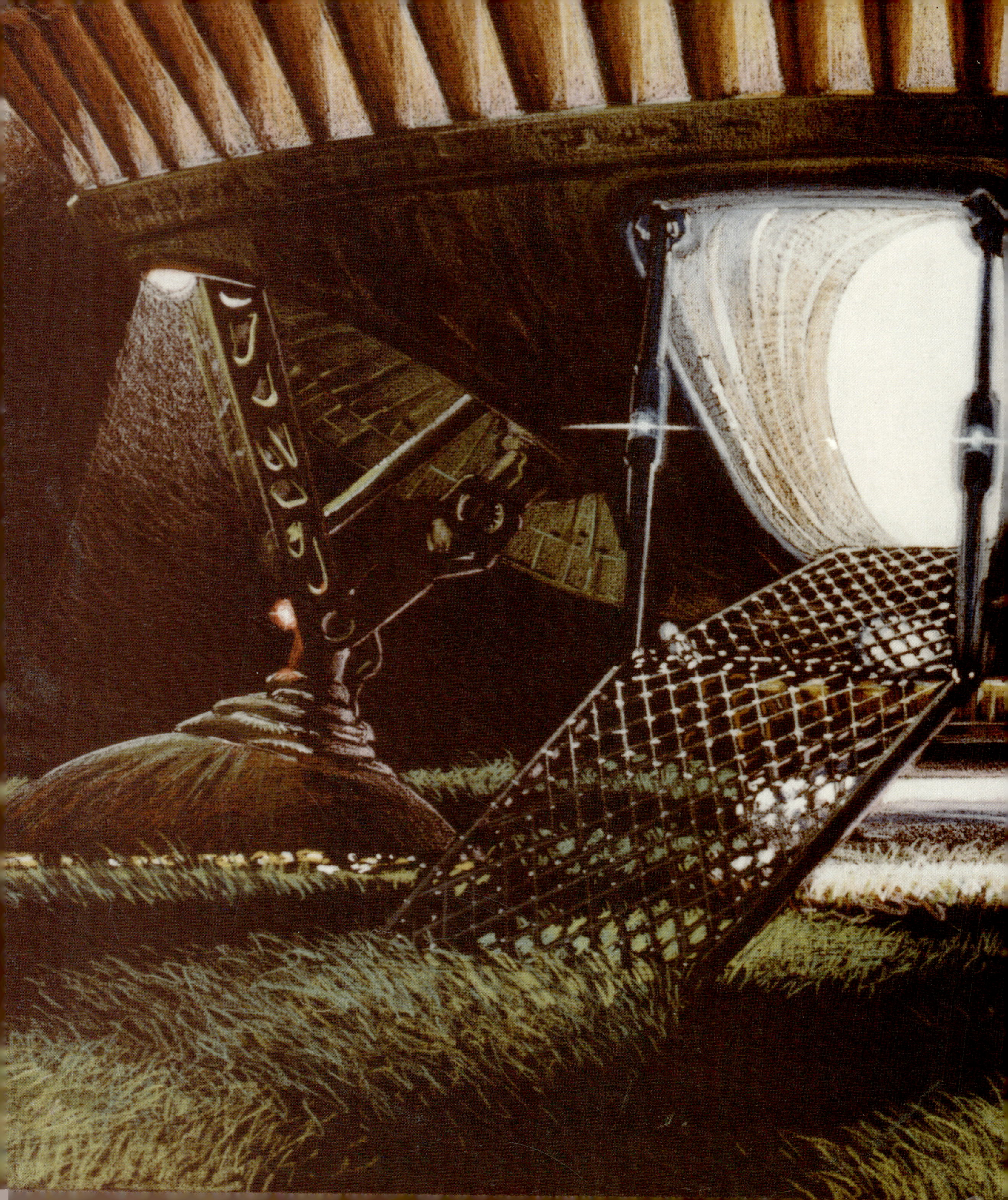

PART ONE: FROM CONCEPT TO CASTING

The NIGHT SKIES of a BOY'S LIFE

In the Beginning There Was *Night Skies*

One of the things that really inspired me to work with Steven was *Close Encounters of the Third Kind*. The movie had a profound effect on me and, more than anything, was the catalyst that convinced me I wanted to make movies as a career. When I did, in fact, find myself eventually working with Steven, one of the things we discussed was the research he had done with a scientist and astronomer named J. Allen Hynek during the making of *Close Encounters*.

Steven asked me to investigate a particular case about a farm family that was terrorized one evening by gremlin-like, extraterrestrials. They supposedly surrounded the house, trying to get access. They also rode the cows through the barnyard and made the people crazy.

—Kathleen Kennedy, Producer

When I read an early draft about the farm family case [*Night Skies*], I didn't feel it was a movie I wanted to direct. It was too violent and went against my own beliefs that aliens would come to earth with bad intentions. Personally, I never thought that would be the case. I thought they would come here to either observe at a distance or to interact in some kind of healthy way.

It went against my grain as a filmmaker and story teller to tell an aggressive, scary story about aliens attacking a farm house. That's when everything changed in my mind and I realized I was not going to make that movie, but I might make another movie about an alien who gets left behind on earth, an idea that came from the ending of *Close Encounters* when the spaceship door closes.

—Steven Spielberg, Director/Producer

Previous page: An original painting by Ed Verreaux of the landing of E.T.'s spaceship. Above: Producer Kathleen Kennedy and director Steven Spielberg wearing hard hats during the filming of the movie. Left: Early concept for a poster of the 1982 release.

The Concept: How *E.T.* Got Started

I'd always wanted to tell the story of a disenfranchised and lonely boy in a relationship with his siblings. I also wanted to tell a story about a young child's reaction to his parents' divorce and how that impacts him for the rest of his life. So the story was on my mind for maybe fifteen or twenty years. Also, it was a childhood fantasy of mine to tell the story of a special, best friend who rescues a young boy from the sadness of a divorce. So, *E.T.* came about in stages for me.

Sometime in 1979 or 1980, we were shooting *Raiders of the Lost Ark* in Tunisia and, during one of the long set ups, I was walking in the desert, picking up prehistoric sea shells, and trying to figure out how I could tell the story of this lonely boy. At the time I was feeling kind of separate from myself, which often happens when you are directing. You go into a kind of fugue state to make a movie. So I was in one of these states of mind when, bang, this concept hit me and the story began to flood into my mind. For the next couple of days, during the shooting of *Raiders*, the bones of the story began to fall into place.

It took me two or three days to figure out the beginning, the middle, and the end of the story. Then I remembered loving this movie called *The Black Stallion* which had been co-authored by Melissa Mathison, who was on the set of *Raiders* with Harrison Ford.

I asked Melissa to write the script, but she was reluctant at first so I started nagging her about it. I went to Harrison and said, "Harrison, talk to Melissa, I think she should write this movie." Then Kathy Kennedy talked to Melissa. The two of them, Kathy and Harrison, convinced Melissa to at least do a first draft for me. And that's how it all got started.
—STEVEN SPIELBERG

ABOVE: Producer Kathleen Kennedy and director Steven Spielberg on the set during the filming of the school scene where Elliott releases the frogs in his science class.

Early Ideas

Many of the scenes from the movie come from my own experiences with children.

I would ask Willard and Benjamin, Harrison's sons, and their friends and other kids what kind of powers they would like from an alien. A lot of the children mentioned the obvious: telepathy or telekinetic powers. But I was struck by the fact that several of them said they would like this magic creature to be able to heal. I thought it was such an incredibly poignant idea to come from a child. They weren't talking about saving someone's life by healing. They were talking about taking the "owies" away. And of course, E.T. heals.

Very early on, Steven Spielberg and I decided that we didn't want to have any adults mucking up the works. This was important for a couple of reasons. First of all, E.T. is this little creature. The earth that he experiences is small and filled with little people his own size. When he returned to his planet, he would be reporting on a planet that was populated by children, which we thought was a poetic idea.

Secondly, Elliott had to have the power in the movie. If even for a moment an adult took away Elliott's power before it became a matter of life and death, then Elliott would have lost all of his magic.

—MELISSA MATHISON, SCREENWRITER/ASSOCIATE PRODUCER

I never wanted to show grown-ups in the movie until the very end. I wanted to suggest them, like in a *Tom & Jerry* cartoon where, when the mom comes in, you only see her from the waist down. I was raised with television and with cartoons so this made sense to me. I didn't want that world contaminated with anything beyond a young teenager's point of view.

I was also very interested in the idea that E.T. could communicate psychically with Elliott. He could reach out to Elliott in school and give him ideas while he was sitting in class. If E.T. got drunk, for example, Elliott got drunk. Elliott would start becoming and feeling E.T.'s psychic spirit inside of him. That was really interesting to me. I didn't know where those ideas were going to fall into the structure of the movie. But these were like my wish list. Can we put this in the movie? Can we put that in the movie?

—STEVEN SPIELBERG

LEFT: *Writer Melissa Mathison and producer Kathleen Kennedy during the filming of the Halloween scenes.* ABOVE RIGHT: *Director Steven Spielberg setting up a shot in Elliott's classroom.*

The Script: Writing the First Draft

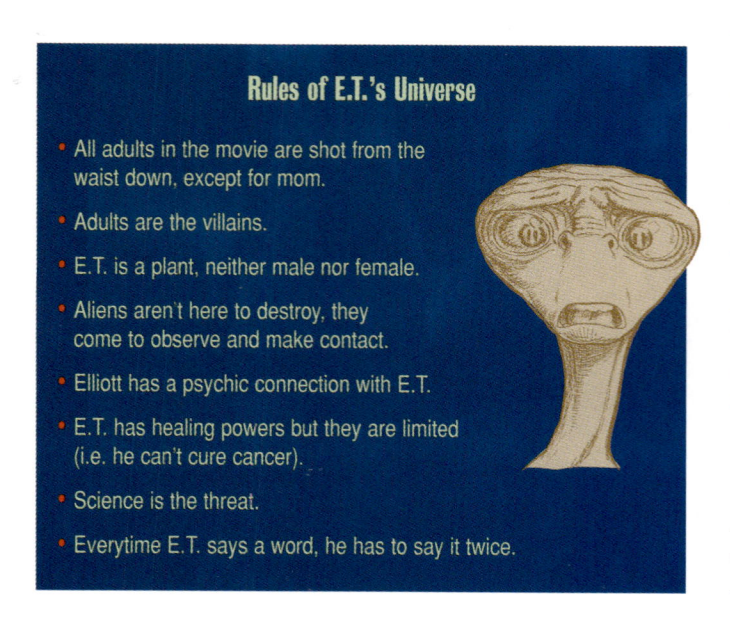

Rules of E.T.'s Universe

- All adults in the movie are shot from the waist down, except for mom.
- Adults are the villains.
- E.T. is a plant, neither male nor female.
- Aliens aren't here to destroy, they come to observe and make contact.
- Elliott has a psychic connection with E.T.
- E.T. has healing powers but they are limited (i.e. he can't cure cancer).
- Science is the threat.
- Everytime E.T. says a word, he has to say it twice.

As I remember it, I would write for four or five days in my little office in Hollywood, and then drive out to Marina Del Rey where Steven Spielberg was editing in a little apartment on the beach. I'd bring him my pages and we'd sit and go through them. We would decide what worked and what didn't and where we'd go from there. Then we would talk about the next hunk that should be written. I'd go back to my little office and do my writing and come back again a few days later to meet him.

It took eight weeks for us to get the first draft, which was quite fast, I think.

—MELISSA MATHISON

Melissa delivered this 107-page first draft to me and I read it in about an hour. I was just knocked out. It was a script I was willing to shoot the next day. It was so honest, and Melissa's voice made a direct connection with my heart.

—STEVEN SPIELBERG

I was having lunch with an executive at MGM. In fact, we were discussing *Poltergeist* which we were making at the time. Steven came running into the commissary with this screenplay and he said, "I've just read Melissa's first draft. We could shoot this tomorrow. It's the best first draft I've ever read." I think, in many respects, Steven would say that that's still true, even today.

—KATHLEEN KENNEDY

RIGHT: Producer Kathleen Kennedy poses with the star of the movie during the first release of the movie. ABOVE: Writer Melissa Mathison clowning around on the set with actor Henry Thomas.

16

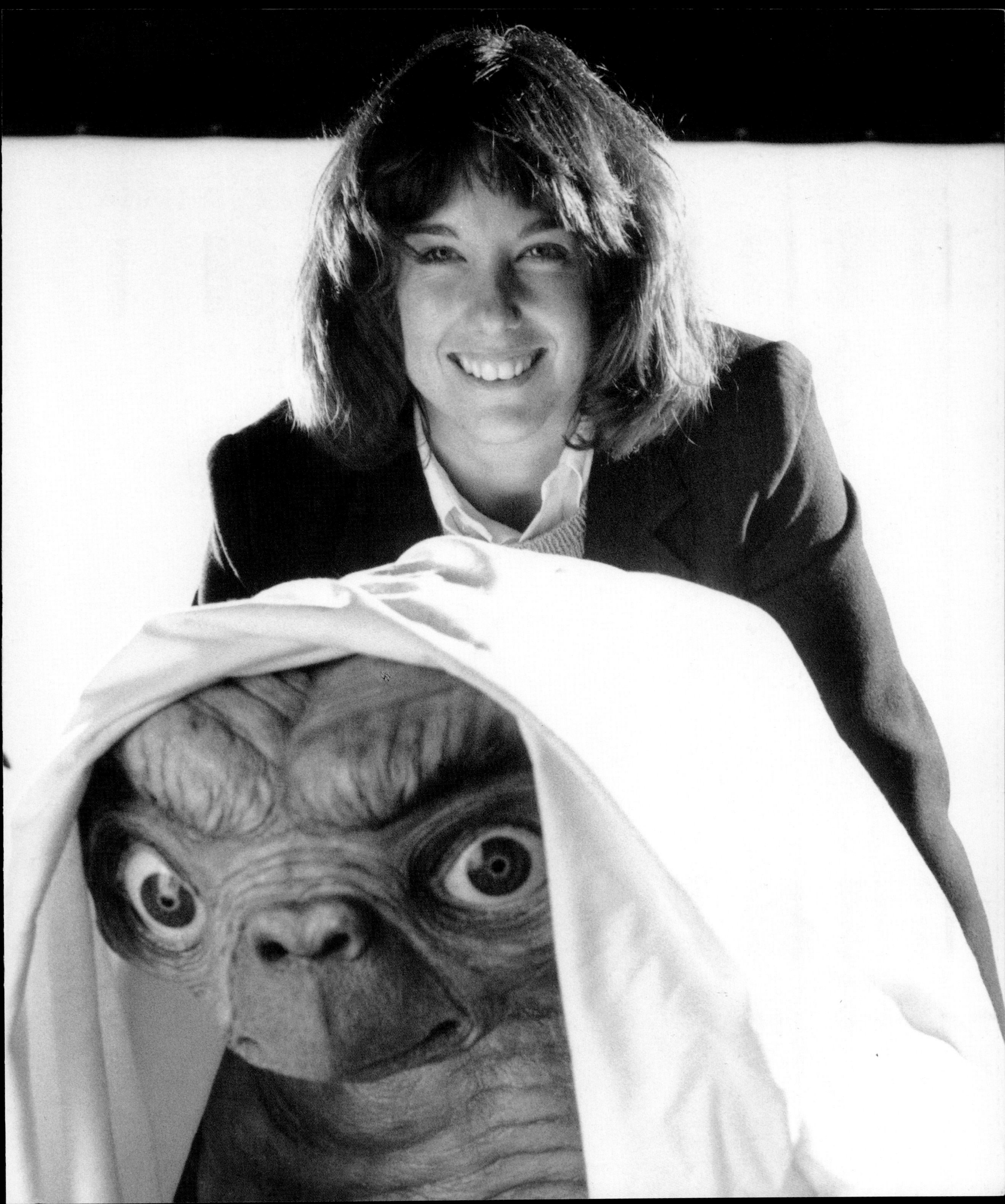

CREATING the CREATURE

Shopping for a Designer

I went to several designers to find my single creature. I had one concept for E.T. that was pretty consistent with all the designers. I didn't want anybody to think that E.T. was anything other than an actual extraterrestrial. Therefore, it couldn't look like there was somebody in a suit. I wanted him to be only three feet tall. So, I needed him to have a small neck and I want the neck to telescope, like a turtle coming out of his shell. The neck defied the idea of a human being being inside that suit. That was a concept I came up with even back during *Close Encounters*.

Ed Verreaux did some sketching for me and we gave Carlo Rambaldi some of the sketches. Carlo had created one of the creatures in *Close Encounters of the Third Kind*. He designed Puck with a very tiny neck. I love Carlo's designs.
—STEVEN SPIELBERG

In the early stages, we didn't really know what E.T. was going to look like because we were just sort of talking about him. At some point, fairly early on, we set down some ground rules. First, that E.T. isn't a monster.

The thing I really remember very specifically working with Steven was going into his office and looking at all these books. He would say, those are neat eyes, that's a neat mouth. Look at this person. They were really interesting because they would be some very, very, very old people with these very old, wizened eyes.

Then Carlo and I would go away for a day or two and we would draw a lot of stuff. We would just basic shotgun. Then we would go back to Steven's office and pin the stuff up on the wall. Steven would look at them and tell us what he liked and didn't like.
—ED VERREAUX

LEFT: *E.T. as photographed in the 1982 release of the movie.*
ABOVE: *Carlo Rambaldi pointing to the original sketches of the extraterrestrial.*

I came to America about twenty-five years ago to work on the remake of *King Kong* for Dino De Laurentiis. When I was finished, I got a call from Steven Spielberg. He explained that he wasn't happy with the look of one of his aliens in *Close Encounters of the Third Kind*, and asked me to come up with some ideas. I ended up doing something that Steven liked, and a few years later, he called me to work on *E.T.* I did not do many sketches at first, but I did look at an abstract painting called *Women of Delta* that I had done for the Academy of Fine Arts in Italy, showing women with very long necks. And that was a departure for me. Steven then came to my shop many times, and we worked together. We had different types of E.T.s, different heads, and several ways to approach each scene, including using little people, a boy with no legs in a suit, and a mime for the arms and hands in some cases.

When we were working with the mechanical E.T., using levers, the cables were hidden underneath the floor, and I would be standing off-stage with several other puppeteers, watching E.T. on a video screen and trying to improve his great performance. It was challenging because it was difficult to see the image clearly on the video monitor, but we managed and I think Steven was happy.

During the shooting, everyone who worked with us showed a lot of respect for E.T. Everyone seemed to forget that he was not real, and they definitely treated him like another actor. To me, E.T. was always a boy. He was very innocent, and one thing I tried to avoid was making him look old. For instance, the wrinkles on his face were designed to be like ornaments and nothing like wrinkles on the face of a human being. I just wanted him to look like a happy face.

I remember going to see *E.T.* at the Cineramadome with my (Italian) family when it came out. It was just phenomenal, and I was very excited to win my second Oscar for this film, which I shared with ILM. And it's a thrill that twenty years later *E.T.* feels like a new movie.

— CARLO RAMBALDI, E.T. CREATOR

Carlo did a number of versions in clay, and I worked with him. I'm not an artist, so I didn't touch the clay but I would say, "Too scary. Too Disney. Too sweet."

Finally, this creature emerged from clay which, after a couple of weeks, became E.T.
—STEVEN SPIELBERG

LEFT: *Carlo Rambaldi adjusting E.T.'s mouth for the filming of the scene in Elliott's room.* ABOVE: *Workroom with several versions of the E.T. costume.*

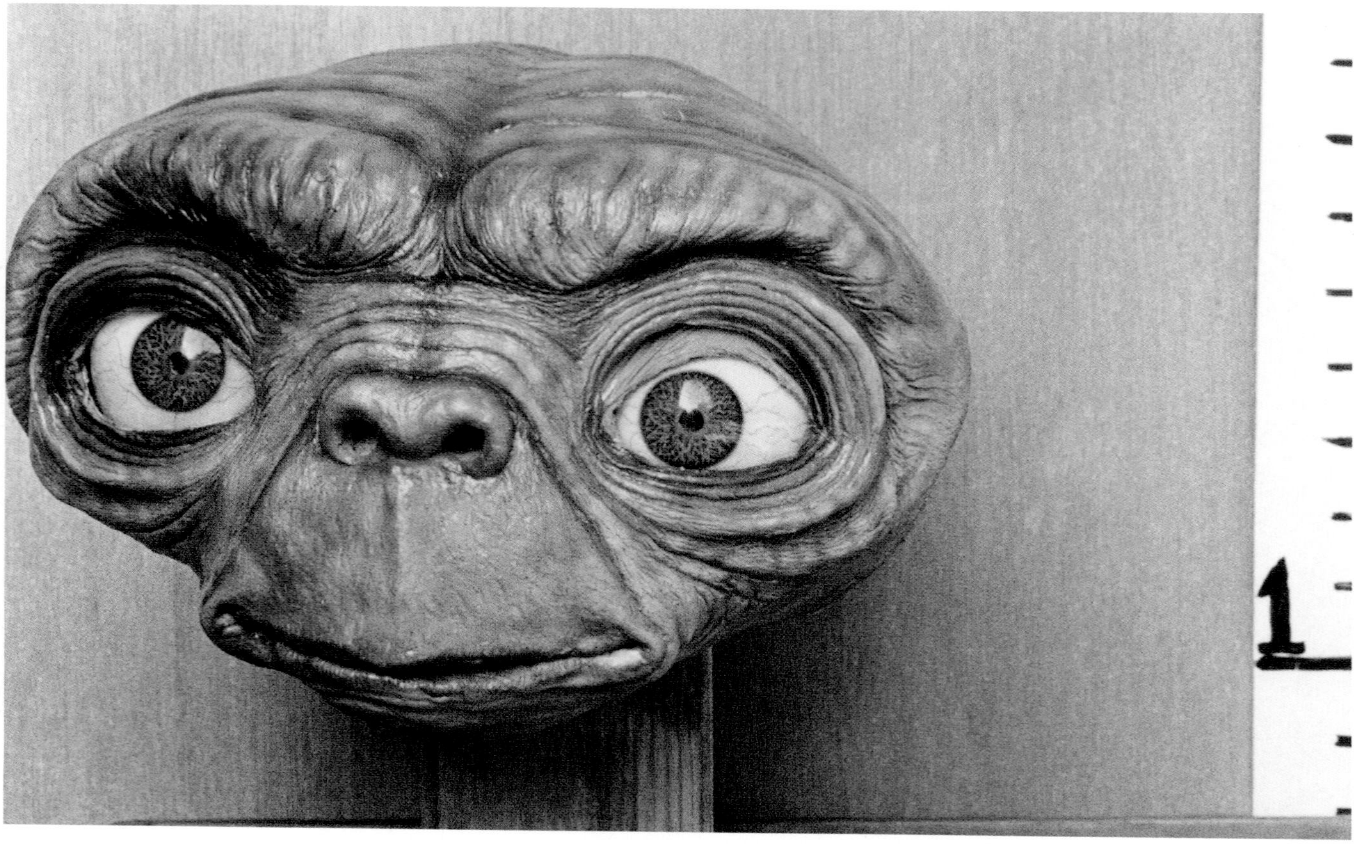
1

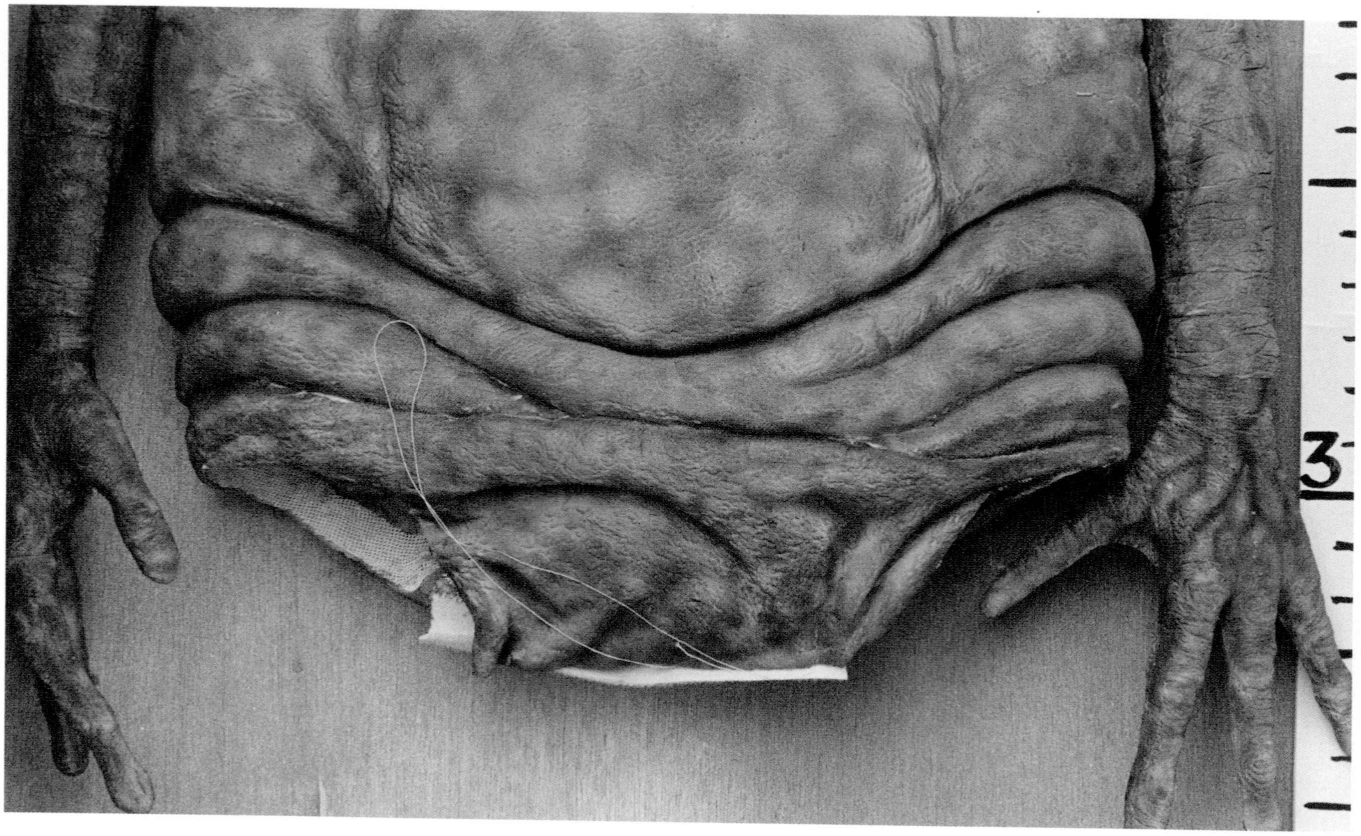
3

Details and measurements of the different sections of the E.T. costume. BOTTOM RIGHT: *An E.T. technician working with the creature during the filming of the movie.*

The Eyes

The eyes of Albert Einstein...

...Ernest Hemingway...

...and Carl Sandburg.

I remember showing Carlo some pictures of Albert Einstein, Ernest Hemingway and Carl Sandburg. I loved their eyes and wanted E.T.'s eyes to be as frivolous and wizened and sad as those three icons.

I was not happy with any of the eye work that we were doing on E.T. The eyes looked like they were painted and didn't have any depth or authenticity. I kept saying, "Who does glass eyes?" Glass eyes look real. You can only spot the glass one because it stays fixed and the real one wanders. I asked Kathy to find somebody who makes glass eyes and give them a job working on E.T.

Kathy found Beverly Hoffman, who worked at the Jules Stein Eye Institute. Beverly came on board and did a wonderful job making over-sized glass eyes for us.
—STEVEN SPIELBERG

BELOW: *E.T.'s eyes were spaced so far apart that the kid actors could only look in one eye at a time. They decided they would all look in the same eye at the same time and, for different scenes, choose alternate eyes.*

BELOW: *Carlo Rambaldi works on the skull of E.T.* OPPOSITE: *Sketches showing the expressions of E.T.'s nose, eyes, and brow and how they should move.*

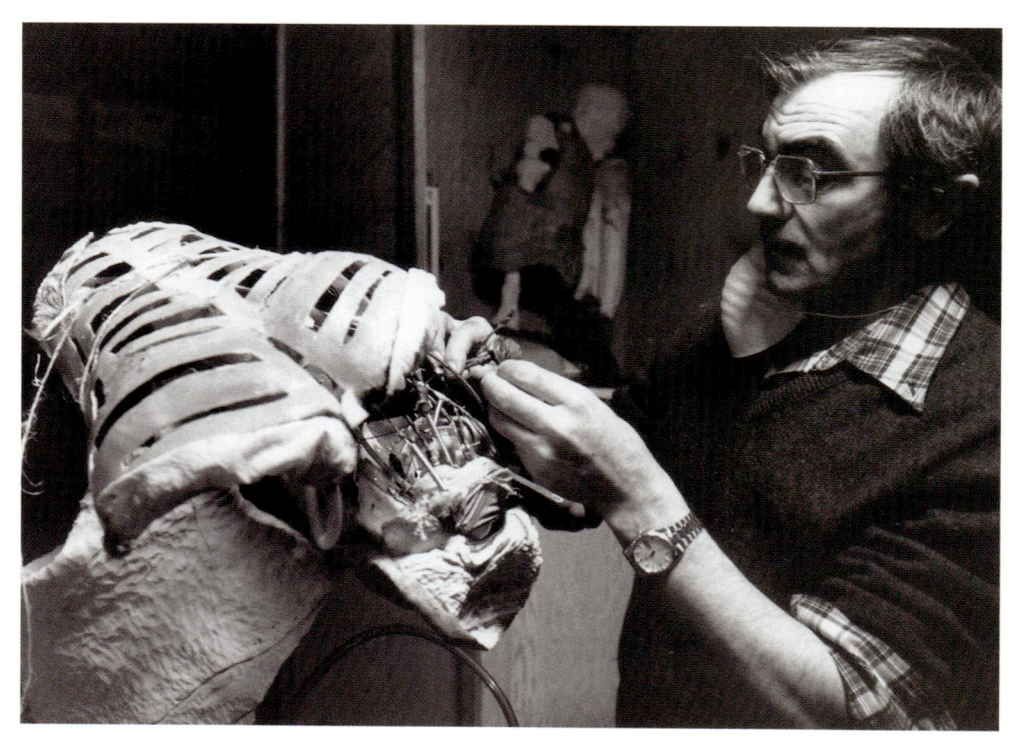

F. NOSE

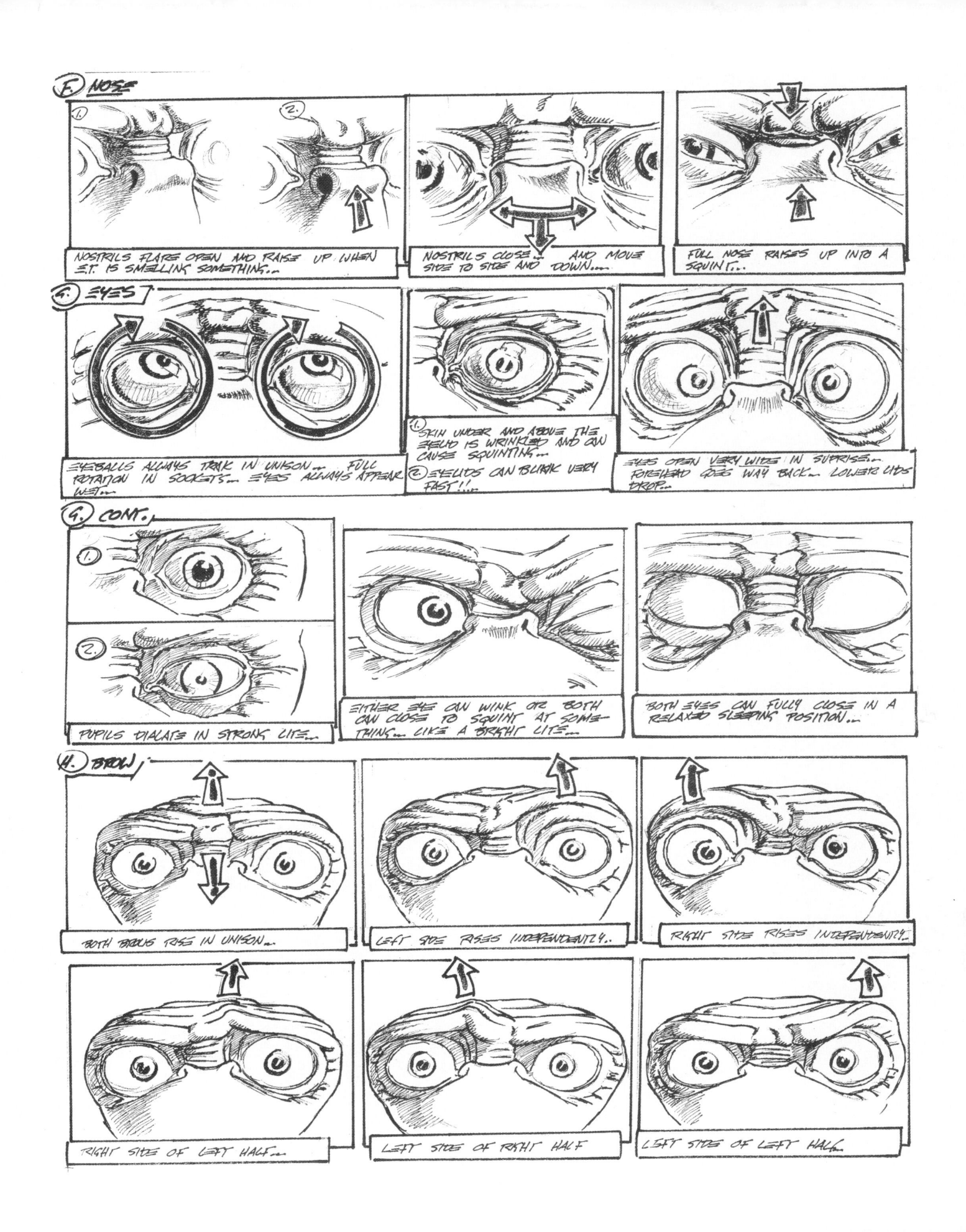

- NOSTRILS FLARE OPEN AND RAISE UP WHEN E.T. IS SMELLING SOMETHING...
- NOSTRILS CLOSE... AND MOVE SIDE TO SIDE AND DOWN...
- FULL NOSE RAISES UP INTO A SQUINT...

G. EYES

- EYEBALLS ALWAYS TRACK IN UNISON... FULL ROTATION IN SOCKETS... EYES ALWAYS APPEAR WET...
- 1. SKIN UNDER AND ABOVE THE EYELID IS WRINKLED AND CAN CAUSE SQUINTING...
- 2. EYELIDS CAN BLINK VERY FAST!!
- EYES OPEN VERY WIDE IN SURPRISE... FOREHEAD GOES WAY BACK... LOWER LIDS DROP...

G. CONT.

- 1. & 2. PUPILS DIALATE IN STRONG LITE...
- EITHER EYE CAN WINK OR BOTH CAN CLOSE TO SQUINT AT SOMETHING... LIKE A BRIGHT LITE...
- BOTH EYES CAN FULLY CLOSE IN A RELAXED SLEEPING POSITION...

H. BROW

- BOTH BROWS RISE IN UNISON...
- LEFT SIDE RISES INDEPENDENTLY...
- RIGHT SIDE RISES INDEPENDENTLY...
- RIGHT SIDE OF LEFT HALF...
- LEFT SIDE OF RIGHT HALF
- LEFT SIDE OF LEFT HALF

The Hands

Partial List of Things E.T. Carries Based on the Early Script*
[Out of sequence]

- A flowering weed
- A miniature redwood
- Pulls back a leafy limb
- Hands move in to cover red light
- Breaks branch from shrub
- Opens hand—a red M&M's candy inside.
- Picks up M&M's
- Eats an orange without peeling it
- Rolls balls of clay
- Picks up ABC book, turns pages
- Strums fingers on drawings
- Lifts comics
- Lifts Speak & Spell
- Takes walkie talkie, removes casing, pulls out speakers
- Searches the refrigerator.
- Pulls out a six-pack of beer and drinks a bottle—and another and another
- With beer in hand, staggers to the T.V.
- Lifts phone receiver.
- Changes channels on T.V. with remote

*Original note prior to clearances

The mechanical arms that Carlo designed were really great but this was 1980s technology and the arms were very jerky when they worked. The fingers could move but almost too thoughtfully.

The arms had what I called *wagga wagga*. An arm would stop and go *wagga wagga wagga*. They were ungainly. E.T.'s arms and hands had to move like a dancers. I thought we should hire a mime and put E.T. hand make-up on her, so that she could really be graceful about picking things up or touching and reaching out to the children. This was why Caprice Rothe, a wonderful mime artist, came to work with us.

I remember a wonderful moment after Caprice had a lot of coffee one morning. We came to work early and her hands were actually shaking. I thought she was doing it on purpose because she had found something about E.T.'s character.

In that same scene was a wonderful moment where E.T. was eating some watermelon. There was a little bit of watermelon on the lip. Caprice always had a monitor that she could look at.

She did the most natural thing in the world. She reached up and took this little piece of watermelon off of E.T.'s lip. Only someone who was very in touch with human behavior would've thought of that gesture. Caprice had a great understanding of the way the human body moves and what we do with our hands and our face and our bodies. I know it's a tiny moment people don't even recognize in the movie, but I'm really proud of what she brought to that scene.

She really brought E.T. to life in that moment. He was alive. Completely alive. Nobody was running him. There were no wires. There were no servers running. E.T. was really an organism from somewhere else.

—STEVEN SPIELBERG

RIGHT: *Caprice Rothe, a mime artist, brought E.T.'s hands to life.*
ABOVE: *Wearing the E.T. hand gloves and watching the monitor of E.T.'s face, Rothe gives emotional expression to the creature.*

③ FACE/MOUTH

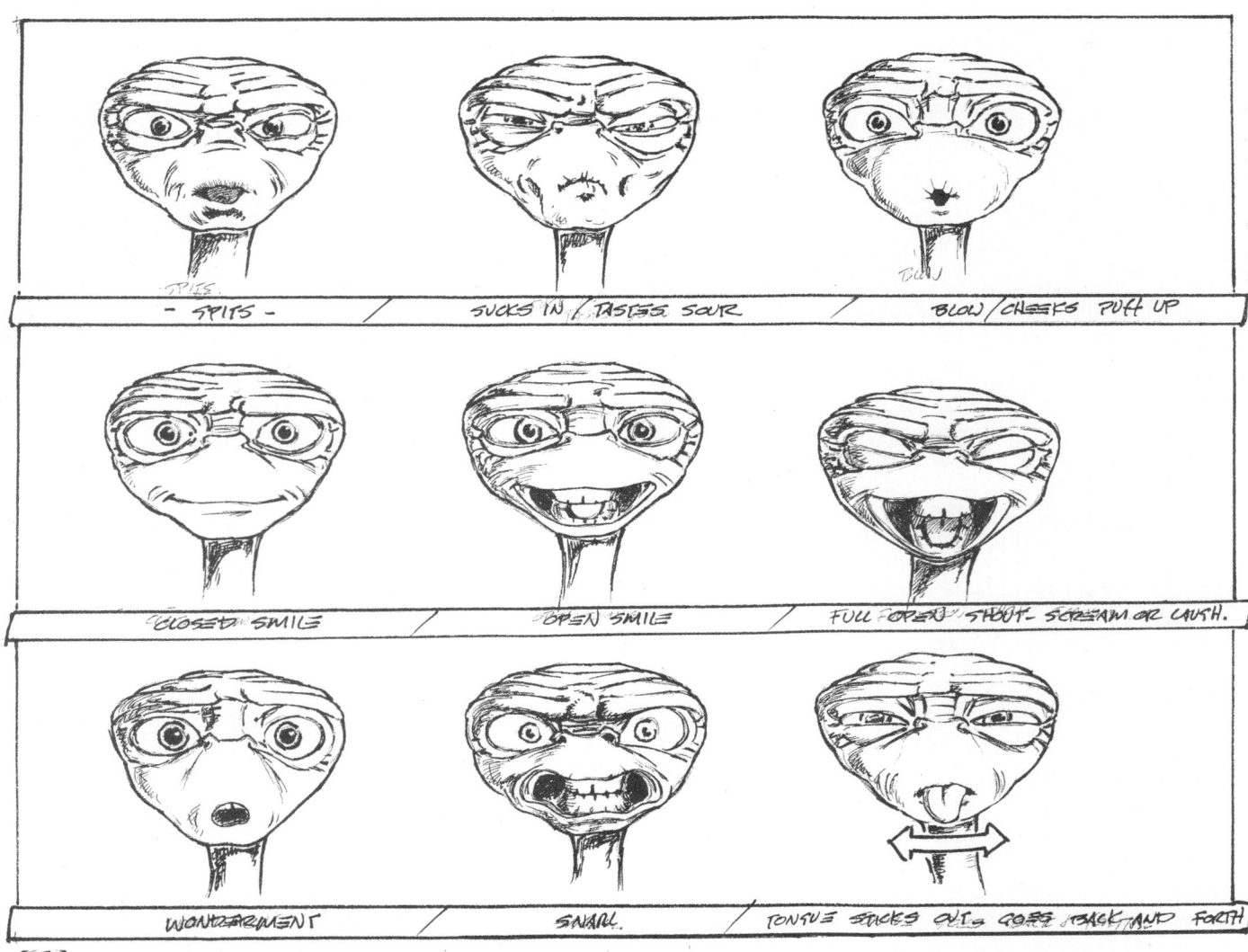

SPITS	SUCKS IN / TASTES SOUR	BLOW / CHEEKS PUFF UP
CLOSED SMILE	OPEN SMILE	FULL OPEN SHOUT, SCREAM OR LAUGH.
WONDERMENT	SNARL	TONGUE STICKS OUT & GOES BACK AND FORTH

③ CONT.

| MAKES 'F' SOUND | KISS |

A great deal of time and effort went into giving emotional expression to E.T. Here are some of the thousands of sketches that were created to show the position of the creature's face, eyes, and mouth during various activities: kissing, spitting, smiling, etc. RIGHT: Memo from producer Kathleen Kennedy to special artist consultant Craig Reardon regarding E.T.'s gums.

MEMO

EXTRA-TERRESTRIAL PRODUCTIONS
Culver City, California

TO: Craig Reardon
FROM: Kathy Kennedy
DATE: August 26, 1981

RE: E.T.'s Head   Culver City, California

. . . I mentioned to Carlo and thought you might have some thoughts, regarding the consistency of the gums inside E.T.'s mouth. Steven is very concerned that these have a very fleshy, gooey consistency similar to a human mouth. This has become even more apparent since seeing the film test. Perhaps some kind of silicone application or whatever. I just thought perhaps you and Carlo could put your heads together on this.

Thanks.

Regards,
Kathy Kennedy

old. I told him we needed to test the creature. I asked Harold to bring Rachel to Carlo's shop, and he said okay.

By the time he arrived, this four-year-old was hysterically crying and was not into doing this at all. Harold says to me, "I don't know if this is going to work, I've tried to bribe her with two McDonald's burgers but it's not working. She doesn't want to do it."

I went over and talked to Rachel. She calmed down a little bit and got into the suit. But by the time we get the head on, she is completely hysterical again. She's jumping up and down and screaming and crying. Harold said, "Just roll tape."

So we roll tape and end up having to show Steven this hysterical, crying four-year-old in the suit.

But he bought it. He said, "Okay, this may be the way we have to go."

—KATHLEEN KENNEDY

E.T. Walks

We did get to a point where I finally threw up my hands and said, "I don't know how in the world we're ever going to get E.T. to move in a believable way, without putting somebody in a suit."

I knew Steven would never agree unless we could show him that it would work. I thought that if I could videotape somebody in a suit maybe I could show Steven that it works on some level. We certainly didn't have to rely solely on this, but we could use it for some shots at least.

So I called Harold Brown, Steven's attorney, because, at the time, his daughter was four years

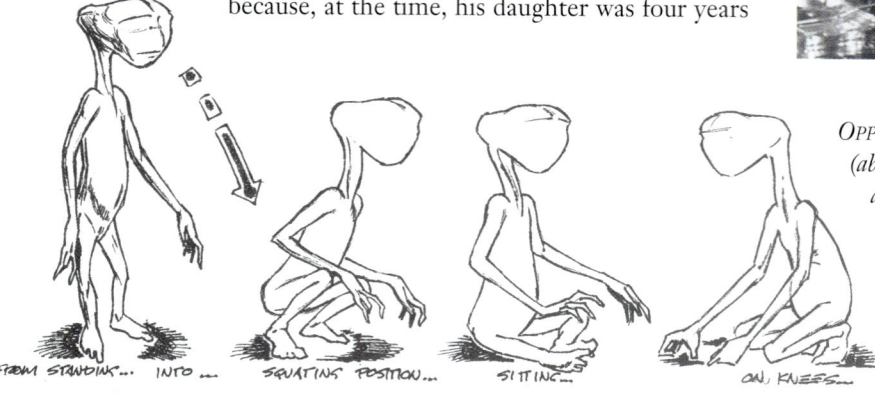

OPPOSITE: Two of the actors inside the creature: Pat Bilon (above) and Tamara De Treaux (below). Bilon was 2'10" tall and weighed 45 pounds. De Treaux was an actress from Los Angeles, while Bilon was a former sheriff's dispatcher from Youngstown, Ohio. ABOVE RIGHT: Steven Spielberg and E.T. during filming. LEFT: Initial sketches of E.T. sitting down from a standing position. In these early sketches E.T. had long legs. In the final design, the creature had short, squat legs, as shown in the top left photo.

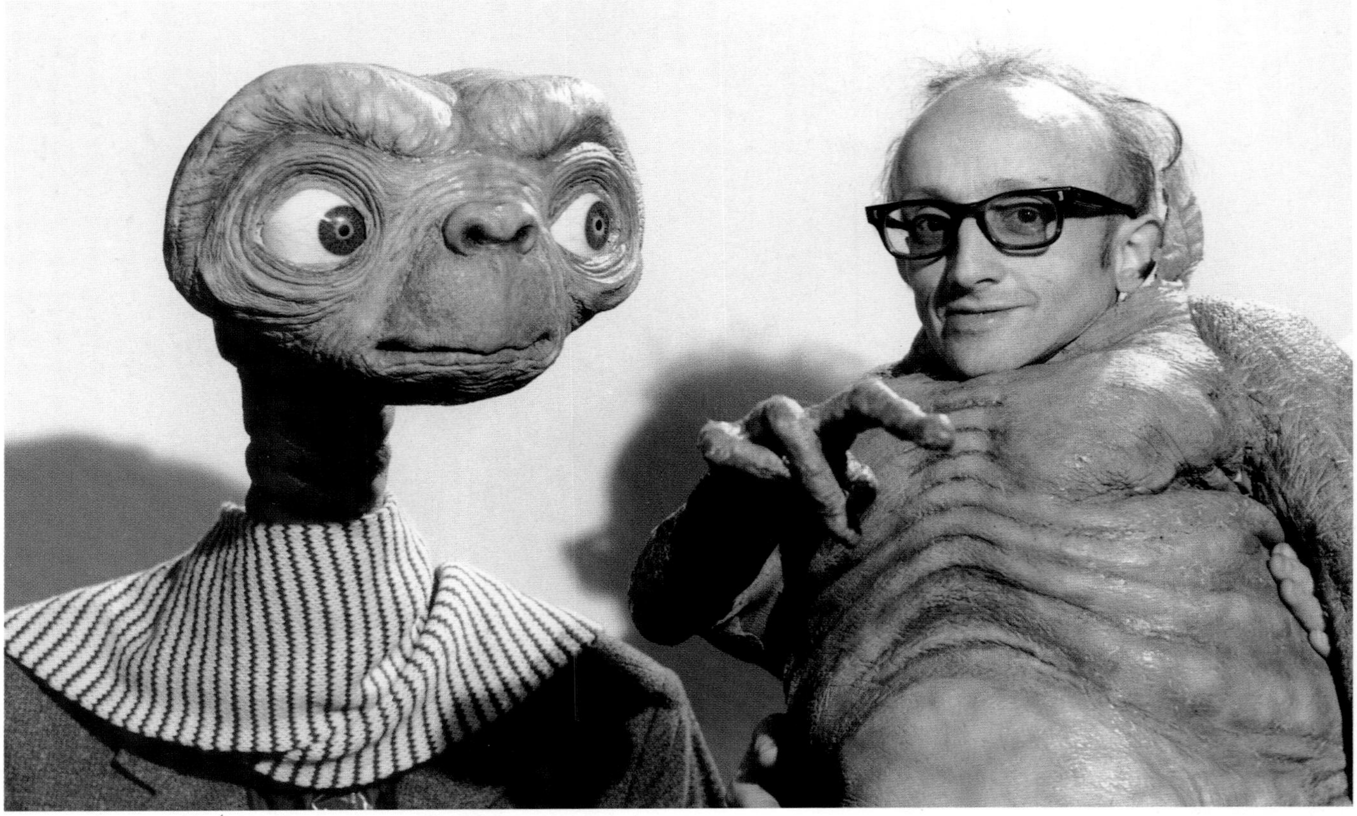

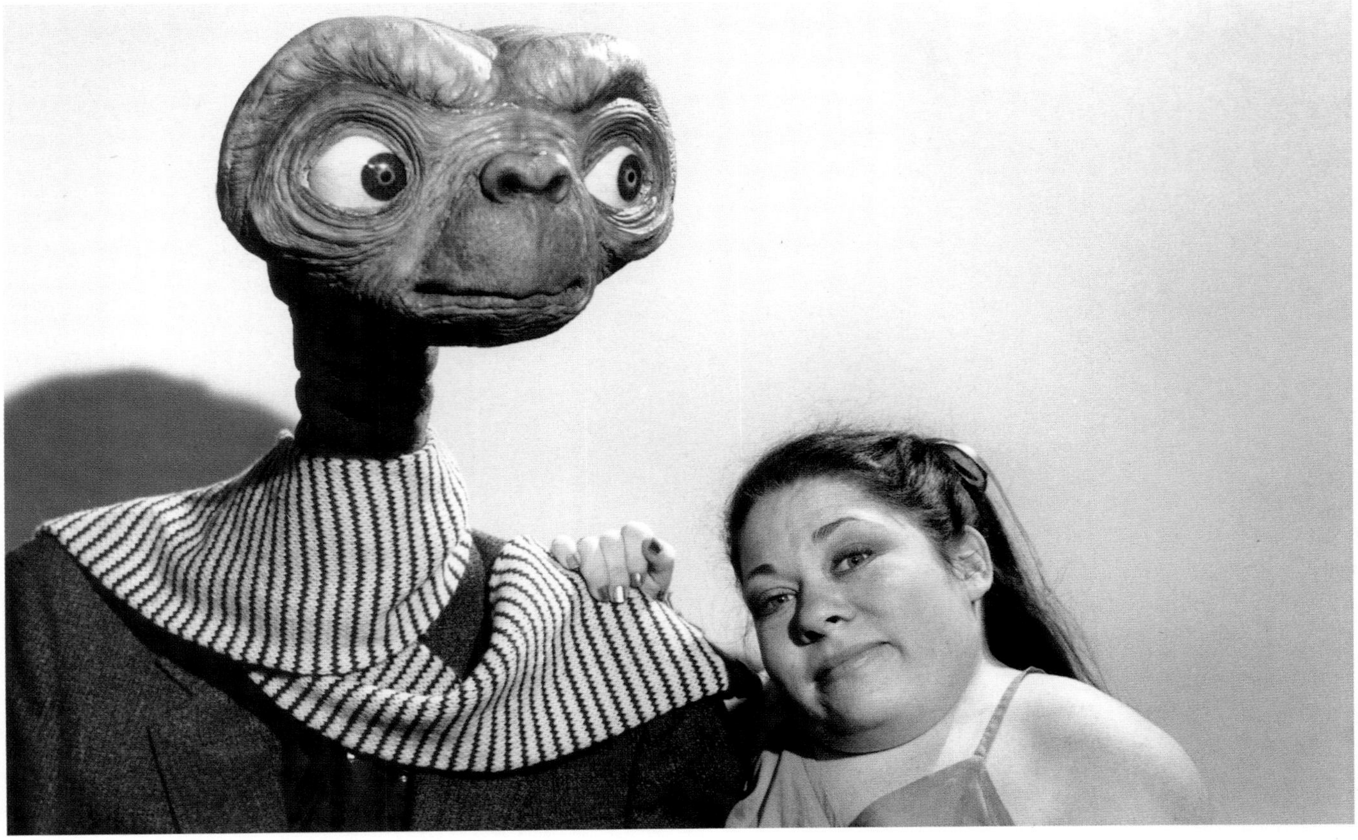

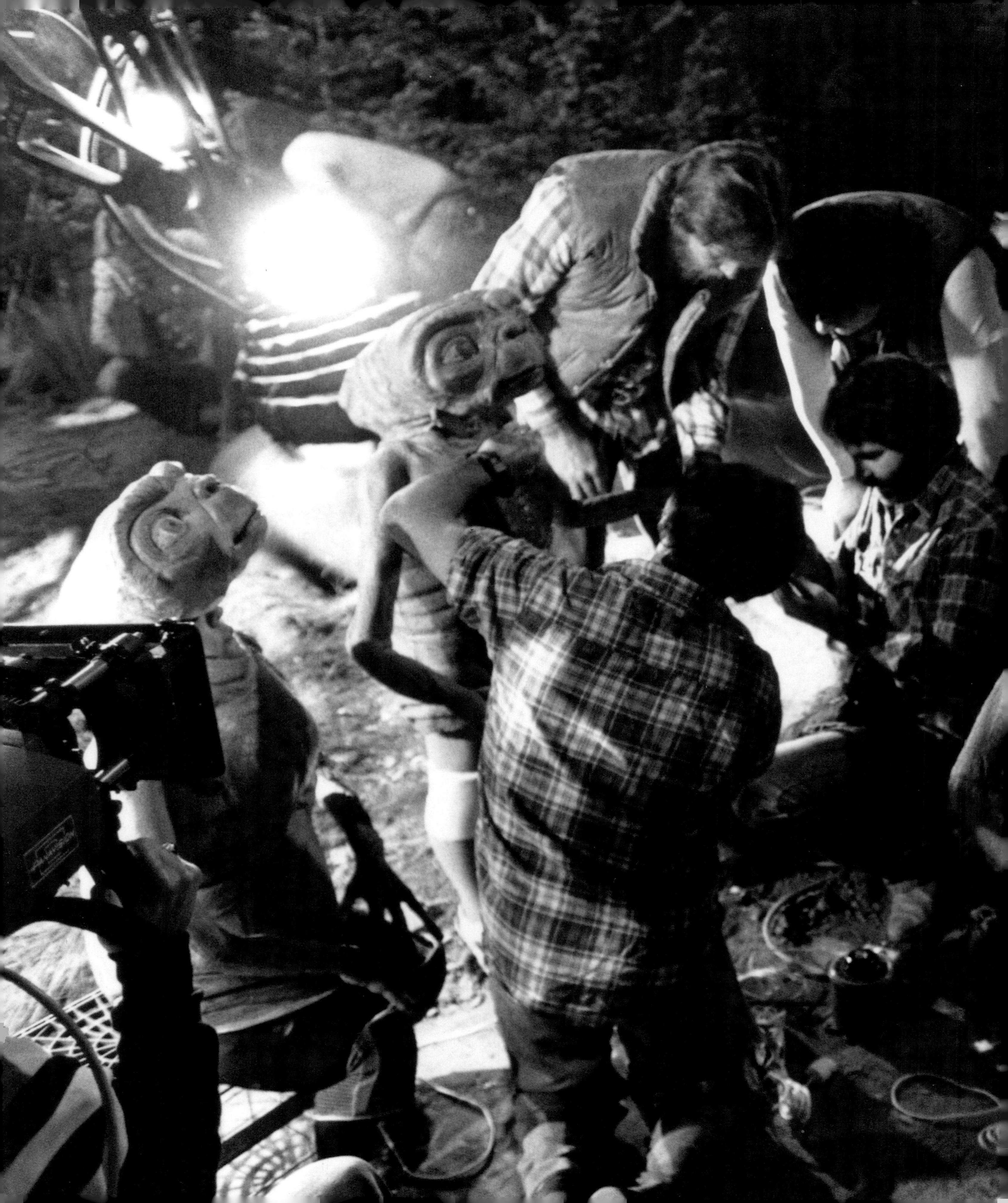

I remember saying to Carlo Rambaldi that E.T. should kind of waddle when he walks like Chaplin with his cane. He should also look like Bambi slipping on the ice, where Bambi couldn't find his footing. When E.T. starts to walk on earth, he is ungainly and insecure.

Pat Bilon made the strongest contributions to E.T.'s walking scenes. But there were other people who also contributed. A wonderful young boy, Matthew De Meritt, who didn't have legs, was able to walk on his hands. He did the most memorable sequence when E.T. walks into the room, having had a few too many beers, and stumbles and falls on his face. Then Gertie knocks him over when she opens the refrigerator door and he falls over backwards. All of these were Matthew's contributions.

Tamara De Treaux did the very opening scene where E.T. comes out of the woodshed and places the Reese's Pieces on Elliott's sleeping bag. Tamara also did the last scene in the movie, where E.T. walks up the gangway, holding the flowers from Gertie.
—STEVEN SPIELBERG

LEFT: *On the set during the filming of the opening scenes where the extraterrestrials are researching the plant life in the California hills.* ABOVE: *An actor on the 1981 set being fit with the E.T. suit.*

Inside E.T.

I wanted to be able to see inside E.T. I wanted to see his organs when he turns on his heart light. I thought the organs should be moving in a strange way and we should see E.T. breathing. I think it was Craig Reardon who said, "I understand from your script that you think E.T. is a plant."

I said, "I don't think he's a mammal, he's not a bird, he's not a fish. I think he's a vegetable."

They suggested this concept of making E.T.'s insides look like a plant. I thought that was fantastic and they went ahead with that idea.

—STEVEN SPIELBERG

Three E.T.s

During the filming, three different types of E.T.s were used. The models and the different heads cost about $1,400,000. The electronic parts accounted for about $400,000 of that amount.

1) A MECHANICAL MODEL: The mechanical E.T. was operated by twelve men who were connected to the model by twenty-foot cables. Each operator controlled a different function on the model. Four people controlled the face alone. Spielberg called the operators, "E.T.'s Twelve Hearts."

2) AN ELECTRONIC MODEL: This model was operated by radio control. Both the electronic and the mechanical model had eighty-seven points of movement including ten points in the face alone.

3) E.T. SUITS: Actors were put inside costumes for the walking scenes, and a mime wore E.T. gloves for specific scenes involving his hands and arms.

MEMORANDUM
EXTRA-TERRESTRIAL PRODUCTIONS
Culver City, California

Mr. Carlo Rambaldi
Northridge, California 91324

RE: RED LIGHT – E.T.   1st July 1981

If you will recall, Steven has always emphasized that the heart light should be organic, have depth and movement and the light should have the characteristics of a bright fluoroscope.

I should also mention that Steven up until now expected all E.T.'s to have the red light capability. If that is not possible, I will need to let him know his limitations right away.

Thank you.

Yours sincerely,
KATHY KENNEDY

MEMORANDUM
EXTRA-TERRESTRIAL PRODUCTIONS
Culver City, California

FROM: Ed Verreaux
TO: Craig Reardon
DATE: July 31, 1981
SUBJECT: E.T. HEART LIGHT

Aside from color:

A) Since this is an animated effect, light intensity should be variable according to conditions. . . .it shouldn't just snap on like a light switch but rather be able to increase or decrease in brightness from very dim (very slight like a light sunburn) to very bright (shining through the hospital bed sheets. . . hiding from Keys and his men in the ditch) and any position in between.

B) While E.T.'s skin is not totally transparent in the heart light area, we should be able to see some internal organ activity (always movement) when the light is on. The pulsing of the heart (two-three hearts?), intestinal contraction, changes in the density of viscera, lung expansions and contractions. The rib cage will block out light but the skin should be diffuse enough to allow some light to bleed through. Also, we should be able to see some vein activity in front of the light radiating out toward the limbs, not necessarily with bubbles of E.T.'s blood pumping through, but some lines to indicate blood vessels.

If you have any questions, please call me at the office.

Best regards,
ED VERREAUX

cc: Kathy Kennedy, Melissa Mathison, Steven Spielberg, Mitch Suskin

---

BELOW: Four of the dozen operators (Steven Spielberg called them "E.T.'s Twelve Hearts") working in unison to bring life to the creature.

Almost every member of the cast and crew wanted a portrait with the star of the movie. THIS PAGE: Among those who posed with E.T. are Carlo Rambaldi (26A) lighting a politically incorrect cigarette for the alien. OPPOSITE PAGE: Allen Daviau (25A), Robert Macnaughton (20A), and Henry Thomas (32A).

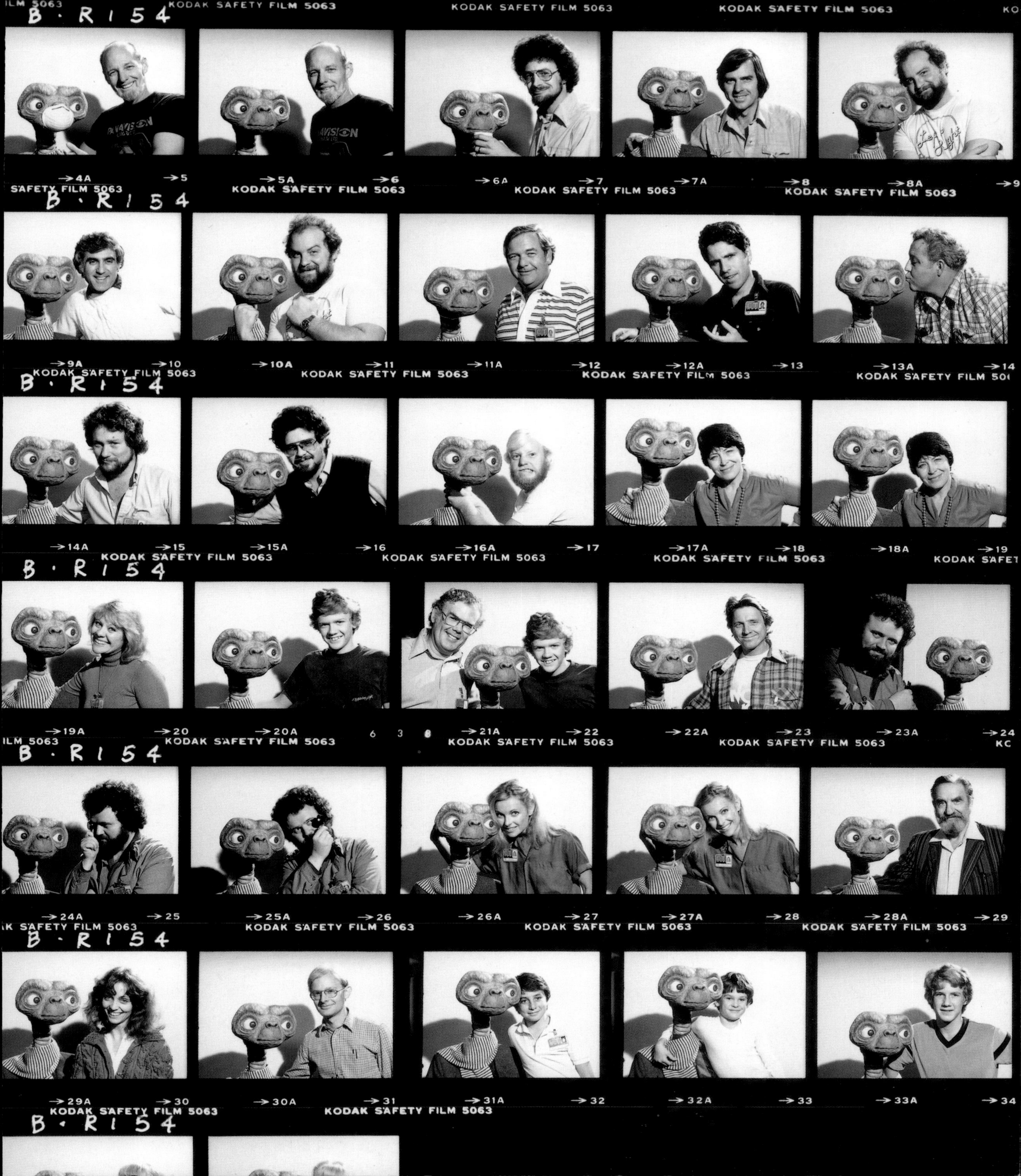
B · R154
KODAK SAFETY FILM 5063

ASSEMBLING the CAST

Casting ELLIOTT

I think, in a funny way, with children, you almost know the minute they walk into the room whether you're in fact looking at the character, because they do come in and claim the role in some way. Usually that's because you're casting some element of their existing personality. And that's what you're looking for in terms of trying to find the character.
—Kathleen Kennedy

I could not find an Elliott. I looked for a long time, at least six months. Actually, I made an offer to a boy who I thought was Elliott, but that fell through. I was really only about a month away from shooting the movie and still did not have an Elliott.

Then I heard from Jack Fisk. He had just made a movie called *Raggedy Man* and he used this kid named Henry Thomas. Jack recommended Henry to our casting person.
—Steven Spielberg

My audition was kind of scary. I was reading these two random scenes, but I hadn't read the whole script and I didn't even know the story. So I read these two pages three or four times, and it was really bad. I remember thinking, I'm not reading very well. This is horrible, I'm not going to get this part.

Steven said we should do an improvisation. Here's the situation: You just found this creature and you love it. It's like your dog. It's your pet and the government wants to take it away from you and do experiments on him.
—Henry Thomas

I got behind the video camera, turned it on, and that's how Henry convinced me that he was Elliott. Everybody in the room was in tears. I just remember turning to Henry and saying, "Okay, kid, you got the part."
—Steven Spielberg

Above: Henry Thomas poses with E.T. and his mom.
Opposite: Drew Barrymore rides atop Steven Spielberg's shoulders during filming.

Casting GERTIE

I auditioned for *Poltergeist* and Steven said, "No, you're not right for this, you're right for this other movie. So come back."

I came in a lot of times. I was so happy to have a grown-up who listened to me talk. He believed in my stories; he loved them. It made me feel so good and so alive.
—Drew Barrymore

I met a lot of Gerties, but Drew had the part the minute she stepped into the room.

She began making up these stories that she was a punk rocker, she had a punk rock band, and she was going on the road. She's six years old and she's telling me that she's going to do a twenty-city tour in America with her punk rock band. Her stories kept getting bigger and bigger and wilder and wilder. She just blew me away. I mean, there was no second choice.
—Steven Spielberg

Casting Elliott's BIG BROTHER

When I first heard of E.T., it was called *A Boy's Life*. I was doing a play in New York at the time, and I came to L.A. to read for a movie called *The Entity*. I didn't get that part, but the casting director mentioned that there was something going on over at Spielberg's office. I ended up getting in on a late audition. I remember the day of the audition because it wasn't really an audition. They wouldn't allow the script to be seen. So it was more of an interview with Steven himself.

—Robert Macnaughton

I thought Robert was a really good actor. He had stage experience and was the most professional of all the kids. He was the anchor because he had worked and acted before in front of people. He was really solid.

—Steven Spielberg

Casting KEYS

The first time I met Steven, I was brought in by a casting agent named Mike Fenton who really helped me at the start of my career. Mike wanted me to meet Steven for Indiana Jones.

Mike asked me if I could wear a hat. I said, "I wear hats all the time." So he gave me this fedora and said that I was going to be a swashbuckling adventurer. He said I should just go in and meet Steven.

I walked into the room and tripped over a lamp stand.
—PETER COYOTE

If *Raiders* was a comedy, I would've cast Peter Coyote to play Indiana Jones because he was kind of awkward and clumsy. But he made a good impression on me because I remembered him.

When we were casting the part of Keys, I said, "Whatever happened to that guy that kept knocking things down when he came into audition for me and George [Lucas] for *Raiders*?"

I gave him the part.
—STEVEN SPIELBERG

Casting MOM

Steven is a master at casting. He watches people and has a real talent for taking their quality and putting them in the role that's right for them. He originally saw me doing hookers and call girls and put me into his mother.
—DEE WALLACE STONE

I chose Dee Wallace because Dee was like a kid herself. I didn't feel I was violating my rule not to have adults in the film until the very end.
—STEVEN SPIELBERG

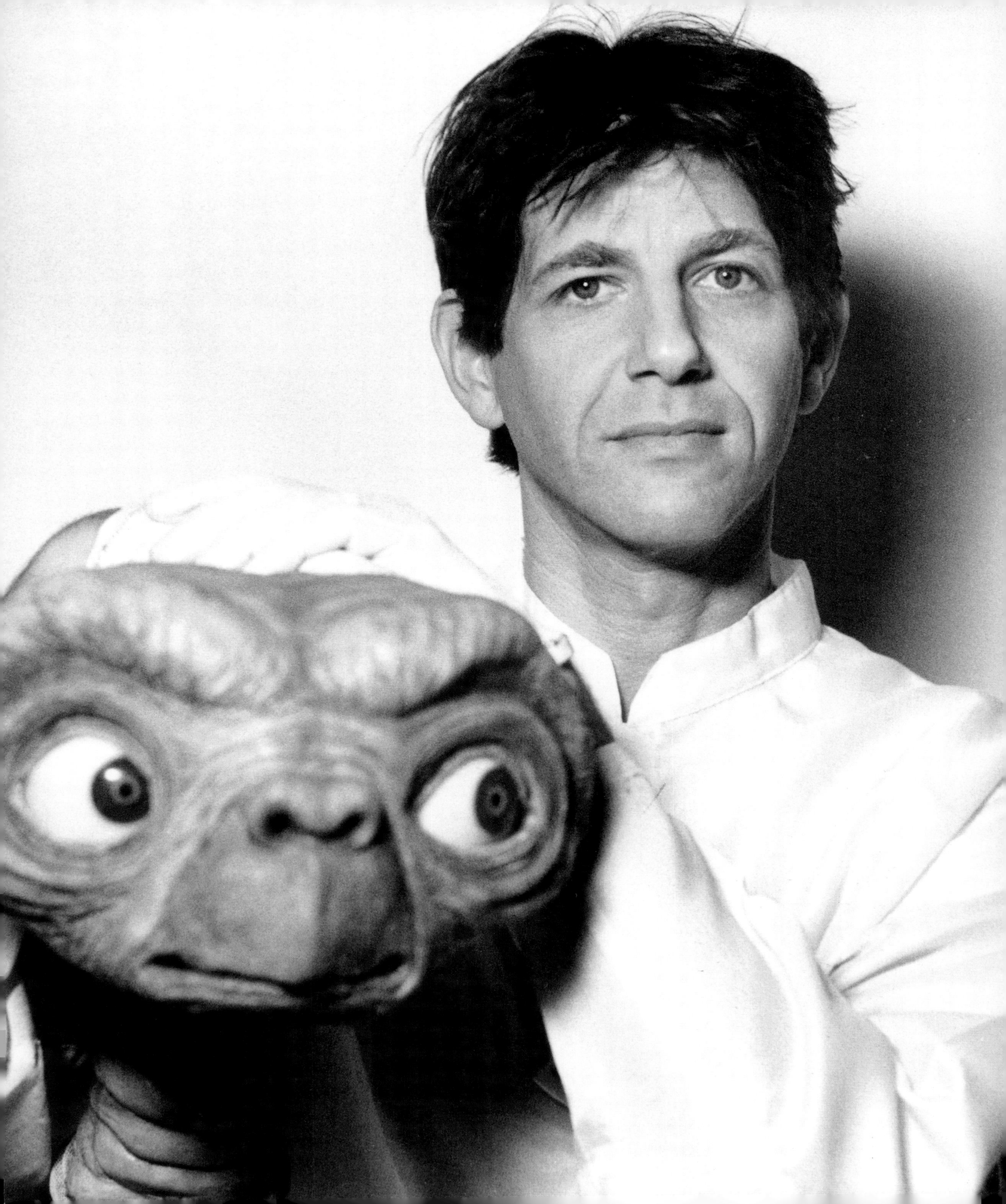

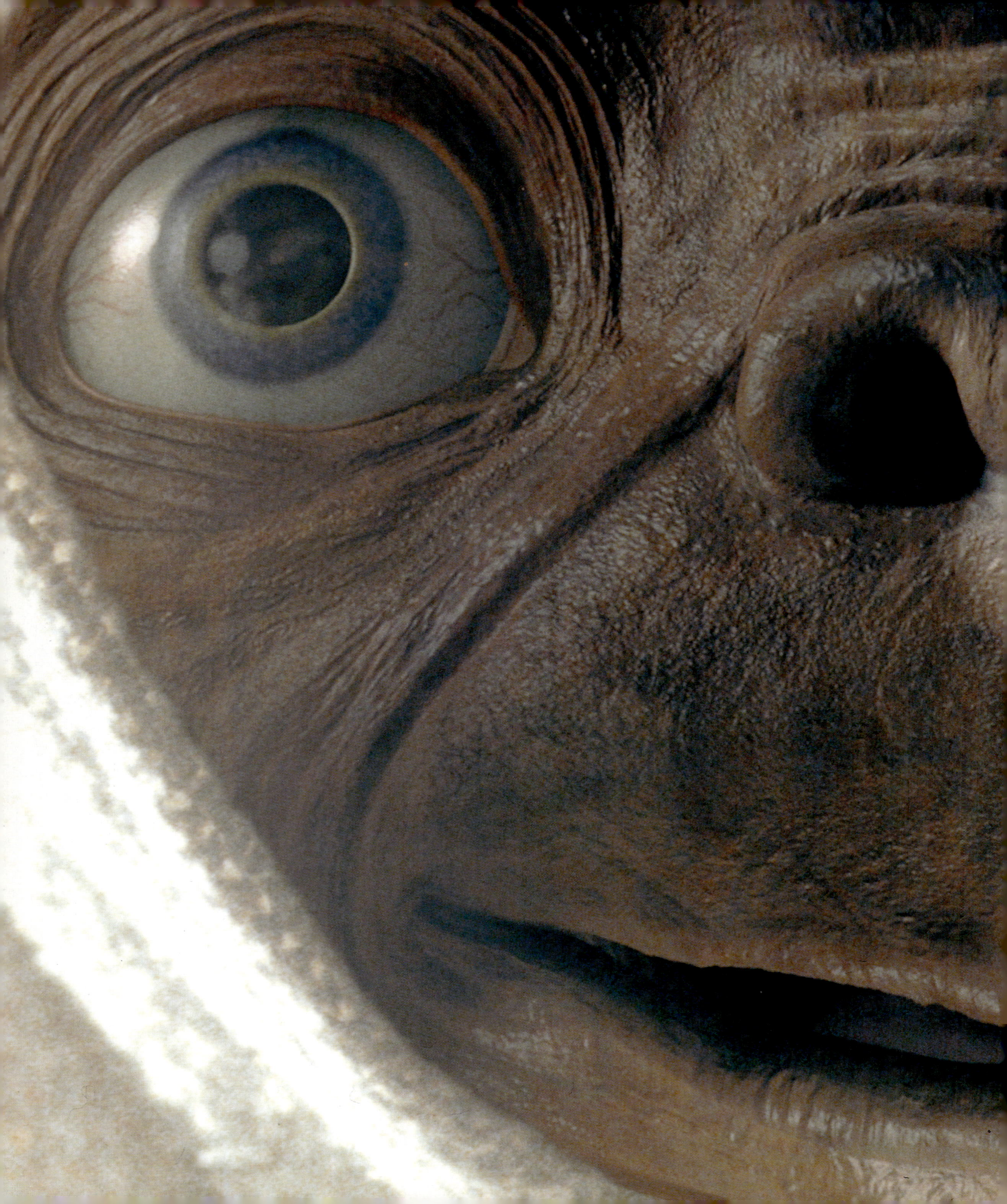

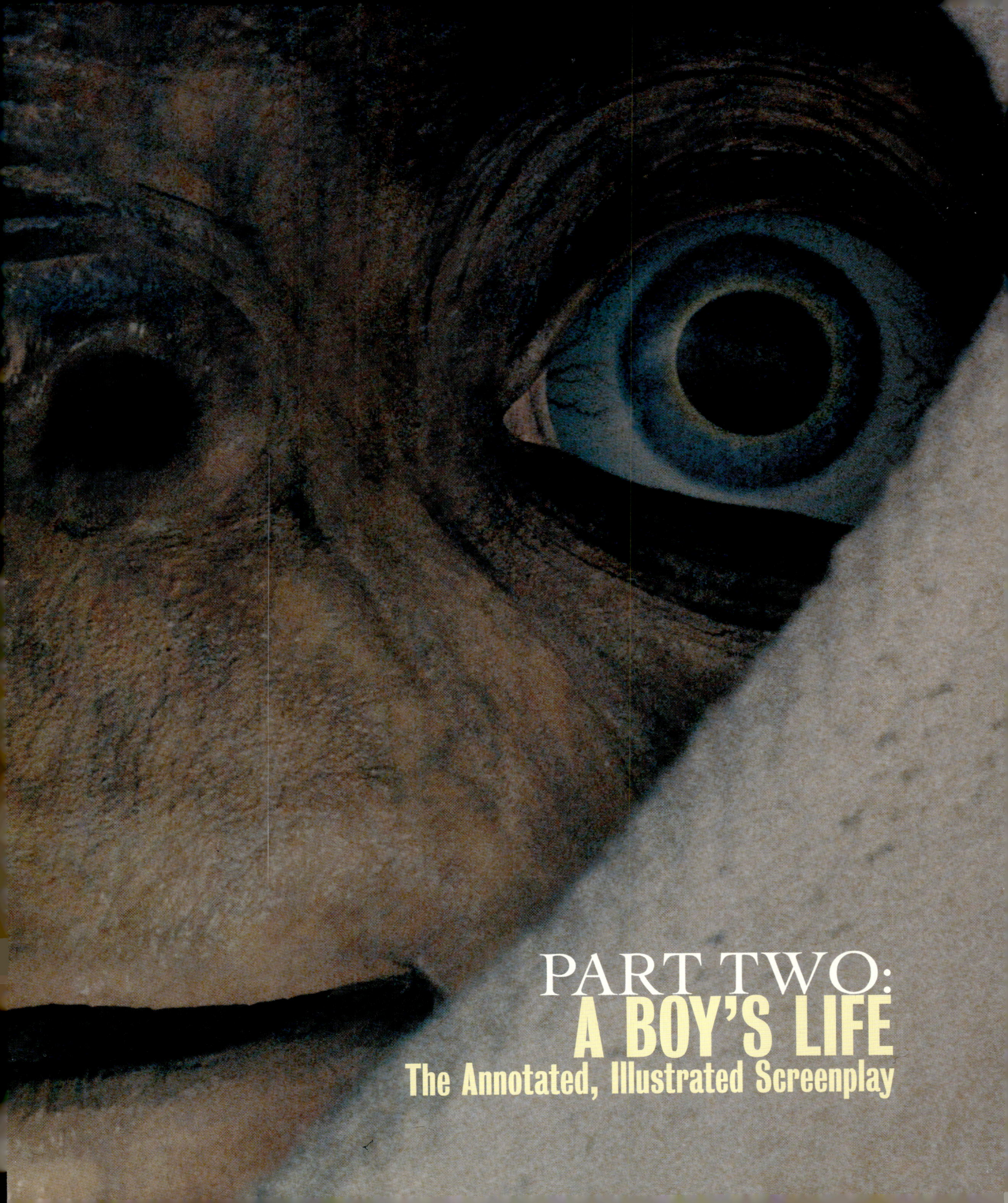

PART TWO:
A BOY'S LIFE
The Annotated, Illustrated Screenplay

SCENE
TAKE
"A"
CAM
244A
4
PROD.
A BOY'S LIFE
DIR.
Spielberg
CAM.
Daviau
DAY
DATE 10-2-81
SOUND

The view comes to rest on a freak clearing, a barren meadow, nestled among the towering trees.

It is here that we see the spaceship.

END MAIN TITLES

EXT. THE LANDING SITE – NIGHT

The spaceship is not large. It slightly resembles a reflective hot-air balloon, a Christmas tree ornament, inscribed with a delicate gothic design. An open hatch door stretches down to the landing site. Soft pastel light spills from the interior of the ship, and in this light, we make out the movements of creatures.

The creatures are short, stocky, humanoid, but our distance and the misty atmosphere prevent any close identification of features. The creatures are banded together, working with strange, antiquated tools, probing the earth. Their jerky movements and their reaction to the slightest sound reveal their hesitancy and fear.

A smoky, camouflaging mist seems to emanate from the creatures themselves, on an inhale-exhale rhythm, as if their hot breath was consolidating in the cool night air, blanketing their tracks with fog.

A creature moves up the gangplank as we follow two creatures as they move along.

Another creature moves up the gangplank, and we see creatures' hands reach up and pull on a branch.

The Space Program

E.T. is my response to the stalled space program. If the government won't fund the space program, to allow people's imagination to soar, then all I can do is make movies that bring space down to earth and make it more accessible to the imagination.

—STEVEN SPIELBERG, 1981

LEFT: *Henry Thomas in the Halloween scene when the movie was still known as* A Boy's Life. ABOVE: *Charlie Bailey, chief model maker responsible for the spaceship.* BELOW: *Drawing by Ralph McQuarrie.*

Drawing by Ed Verreaux of the spaceship landing on earth.

PRODUCTION NOTES
Ideas for the Landing of the Spaceship

1. Initially, one of the ideas was to have Elliott witness the landing, along with other people.

2. At one point, there was talk of adding another character to the movie, a kind of Mr. Wizard, who would also see the ship and be the one adult who believes Elliott.

3. Steven Spielberg thought the ship could land in a vacant lot, but Melissa Mathison thought a forest would be more magical.

4. The opening scene was shot in the redwood forest area near Crescent City in northern California. Hit hard with rain, the landing site was completely flooded and, at a new location that was found, cows ate all of the grass. Greenery was gathered from other locations to fake the bottle grass.

INT. SPACESHIP – NIGHT

A soft-white den of mist. We hear clearly now the unique breathing pattern of the creature as we see his obscured form enter the ship through plant branches.

We are in a greenhouse — a Gothic cathedral of a structure. Heavy precipitation drips from the strange and varied plants. The creature moves toward the far end of the greenhouse.

EXT. THE LANDING SITE – NIGHT

An owl hoots. The creatures freeze. The danger passes. Work is resumed.

A SAPLING – NIGHT

On the ground in front of ferns, a tiny sapling stands. A creature's hands uproots it and moves it out of sight.

EXT. FOREST – NIGHT

THE CREATURE
The creature walks into the forest. His heart also begins to shine through, and the ruby glow pinpoints

47

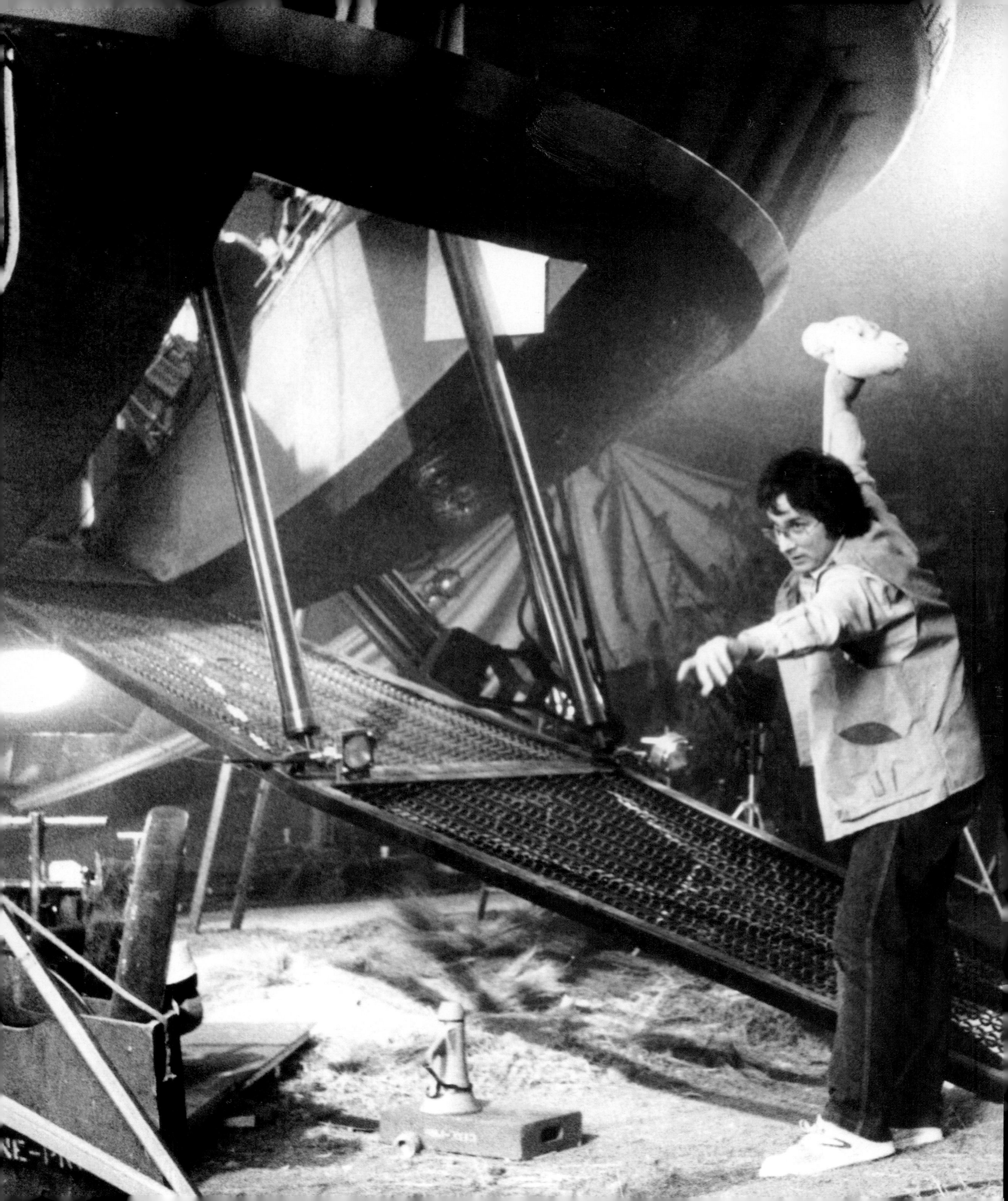

> **PRODUCTION NOTES**
>
> **Inside the Spaceship**
>
> 1. An elaborate sprinkler system was installed on the interior set so there was always a thin mist of water.
> 2. Gardening tools were designed but never used.
> 3. Flowers were designed for the ship including watermelon-like blossoms.
> 4. Steven Spielberg remembered a movie called *The Day of the Triffids* and asked production designer James D. Bissell to include one in this scene. He produced a four-foot foam latex figure with a moveable armature.
> 5. The lab contained two dueling, hand puppet cobra plants with whip-like antennas which were filmed but cut during editing.

him: a small awkward creature, alone in the gigantic redwood forest under a starry sky.

EXT. FOREST – NIGHT – POV

The sounds of the forest rise, and we see the height of the trees from the creature's POV as the creature moves deeper into the forest.

The creature moves along, looking up and around.

EXT. HILL LOOKOUT – NIGHT – POV

To the sound of heavy breathing and an awkward tread, we see the creature's hand reach out and pull back a leafy limb.

THE VIEW: THE SOURCE OF LIGHT – POV

The source of light — a suburban neighborhood, edging up against the base of the mountains and the border of the forest.

THE CREATURE

We cannot see his face. He turns his head to look down the road.

THE VIEW: THE SOURCE OF LIGHT – POV

A sea of yellow house lights lies below him.

LEFT: Steven Spielberg directing a scene from the beginning of the film.

THE CREATURE

Following his reaction, we hear the sound of a motor, and with no further warning, harsh blinding white lights streak around the corner.

THE APPROACHING CAR pulls to a stop. The creature runs across the road, partially hidden by the forest ferns.

MORE CARS

converge on the scene. We see bright headlights. The creature hidden in a clump of ferns looks on, as we hear the slamming of doors and muffled voices.

A PUDDLE OF WATER

just in front of where the creature stands hidden. The feet of the moving men step into the puddle as they move past him.

NEAR A VEHICLE

We see a man step out. Seen only from the waist down, a ring of keys hangs from his belt. The keys make a tremendous racket, displacing all other sounds of the night. He moves to where the other men stand hovering over the map on the hood of a car.

EXT. THE LANDING SITE – NIGHT

The ship is looking deserted. All hands are on board.

The fellow creature remains in the door opening, his heart light sending frantic signals into the dark forest.

THE CREATURE

His red light comes on as he watches. His hand moves in to cover it.

EXT. THE FOREST – NIGHT

The men turn toward the clump of ferns the creature is standing in, and with their flashlights lighting their way, move toward his hiding place. Again we hear the sound of keys.

The creature moves quickly zigzagging invisibly through the tall ferns.

The movement alerts the men, and they move in the direction of it, flashlights sweeping everywhere.

Lights start flashing in the spaceship.

We see the creature gliding through the forest ferns, his ruby-red beacon throbbing.

The men are not far behind.

The chase continues; the creature leads the way.

CREATURE'S POV

The ferns in his foreground are lit by his own light part in his path. The men follow persistently.

Back in the spaceship, a creature waits; his heart light beaming.

They are on his trail. One man jumps through a V-shaped tree, taking the lead as the other men follow, flashing their lights.

The man with the keys moves amid the other men. His keys jangle horrifically as they move forward.

The creature is nearing the landing site. He crosses a road. All we can see is his red light signaling his position to his pursuers, as he moves into another part of the forest.

The pursuers continue their chase.

The landing site is almost in view. He races toward it, the men hot on his heels.

CREATURE'S POV

Again the ferns part as he races toward the ship.

EXT. THE LANDING SITE – NIGHT

The hatch door lifts. The last image from the interior of the ship is the fellow creature's red light as the door closes and we hear a panicked group breath.

**SLOPE NEAR THE LANDING SITE
(WHERE THERE IS A GATE)**

The creature almost flies down the slope he is moving so rapidly.

EXT. THE LANDING SITE – NIGHT

The ship hovers, then departs quickly, spinning above the treetops and disappearing into the night sky.

SLOPE NEAR THE LANDING SITE

The men come racing toward the light. They stop and raise their flashlights to the sky. They move forward still hoping to find whatever it was they were following.

CLOSER: THE CREATURE

The creature stands. The creature cries out — a sound of desperation, disbelief, and fear.

SLOPE NEAR THE LANDING SITE

The creature stranded on earth moves back up the slope toward the forest, looking around at his new planet. He moves down toward the suburban lights.

THE MEN
move into the area where the ship had been frantically looking about, flashing flashlights.

INT. ELLIOTT'S HOUSE – NIGHT

CAMERA has pulled back now, REVEALING four boys seated around a kitchen table. They are into the final hours of late night "fantasy role-playing game." The table is cluttered with pop cans, potato chips, calculators, books, and a domino maze which is being used to signify the route of tonight's adventure.

MICHAEL – fourteen, tall, lanky. The oldest of the three children who live in this home.

Ideas Cut from the Script

Melissa Mathison and Steven Spielberg had many, many ideas for the script and here are a few that they ultimately rejected:

1) E.T. goes into a fox den and sees several cubs and their mother.

2) It's a belt, not a heart light, that lights up.

3) Elliott's father is in the movie.

4) Elliott tries to bait E.T. with Reddi-wip.

5) At a football game, E.T. gives Michael the power to win big.

6) Mom meets E.T. when Elliott gives him a shower.

7) There's a character in the movie named Mr. Pfister, a Mr. Wizard type, who helps the kids.

8) There's a character in the movie named Lance, an evil kid who wants to make a profit from E.T. Melissa Mathison was thinking that Lance would be Elliott's alter ego.

9) E.T. has a little pouch, like a kangaroo, and carries stuff around with him.

10) There's a parrot in the house who knows how to talk. The kids teach E.T. to talk the same way they taught the parrot and, when E.T. does finally speak, the mom thinks it is the parrot.

11) Harvey, the dog, gets hit by a car and E.T. heals him.

12) E.T. heals the J.R. character on the television show "Dallas."

ABOVE: E.T. was acclaimed for its realistic portrayal of family life and the conflicts between family members.

> **SCRIPT NOTES**
> In the original script, the boys were playing *Dungeons and Dragons* in the opening of the movie. This had to be changed when the production company was not allowed to use the name.

TYLER – Michael's friend, cute, sassy, wise beyond his years.

STEVE – the game master, meticulous, inscrutable.

GREG – on the phone.

A fifth boy stands behind the bar by the table. He is Elliott, nine or ten.

ELLIOTT
Steve.

STEVE
Five.

MICHAEL
Oh, great.

ELLIOTT
Steve.

STEVE
So you got an arrow right in your chest, and you're out ten more rounds. Ten more rounds.

ELLIOTT
I'm ready to play.

TYLER
Oh, no.

The boy, Elliott, is trying to get a word in. He is being ignored.

GREG
Don't worry about it, Mike. I got resurrection. I'll bring you back.

ELLIOTT
I'm ready to play, Steve.

MICHAEL
I'm already one of the undead, Greg. I can still throw death spells, huh, Steve?

GREG
I'm just trying to help you out, man. Don't be so cranky.

STEVE
Yeah.

ELLIOTT
Steve.

TYLER
Hows 'bout throwing a spell over the pizza man? Where's our pizza, man? Get it? Huh?

Elliott has waited long enough. He interrupts finally.

ELLIOTT
Well, I'm ready now to play.

STEVE
You can't have a fight now. You're a thief.

TYLER
But I haven't gone yet.

ELLIOTT
I'm ready to play now, you guys!

STEVE
It's coming around to you.

GREG
We're in the middle, Elliott. You can't just join any universe in the middle. I got him! I got him! Mm. Hey, what am I asking him for, you guys?

MICHAEL
Did you say ten more rounds?

TYLER
"Papa Oom Mow Mow."

MICHAEL
"Papa Oom Mow Mow."

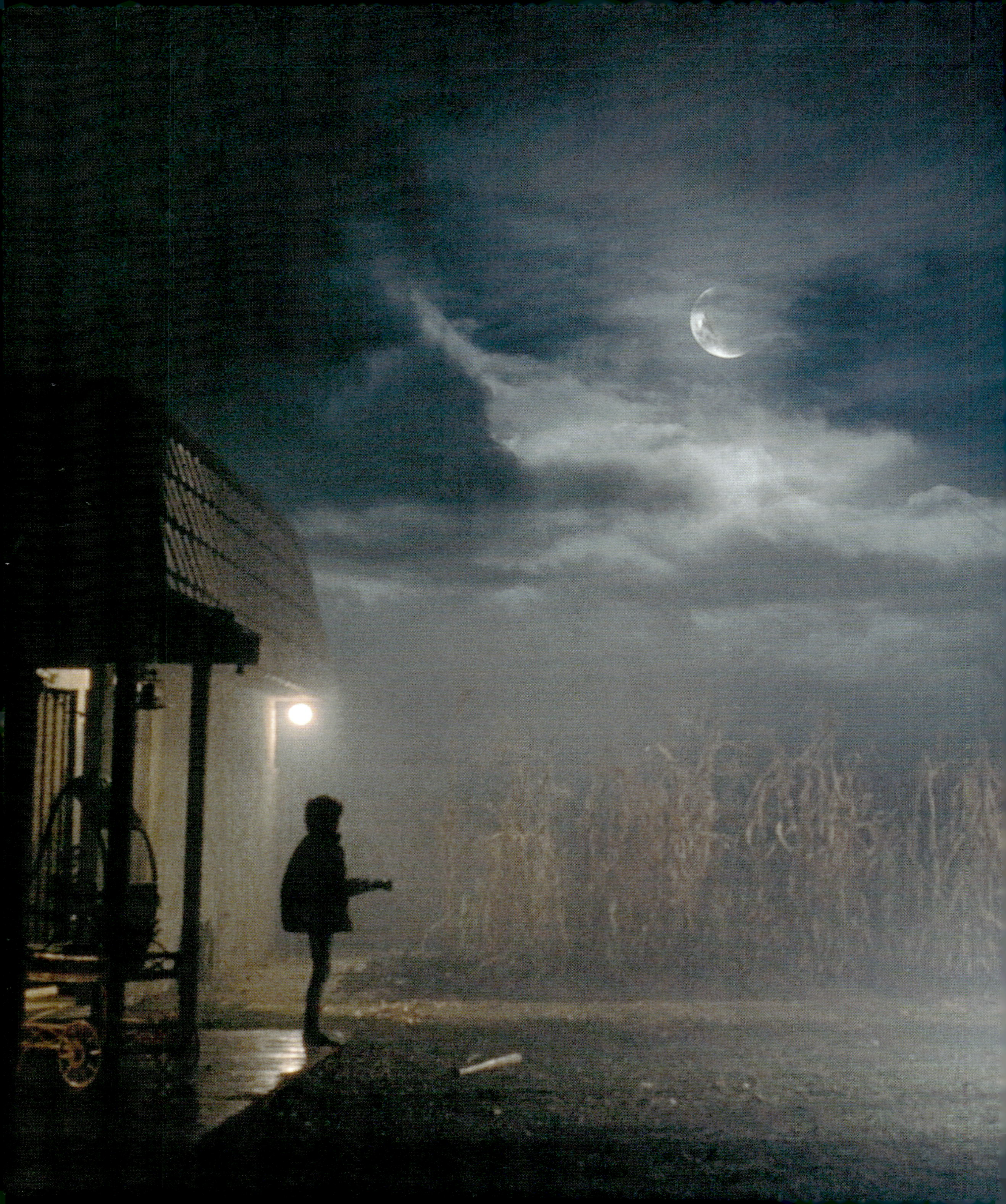

GREG
Mm-hm. All right. Okay. (*into telephone*) "Papa Oom Mow Mow." Yeah.

MICHAEL
Ten more rounds.

GREG
Yeah.

ELLIOTT
Mike?

GREG
I know. It's not for us. It's for his mother.

ELLIOTT
Mike?

GREG
"Papa Oom Mow Mow."

MICHAEL
You have to ask Steve. He's game master. He has absolute power.

GREG
"Papa Oom Mow Mow."

ELLIOTT
Steve?

GREG
Thanks a lot. Okay, bye.

TYLER
Steve, can I play now?

STEVE
Go wait for the pizza first.

ELLIOTT
Then I'm in?

STEVE
Yeah, you're in. But figure out your strategy, 'cause you're playing after Greg.

GREG
With plenty of sausage and pepperonis!

TYLER
Everything but the little fishies.

EXT. FRONT OF ELLIOTT'S HOUSE – NIGHT

Elliott stands in the driveway playing with a baseball. He has a mitt on. His house is at the top of a cul-de-sac, the last house before the onslaught of forest and mountains. A Volkswagen pulls up next to him.

ELLIOTT meets the Volkswagen and collects the pizza.

Elliott climbs the driveway, balancing the pizza on one hand.

EXT. FRONT YARD – NIGHT

As he heads for the door, there is a sudden, loud, crashing noise from the backyard.

Elliott halts.

ELLIOTT
Harvey? Harvey, is that you, boy?

The Music

Steven Spielberg made *Close Encounters of the Third Kind* about four years before *E.T.* and, in the broadest sense, they have similar themes. I think that what makes them both successful is that they affirm the fact that we are not alone in the universe. In the case of *Close Encounters*, the beginning of the film is much more terrifying because we don't know who these aliens are. But there's a great kind of uplifting feeling of almost religiosity, I think, at the end when we suddenly recognize that we have brothers and sisters. And so, there's a relief in the music. *E.T.* is also a bit scary in the beginning, but the minute we meet this little creature, the film becomes much more of a love story. That makes for a very different kind of musical challenge in *E.T.* as compared with *Close Encounters*.

Music is, of course, very difficult to verbalize for all of us. I could just parenthetically point out something that we've all been told but it can bear repeating. The one thing that perhaps every culture on earth shares, even before language, is music. When tribes couldn't speak to each other, they would beat a drum to organize a war or sing a song to celebrate a birth, or wail something at a funeral. There's a very basic human, non-verbal aspect to our need to make music and use it as part of our human expression. It doesn't have to do with body movements, it doesn't have to do with articulation of a language, but with something spiritual. So, for a composer like myself and a director like Steven Spielberg, it's very difficult to say: "What do we really want?" The simplest answer about my relationship with Steven Spielberg is that we talk a lot and we talk about tempo, not so much in a harmonic or melodic context, but how fast or how slow the music should be. Tempo is the first thing a composer has to get right. The next thing has to do with how loud or how soft the music should be. Then, we determine the harmonic ambiance and talk about emotion and texture.

—JOHN WILLIAMS

ABOVE: John Williams and the star of E.T. at a concert.

INT. KITCHEN – NIGHT

Mary moves with some dishes from the stove to the dishwasher. She is swaying with the music as she bends over to put the dishes into the dishwasher.

          MICHAEL
Oh, this is really great, Ty, you destroyed the dungeon. Thank you.

          GREG
Is this the one I asked for?

          STEVE
Yeah, that's the one you asked for.

          GREG
Yeah.

          MICHAEL
Stop it!

          GREG
All right.

          TYLER
Sorry.

EXT. BACKYARD – NIGHT

Elliott continues calling his dog until he reaches the backyard. A roomy, grassy stretch of land with a vegetable garden and a lattice toolshed. A red light is hanging over the fence gate. The gate is blowing in the wind. We hear what sounds like a sharp inhalation and see what looks like a sucking of mist through the toolshed door.

          ELLIOTT
Harvey?

Elliott walks to the tool shed. He stops and puts the pizza on the ground, then throws the baseball into the toolshed. Wait a beat, then the ball comes hurtling back out at him.

Elliott, turns to run, trips over the pizza, and continues toward the back door.

INT. KITCHEN – NIGHT

Mary has turned to the table. Her hand on her hip.

          TYLER
All's you can get is those forty-year-olds.

          MARY
So, how do you win this game, anyway?

          GREG
Fine. So who got Lisa last year, huh?

          STEVE
There's no winning. It's like life. You don't win at life.

          GREG
Money helps.

          STEVE
Yeah, but....

          ELLIOTT
Mom! Mom! There's something out—!

          TYLER
All right. Where's the pizza?

          ELLIOTT
Mom! Mom! There's something out there!

          MARY
Hey, now...

          ELLIOTT
It's in the...

          MARY
...calm down. Calm down.

          ELLIOTT
...toolshed! It threw the ball at me.

          TYLER
There's something out there. Mom, Mom.

          GREG
Yeah, I know where it can go.

               MARY
Cool it.

               TYLER
It threw the ball at...at me.

               ELLIOTT
Quiet! Nobody go out there.

               MARY
Stop now! You guys stay right here!

All the boys are now intent on defying Elliott. They rise to move outside. Greg and Tyler take a knife from near the stove and move out. Steve is in the lead. They continue out. Michael passing his mother says:

               MICHAEL
You stay here, Mom. We'll check it out!

               MARY
And put those knives back!

               ELLIOTT
Come on, Mom. Mom, I swear, there was something there.

               MARY
Okay, Elliott.

               ELLIOTT
It's out in the... toolshed.

> **FACTS AND FIGURES**
> **The Shoot**
> 1) The shooting schedule for *E.T.* was sixty-five days and began on September 8, 1981.
> 2) The movie was shot at the Laird Studios in Culver City and in the suburbs of Tujunga and Northridge. The final scene was shot in the red forest in northern California, near the Oregon border.
> 3) Elliott's house was owned by a former executive of the Bell Telephone Company. The production company commissioned the house for six weeks but ended up using it for almost four months.

               MARY
I'll get the flashlight. Hold it. Wait a... minute, come on.

As they all go toward the door, Mary and Elliott move behind them.

               ELLIOTT
Mom.

               GREG
You little creep. Creepy.

EXT. BACKYARD – NIGHT

The army of boys are on the patio. Mary takes the lead with Elliott beside her.

               MARY
What exactly did you see?

               TYLER
It's dark out here.

               ELLIOTT
It's in there.

               STEVE
It's scary.

               MARY
There's nothing in here.

               MICHAEL
The gate's open.

Tyler moves into the toolshed and kneels, noticing something.

               TYLER
Look at these.

Michael too crosses in as Mary shines the light on some odd footprints.

               MICHAEL (*on his knee*)
The coyote's come back again, Mom.

               MARY
Okay, party's over. Everybody back inside. Get out. Hurry up. Quick. Hurry up. Come on. Tyler, give me that knife.

58

ABOVE: Steven Spielberg and Henry Thomas working on the scene where Elliott throws his ball into the shed and E.T. throws it back.

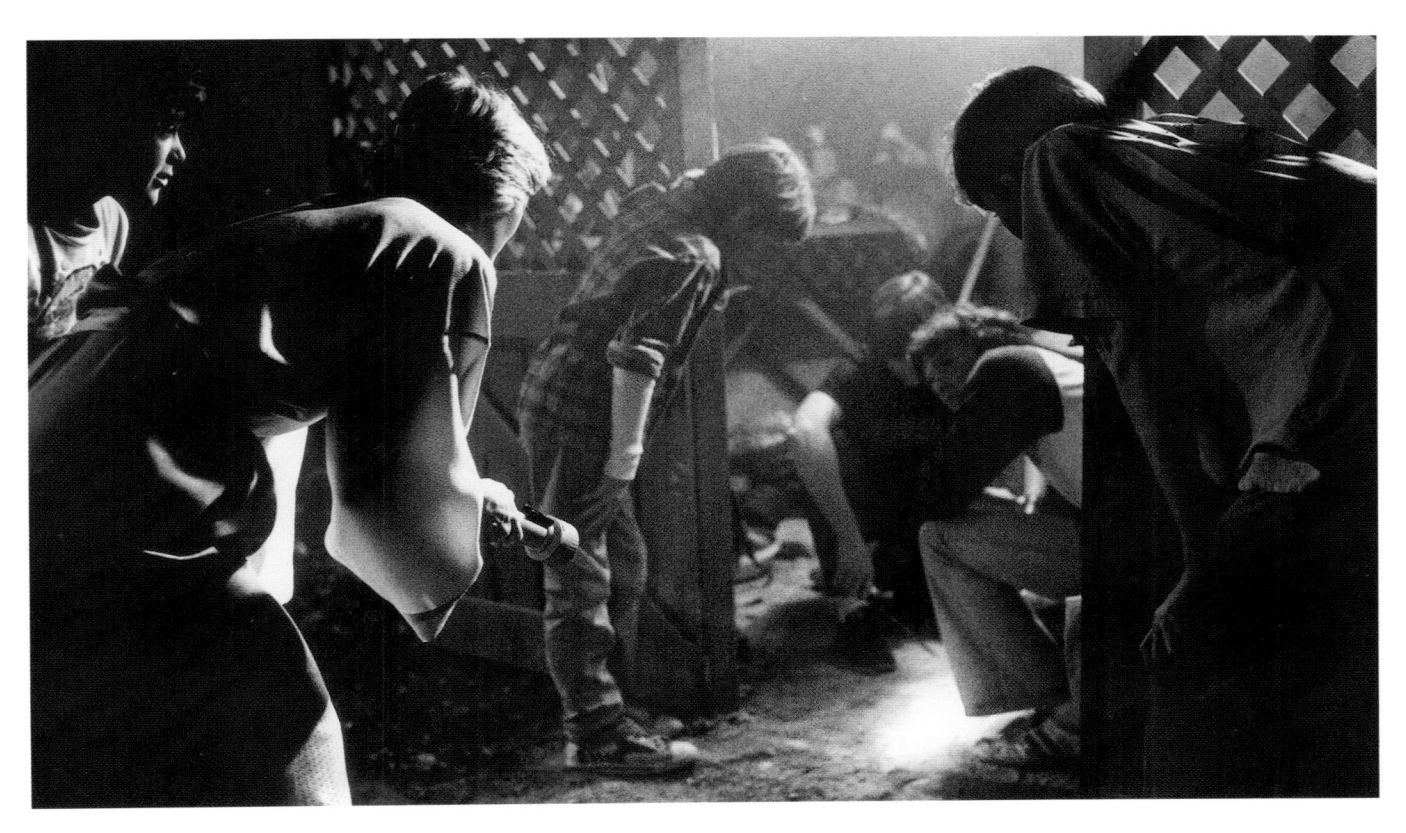

59

Tyler gives her the knife, and kneels to the pizza, opening it and taking a piece from the box and standing.

TYLER
Oh, great. Nice one, Elliott.

ELLIOTT
I–It was an accident.

TYLER
Yeah, accident.

MARY
A pizza? Who said you guys could order a pizza? Huh?

ELLIOTT
Uh, h–him, he—

GREG
Uh, I, but—

She shoos them all toward the house.

MARY
Huh? In the house.

TYLER
You geek, man.

MICHAEL
Hey, Greg.

Elliott, beside Mary.

ELLIOTT
But, Mom, it was real. I swear.

MARY
I know, I know.

TYLER
Douche bag, Elliott.

MARY
(*gently hitting the back of Tyler's head*)
No "douche bag" talk in my house!

ABOVE: Steven Spielberg directs Henry Thomas in the backyard scene.

LEFT: *E.T. as he appeared in the 1982 release.* ABOVE: *For the 2002 release, the creature's features were enhanced.*

                           ELLIOTT
                 There was something. I swear.

                            MARY
                           I know...

They continue toward the door.

The toolshed is quiet; suddenly a hand comes out and holds on to the doorjamb.

INT. ELLIOTT'S ROOM – NIGHT

The clock on the stand beside Elliott's bed reads 2:01 A.M. CAM PANS to Harvey asleep in the lower bunk. A sound is heard, and Harvey reacts to it. He stands and looks toward the window. CAM PANS to upper bunk, and we see Elliott also awake looking toward the sound of the noise outside the window.

EXT. BACKYARD – NIGHT

Elliott descends steps at the back of the house and turns toward garden. Elliott moves cautiously into the yard holding a lit flashlight, muttering and whistling to himself in fear.

He approaches the vegetable garden, coming from the side of the house. He moves through a row of cornstalks, looking around from side to side.

                           ELLIOTT
                     Elliott, you're crazy.

He hears a soft crushing sound, and is momentarily startled. He continues on. He turns, and then he notices the footprints. He follows them until they come to an abrupt end. He is staring at a clump of cornstalks. He gently pulls them apart, and shines the flashlight between them.

E.T.'s face comes bursting through the cornstalks.

It is a terrible sight, like nothing we have ever seen before. E.T.'s wide head is tightened back in leathery creases and furrows. His thick lips are parted in a horrible grimace. His large round eyes are wide, the pupils dilated to an enormous size. Tiny teeth are bared as E.T. makes a terrifying sound — an imitative noise — the SOUND OF KEYS.

Elliott screams and hits the ground. The flashlight rolls to the side, flashing a light across his face.

He sees the movement of the cornstalks as though something were passing by them, but cannot see E.T. again. He rises.

ELLIOTT carefully moves out of the garden toward the hill and back gate. The swings are moving, but E.T. is gone.

He holds onto a swinging bar (part of the swing) and looks up the hill.

The garbage cans come rolling down, and then the gate, which is open, closes.

Elliott looks on in wonderment.

INT. GARAGE – DAWN

Elliott, now fully dressed, kicks up the kickstand, jumps onto his bicycle, and moves down the driveway and off onto the street.

EXT. THE STREET – DAWN

Elliott rides down a hilly street on his bicycle, looking around for the creature.

EXT. FIRE ROAD – DAY

Elliott is huffing and puffing up the fire road.

EXT. FOREST – DAY

Elliott pours some Reese's Pieces in his path.

>   **ELLIOTT**
> (whistles) Hello?

NEAR THE LANDING SIGHT

Elliott rides his bike around a rock. He gets off and moves to the road, tossing Reese's Pieces.

>   **ELLIOTT**
> Hello?

Elliott spots a man down the road and moves back to behind the rock, watching the man.

We see only the man's back — Keys. We hear the steady, annoying sound of keys.

NEAR THE LANDING SIGHT

Elliott moves back to his bike and rides out.

He rides on the forest path. In a tree branch, we spot the strange hand of the creature, who has been watching Elliott.

INT. KITCHEN – NIGHT

The family is having dinner. Elliott is slumped over his plate, a look of depression on his face as he picks at his food.

Gertie, the last child in the family — a five-year-old girl, tomboy, innocent, and "nobody's fool" — sits near Elliott.

>   **GERTIE**
> What are you going as for Halloween?

>   **ELLIOTT**
> I'm not going to stupid Halloween.

>   **MICHAEL**
> Why don't you go as a goblin?

>   **ELLIOTT**
> Shut up.

>   **MARY**
> It's not that we don't believe you, honey.

>   **ELLIOTT**
> Well, it was real, I swear!

>   **MARY**
> What are you going as, Gert?

>   **GERTIE**
> I'm going as a cowgirl.

>   **ELLIOTT**
> So what else is new?

>   **MICHAEL**
> Maybe it was an iguana.

>   **ELLIOTT**
> It was no iguana.

SCRIPT NOTES

Originally, the script included the use of M&M's, but Mars would not allow their product to be used because several executives thought E.T. was "too ugly" and would frighten children. The Hershey Food Corporation agreed to allow the use of a new candy product called Reese's Pieces. As a result of the movie, sales of Reese's Pieces increased by 65 percent.

"It was nothing like that, penis-breath!"

I had been brought up where kids just didn't say those kind of things that we said in the movie. I had to say "penis-breath" and that wasn't that bad because it was an anatomical term. I thought my Grandma could live with that.
—Henry Thomas

I loved this line in the movie because it showed that Mary was different from other moms. Instead of getting upset, the line cracks her up.
—Dee Wallace Stone

MICHAEL
Maybe a... You know how they say there are, uh, alligators in the sewers?

GERTIE
Alligators in the sewers.

MARY
All we're trying to say is, maybe you just probably imagined that it happened.

ELLIOTT
I couldn't have imagined it!

MICHAEL
Maybe it was a pervert or a deformed kid or something.

GERTIE
A deformed kid.

MICHAEL
Maybe a, an elf or a leprechaun.

ELLIOTT
It was nothing like that, penis-breath!

MARY
Elliott! Sit down.

ELLIOTT
Dad would believe me.

MARY
Maybe you ought to call your father and tell him about it.

ELLIOTT
I can't. He's in Mexico with Sally.

News to Mary. She sits a moment, then takes her plate and walks to the sink.

GERTIE
Wh–, where's Mexico?

MARY
Excuse me.

MICHAEL
I'm gonna kill you.

> **MARY**
> If you ever see it again, whatever it is, don't touch it. Just...call me, and I'll have somebody come and take it away.

> **GERTIE**
> Like the dogcatcher?

> **ELLIOTT**
> But they'll give it a lobotomy or do experiments on it or something.

> **MARY**
> It's your turn to do the dishes, fellas.

> **MICHAEL**
> I set and cleared.

> **ELLIOTT**
> I set and cleared.

> **MICHAEL**
> I did breakfast.

> **GERTIE**
> I did breakfast.

> **MICHAEL**
> What's the matter, Mom?

> **MARY**
> He hates Mexico.

Mary starts to leave the kitchen; she is in tears.

> **MICHAEL**
> Damn it! Why don't you...grow up? Think how other people feel for a change!

Elliott takes his plate from the table and almost throws it into the sink. He turns the hot water on. Steam covers the window as Elliott stares through it.

EXT. BACKYARD – NIGHT

Elliott sits, wrapped in his bag, in the lounge chair asleep. His flashlight is still lit.

CLOSE ON ELLIOTT sound asleep. His eyes are open, and he looks toward the toolshed.

He sees a shadow approaching.

He sits up.

ON E.T.

He is now at the toolshed entrance and slowly moving toward Elliott. His face is soft now, his eyes wide and gentle, his mouth closed.

E.T. stares at the boy. The boy has wide eyes and is staring back.

> **ELLIOTT**
> Mo–... Mom... Mom. Michael. Michael. Mom.

E.T. is near the lounge chair now, and his hand extends to the sleeping bag near Elliott's feet.

Elliott tries to scream, but only inaudible sounds come out.

Elliott recoils, then sees that E.T. has left something on the bag. He looks, shining his flashlight onto it. It is a Reese's Pieces candy.

INT. HALLWAY NEAR STAIRCASE – NIGHT

Elliott comes from the steps to the landing and lays down some Reese's Pieces. Elliott moves to the doorway of his room and kneels. E.T.'s hands reach for the candy. E.T. comes from the staircase and starts toward Elliott's room.

INT. ELLIOTT'S ROOM – NIGHT

Elliott enters his room and entices E.T. with more Reese's Pieces. E.T. takes them. Elliott's bag of Reese's Pieces is empty. He swiftly moves to the desk in his

---

SCRIPT NOTES

In the original scene, E.T. gives Elliott only one piece of candy. The hand dropping several pieces of candy was an insert shot, filmed after the end of principal photography.

Lighting: The Magic Look

One of the things Steven knew from the very beginning was that E.T. would be a very shadowy, hardly seen figure in the early stages of the film. We would take a while to discover him. So we had to decide: What color should he be? What texture should we make his skin, especially for the initial stages where we were to barely see the outline of this creature?

One of the things we tested was different colors. I remember him being everything from somewhat of a green to the much more purple color that he wound up.

E.T.'s brownish skin with purple overtones evolved out of those early tests. Initially, I was shooting footage of just the head, and I knew that Steven didn't want E.T. lit with too much detail. In those early stages, we evolved the procedure of using a strong back light on him, putting his face largely in shadow with just the glint in the eyes. And that was how we shot the beginning scenes of E.T., other than those brief glimpses with the flashlights in the cornstalks.

Once we had E.T.'s lighting down, we had to decide how to light the scene around him so that it all made sense. One of the first things I said when I read the script was that everything about the house, the neighborhood, and the family had to be very, very real without any false or mysterious feeling.

Everything had to be naturally motivated because the magic would happen only in the presence of E.T. When E.T. entered the house, the house would remain the same but the room or the closet would be transformed into this magic place.

—ALLEN DAVIAU, DIRECTOR OF PHOTOGRAPHY

LEFT: The film crew on location. Allen Daviau, director of photography, is on the far right.

room, searching the drawers for some new bait. He finds an apple and moves quickly back to the door.

E.T. is gone. Suddenly he spots his head and hands, and they are moving behind a table. Elliott scurries along with them, but E.T. upsets a box of pencils, and in throwing his hands back, knocks down a shelf from the shelves behind him.

Elliott runs to the door and closes it, listening a moment to hear whether he has wakened anyone. He sighs a sigh of relief and moves into the room.

E.T. is standing in a corner as Elliott moves into the room as close as he dares to go. Beside him is his bunk bed. He carefully pulls a blanket off the bottom bunk and throws it onto E.T. E.T. briefly reacts, but then feels the warmth of the blanket and pulls it around him.

We get a good look at him. He is three-and-a-half feet tall, and his thin arms, partially covered by the blanket, hang below his narrow hips. His belly is heavy, now covered by the blanket. His head is oblong and flat—some think like a turtle's. His eyes never leave Elliott.

ELLIOTT is astonished, looking at him curiously.

E.T. holding the blanket around him, looks back just as curious.

ELLIOTT scratches his nose and is astonished as E.T. scratches his nose.

ELLIOTT tries an experiment. He touches his mouth and the side of his head, and to his surprise, E.T. touches his mouth, then the side of his head.

ELLIOTT
Wow.

Elliott holds out all five fingers, E.T. holds out all four fingers. Elliott, one finger. E.T., one finger. Elliott rapidly crooks his finger twice; E.T. crooks the same finger. They continue this interrogation of each other until sleep begins to overtake them.

E.T.'s eyes become droopy. Elliott in turn swoons slightly. Trying not to take his eyes off E.T., Elliott moves back to an armchair and sits down, trying to keep his eyes open.

E.T.'s eyes are closed. Elliott falls completely asleep. E.T. opens his eyes and looks around his new surroundings.

EXT. FOREST LANDING SITE – NIGHT

The clearing is lit by lights. An ongoing clandestine operation. The earlier image of alien creatures gently probing the earth is replaced with the crude and lumbering movements of humans, scouring the area with a fine-tooth comb. Flash cameras briefly turn more light on. Portable machines churn and beep, displacing the rustle of leaves and the hum of nocturnal life. Infrared lights flash.

CLOSE ON KEYS

The keys jingle as he bends to the ground. His hand discovers something. It gives him pause.

CAMERA MOVES CLOSER

Keys unearths a few Reese's Pieces. He lifts one from the soil, and we can hear the crunch off camera. His flashlight goes out.

FADE IN:

INT. ELLIOTT'S ROOM – DAY

Elliott is lying on the top bunk bed. Mary takes a thermometer out of his mouth. Elliott appears to be desperately ill. She reads the thermometer.

MARY
Okay, you're hot. I'll be back.

She sticks the thermometer back into Elliott's mouth. She leaves the room. Elliott immediately takes the thermometer out of his mouth, swings a lamp closer to him, and takes the heating pad out from under the covers. He holds the thermometer to the light bulb heating it up, and holds the pad to his face making his face hot.

MICHAEL (*OC*)
Mary, can I back the car out?

MARY (*OC*)
Not one foot past the driveway.

Elliott hears her coming back and puts everything back in place.

MARY moves to the closet, opening the doors.

Villains: Adults and Science

I drew upon the *Close Encounters* experience in having no alien villains whatsoever in that film. The alien visitation was to observe and not destroy. The villains in *E.T.* really should be the adults who do not have the same pure understanding that children have about a situation like this.

The adults would be more frightened than the kids and call the police. The police and the government would not understand at all and would want to experiment on the alien, do a vivisection or such.

So the villain in the story would be the adults and the threat would be science.

—Steven Spielberg

INT. CLOSET

Mary enters the closet.

EXT. FRONT OF HOUSE – DAY

Michael backs the car down the driveway, screeching to a noisy stop past the end of the driveway. He pulls back up into the driveway, just past the sidewalk.

INT. ELLIOTT'S ROOM – DAY

Elliott's face expresses panic as Mary shakes out the quilt. Relief — it is only a quilt. (VARIATION: Elliott is seated up, and the panic is expressed as the thermometer falls out of his mouth. He puts it back in his mouth when he sees it is only a quilt. He lies back down.)

Mary moves back to his side with the quilt.

> **SCRIPT NOTES**
> Steven Spielberg suggested the thermometer trick because this was something he did as a kid to get out of school. He says that his mom always knew he was faking but let him stay home anyway.

INT. ELLIOTT'S ROOM – DAY

MARY
You were outside last night waiting for that thing to come back, weren't you? You gonna live if I go to work?

MARY
Okay. No T.V.

Elliott sighs with relief. Sure she has finally left, he gets out of bed and moves into the closet to check on E.T.'s whereabouts.

EXT. FRONT OF HOUSE – DAY

The car is in the driveway where Michael left it. Mary moves toward the car where Gertie is bending down looking at the skid marks Michael made. As her mother approaches her she rises, tattletaling.

MARY
Come on.

GERTIE
Mommy, look what Michael did. This and that and—

MARY
I see them, Gert, and when I catch him, I'll catch him.

She has opened the back door of the car for Gertie, who enters and immediately moves to the front seat.

INT. ELLIOTT'S ROOM – DAY

Elliott moves into the room from out of the closet. E.T. follows him. He has a blanket wrapped around him.

ELLIOTT
Come on. Don't be afraid. It's all right. Come on. Come on. Come on. Come on. Come on.

They stand looking at each other.

ELLIOTT
Do you talk? You know, talk?

E.T. is silent.

ELLIOTT
Me human. Boy. Elliott. Ell-ee-utt Elliott.

Silence. Then E.T. crosses to the table. Elliott follows and begins explaining things to him.

ELLIOTT
Coke, see? We drink it. It's, uh, it's a drink. You know... food. These are toys. These are little men. This is Greedo, and then this is Hammerhead. See. . . this is Walrus Man. And then this is Snaggletooth. And this is Lando Calrissian. See? And this is Boba Fett. And, look, they can even have wars. Look at this. And look, fish. The

Kid Talk

A lot of the kids found wonderful things to say that came from the truth of themselves and that they were able to put into the movie.
—Steven Spielberg

Steven wasn't afraid to let kids be kids and bring something new to the film. He had this table set up in Elliott's bedroom with all this junk on it — *Star Wars* toys and little gadgets and everything. He said, "Okay, you've brought E.T. to your room and now show him what's on your table. Go down the line and introduce everything you can."
—Henry Thomas

fish eat the fish food. And the shark eats the fish. But nobody eats a shark. See, this is Pez. Candy. See, you eat it. You put the candy in here, and then when you lift up the head, the candy comes out, and you can eat it! You want some? Oh. This is a peanut. You eat it. But you can't eat this one, 'cause this is fake. This is money. See? We put the money in the peanut. You see? Bank. You see? And then this is a car. This is what we get around in. You see? Car.

ELLIOTT
Hey! Hey, wait a second! No! You don't eat 'em. Are you hungry? I'm hungry. Stay.

Elliott moves toward the door.

ELLIOTT
Stay. I'll be right here. Okay? I'll be... right here.

> **SCRIPT NOTES**
> Melissa Mathison's favorite scene in the movie is here where Elliott shows E.T. his toys. All this dialogue was ad-libbed by Henry Thomas.

INT. ELLIOTT'S ROOM

Harvey starts to enters as Elliott opens the door.

ELLIOTT
Harv!

Elliott quickly bends down and holds the dog.

ELLIOTT
No bite! No bite! Come on, Harvey.

Elliott takes Harvey out with him and closes the door.

INT. KITCHEN

Elliott at the refrigerator.

ELLIOTT
He'll like this. This.

INT. ELLIOTT'S ROOM

Left to his devices, E.T. wanders to the umbrella stand. E.T. takes an umbrella out, and it springs open. He quickly drops it.

In the closet, a stuffed animal coyote falls over, and we see the umbrella spinning on the bedroom floor.

INT. KITCHEN – DAY

At the moment of E.T.'s fear of the umbrella, we cut to

69

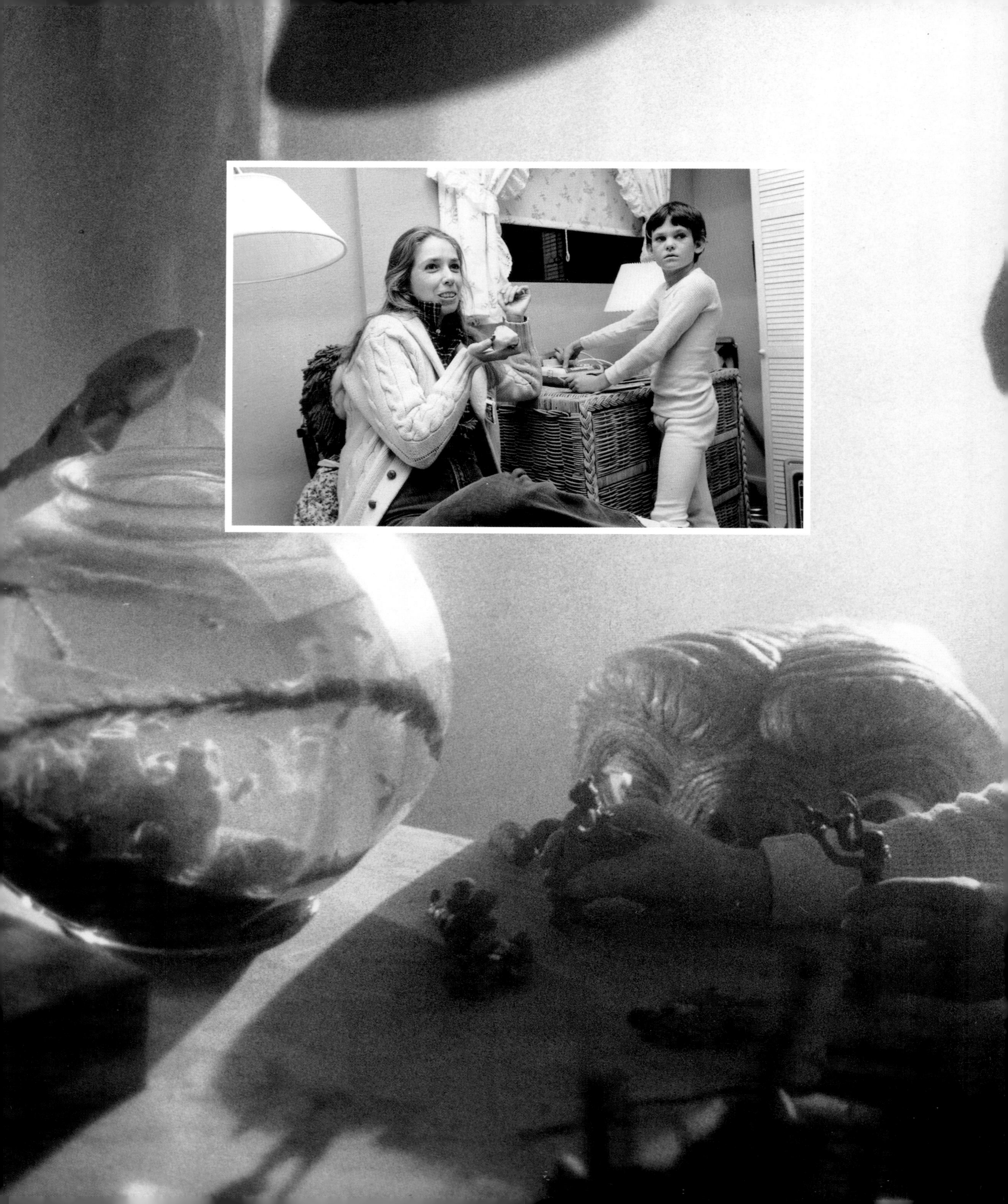

Elliott, standing at the refrigerator. Elliott shrieks and drops a quart of milk and other things he is gathering from the refrigerator.

INT. ELLIOTT'S ROOM – DAY

Elliott moves to the closet.

INT. CLOSET – DAY

Elliott enters still holding the sandwiches and Cokes. He sees a pile of stuffed animals in a corner of the closet.

> **ELLIOTT**
> (*to the pile of stuffed animals*)
> Are you okay?

The animals fall to the floor in foreground of Elliott, revealing E.T. He is shaking.

> **ELLIOTT**
> Too much excitement, huh? You want a Coke?

INT. BATHROOM – DAY

CLOSE: A bathroom scale. We see E.T.'s feet on the scale. The reading is less than forty-five pounds. E.T. steps off.

Elliott is beside him, amazed at the reading.

> **ELLIOTT**
> Thirty-five pounds, thirty-five pounds!!!

E.T. moves to the sink; Elliott follows.

> **ELLIOTT**
> But you're so fat.

They stand at the sink, looking in the mirror. Elliott holds his hand over his own head, then over E.T.'s.

> **ELLIOTT**
> How tall are you? I must be four feet, six inches, you must be around three...

LEFT INSET: *Melissa Mathison and Henry Thomas on the set of Elliott's house. As screenwriter/associate producer, Mathison also helped rehearse the kids.*

Elliott's conversation falls off as E.T.'s neck comes up, making him taller. Elliott, amazed, examines his own neck, as well as E.T.'s.

Elliott moves over to the bathtub. He starts to explain the faucet and water, etc.

ELLIOTT
This is where the water comes from. You see? This is hot, and this is cold. Now, it all comes from a big water tower. It goes through pipes, and sometimes dead bugs, they come through the pipes and land in the bath. But it's real sick. But, anyway, look.

He turns the water on. E.T. has found an opened bottle

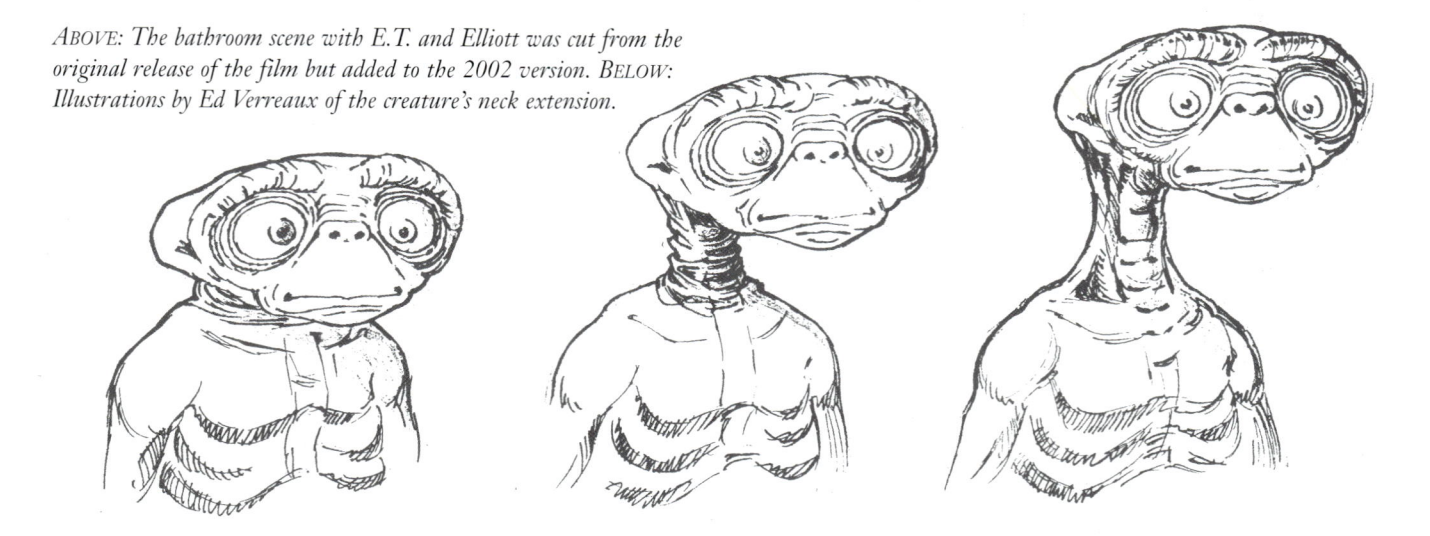

ABOVE: The bathroom scene with E.T. and Elliott was cut from the original release of the film but added to the 2002 version. BELOW: Illustrations by Ed Verreaux of the creature's neck extension.

of perfume. He smells it and sneezes, dropping the bottle into the sink.

Elliott picks up a Coke that is on the tub and moves to E.T. near the sink, still looking in the mirror.

      ELLIOTT
  Are you thirsty? I am.

He opens the Coke, and it squirts all over his face. At that same moment, the telephone in Mary's room rings, surprising them both. Elliott still shocked from the Coke.

      ELLIOTT
  I'll get it.

He moves out of the bathroom.

INT. MARY'S ROOM – DAY

Elliott picks up the phone, and puts the Coke down on the nightstand.

      ELLIOTT
  Hi. Yeah, I'm fine. Sure. Yeah, I still got a
  fever, though. Yeah. Uh-huh.

He moves toward the door and opens it, checking on Harvey who sticks his nose in. Elliott quickly closes the door, keeping Harvey out in the hall.

      ELLIOTT
  Back. I'm fine, Mom. Yeah. Yeah.

He moves toward the nightstand again, trying to get off the phone. In his background, we can see E.T. in the bathroom move from the sink toward the tub. The blanket he is wearing falls off.

      ELLIOTT
  No. Mom, I've gotta get in bed now,
  okay? Good-bye. Mom...Mom, I'm sick.
  Mom, I don't need to go to the doctor!

INT. MARY'S ROOM – DAY

He moves once more toward the door. He is so intent on getting Mary off the phone that he does not see E.T. in his background fall into the tub, which is by now full of water because Elliott forgot to turn it off.

      ELLIOTT
  Mom, I only had a fever of ninety-nine
  today. Okay, and a half. Uh-huh. Yeah,
  Mom. Okay, bye. Mom, I've, I've gotta

BELOW: It's bath time for E.T., helped along by Steven Spielberg.

> ### SCRIPT NOTES
> This bathroom scene was deleted from the original cut of the movie. For the 2002 edition, this entire scene is reinstated. Many of the scenes were digitally enhanced for the new release (see page 174, The Restoration: An E.T. for 2002, for more details on the 2002 release).

throw up. Mom, please. I'm gonna throw up on the phone if...if you don't let me go. Okay, bye. Mom, I've gotta throw up now. Yeah, uh...

He picks up the Coke, pours its contents into the phone, and hangs up.

He moves back toward the bathroom.

INT. BATHROOM – DAY

We can see Elliott from the bathroom. We can also see E.T. under water. Elliott sees E.T. He runs to him, terrified. He pulls him up out of the water.

> **ELLIOTT**
> You could drown in stuff like this.

E.T. pushes Elliott's arm off of him and falls back into the water enjoying it.

> **ELLIOTT**
> Is this your idea of a good time?

INT. KITCHEN – DAY

Michael, wearing his football shoulder pads, enters singing from the playroom. He opens the refrigerator door, takes out a Coke, and continues singing as he exits the kitchen.

> **SCRIPT NOTES**
> The scenes of Elliott giving E.T. a bath were cut from the original 1982 release, and restored to the 2002 release.

INT. ELLIOTT'S ROOM – DAY

Elliott moves to the door of his room and opens it, admitting Michael. He steps back; Michael stays in the doorway.

> **ELLIOTT**
> Mike, Mike, come in.

> **MICHAEL**
> How you feelin', faker?

> **ELLIOTT**
> I'm feeling fine. Look, I've got something really important to tell you.

> **MICHAEL**
> You know what? Tyler said he got 69,000 on Asteroids yesterday. But he pulled the plug.

                    ELLIOTT
Look, remember the goblin?

                    MICHAEL
You're so lame, Elliott.

                    ELLIOTT
Come on, Michael, he came back.

                    MICHAEL
He came back? He came back?!
Oh, my God!

Michael pretends something is pulling his head out the door. His head reenters.

                    ELLIOTT
One thing!

                    ELLIOTT
I have absolute power. Say it. Say it.

                    MICHAEL
What have you got?

                    MICHAEL
Is it the coyote?

Elliott crosses to Michael, closes the door, and leads him to the center of the room, as he says:

                    ELLIOTT
No. Look. Okay, now…swear it. The most excellent promise you can make. Swear as my only brother, on our lives—

                    MICHAEL
Okay, don't get so heavy. I swear.

                    ELLIOTT
Okay, um, stand over there, and, um, you'd better take off your shoulder pads.

He marches Michael over near the table, turning him so he can't see the closet door.

                    MICHAEL
What?!

                    ELLIOTT
You might scare him. And, um, close your eyes.

(*as he enters the closet*)

                    MICHAEL
Don't push it, Elliott.

                    ELLIOTT
I'm not comin' out there until your eyes are closed.

                    MICHAEL
Okay, they're closed. Mom is gonna kill you.

He moves toward the closet. Michael removes his shoulder pads.

SCRIPT NOTES
The shot of Michael coming home from school was done after the end of principal photography with a stand-in for Robert Macnaughton.

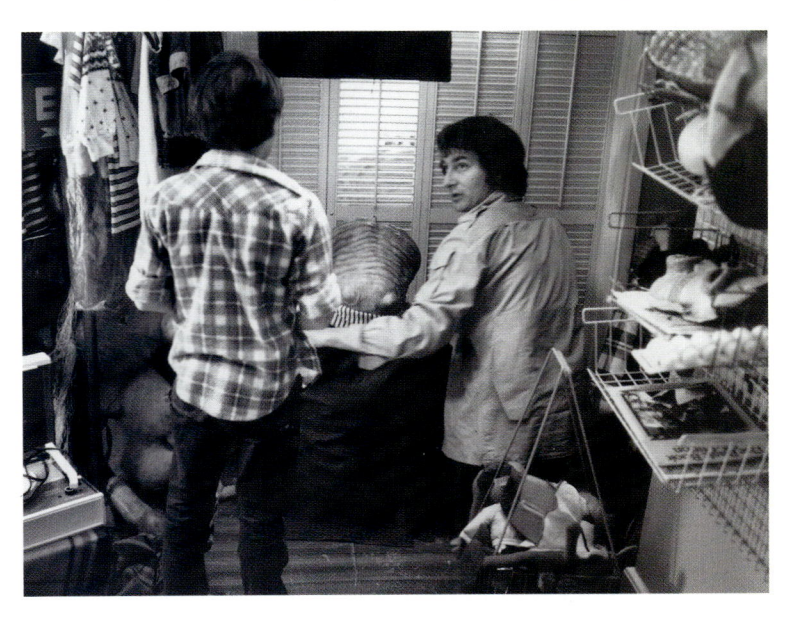

ABOVE: Steven Spielberg and Henry Thomas rehearsing on set.

75

> **SCRIPT NOTES**
>
> A stained glass window was added to the closet to indicate whether it was night or day. The closet, and other interior sets (Elliott's bedroom, the long hallway, Gertie's room and another closet) were all constructed on ten-inch elevated floors so that the cables for E.T. would not be in the way.

ELLIOTT
Okay, um, swear it one more time. I have absolute—

MICHAEL
You have absolute power. Yes.

ELLIOTT and E.T. step out of the closet. Elliott puts his head on E.T.'s shoulder, and nods to the creature reassuringly. He looks to his brother again.

Michael slowly turns to look at what is behind him. He sees E.T. He is stunned. Suddenly the door flies open, and Gertie comes running in.

GERTIE
Elliott, look what I made for you.

She sees E.T. and starts to scream. E.T. screams. Elliott screams.

Then Michael screams and backs into the shelves on the wall, and they come tumbling down.

Elliott catches himself and yells.

ELLIOTT
Stop! Stop!

He moves quickly to Gertie, putting his hand over her mouth, and moves her away from E.T. Michael steps in near them. They hear their mother OC.

MARY
Kids, I'm home! Guys?! Is anybody up there?!

ELLIOTT
Get in the closet. Fast.

INT. CLOSET – DAY   109

Gertie enters closet, followed by Michael, and then E.T. Gertie starts to scream again. Michael puts his hand over her mouth again. The door is closed.

INT. ELLIOTT'S ROOM – DAY

Elliott moves quickly toward the table near the door, and picks up the toy shark and pretends to play with it. Mary enters.

MARY
Anybody home?! Hi, honey, you fee— What happened in here?

She looks around, spotting the shelves on the floor and the rest of the mess. Amazed.

ELLIOTT
Oh. You mean my room.

MARY
(*looking around stunned*)
This is no room. This is an accident.

ELLIOTT
I was, um, reorganizing.

MARY
I can see that. Put those shelves back on the wall, Elliott.

INT. CLOSET – DAY

Michael holds hand over Gertie's mouth, as they stare at E.T.

Mary heads toward the closet, picking up some clothes off a chair and moves toward Elliott. Mike and Gertie watch through the louvred door.

MARY
Let's get the toys off the floor. Make your bed, since you're not using it. Well, you're feeling better, I see. You guys, keep an eye on Gertie for me while I take a shower?

INT. ELLIOTT'S ROOM – DAY

Elliott nods. She kisses his forehead.

            ELLIOTT
Absolutely.

            ELLIOTT
Bye, Mom.

Mary leaves the room, and Elliott sighs relief, drops the shark on the floor, and walks toward the closet.

INT. CLOSET – DAY

Elliott enters, and moves toward E.T. Michael still has his hand over Gertie's mouth.

            MICHAEL
Elliott ——

            ELLIOTT
(*staring at E.T.*)
I'm keeping him.

            GERTIE
(*her voice muffled because of Michael's hand*)
What is it?

            ELLIOTT
He won't hurt you, Gertie. He won't hurt you, Gertie.

            ELLIOTT
We're not gonna hurt you.

Michael removes his hand from her mouth as she begins to move toward Elliott and E.T. Michael moves in too.

            GERTIE
Is he a boy or a girl?

She kneels before E.T.

            ELLIOTT
He's a boy.

            GERTIE
Was he wearing any clothes?

            ELLIOTT
(*kneeling*)
No. But, look, you can't tell. Not even Mom.

            GERTIE
Why not?

            ELLIOTT
Because, um, grown-ups can't see him. Only little kids can see him.

Gertie looks unbelievingly at Elliott.

            GERTIE
Gimme a break.

            ELLIOTT
Well, do you know what's going to happen if you do tell?

He takes the doll she is holding from her and tosses it to Michael.

            ELLIOTT
Do it, Mike. We have to.

Michael takes Gertie's doll, and pretends he is wrenching its arm off.

            MICHAEL
(*in Mr. Bill voice*)
Oh, no, please, no! Don't make me! Please! Somebody help me! Help me!

Gertie runs to him, defending her doll. Gertie's eyes fill with terror.

            MICHAEL
Nooo!

E.T. watches.

Michael gives her the doll back.

SCRIPT NOTES

Originally, Elliott and Michael threatened Gertie's cat, but Steven Spielberg changed it to her doll.

The Kids on Set

I hung out with Robert. I was like the little brother trying to follow the guy around which worked because that was the character in the beginning. Until I find the alien, nobody really wanted to be my friend.
—Henry Thomas

The thing with Drew worked out perfectly because that was supposed to be the relationship in the movie, you know, me torturing her doll or whatever. That's how we treated her. I'm very guilty about it.
—Robert Macnaughton

We did have a lot of fun.
—Drew Barrymore

One of my jobs as associate producer and writer was to rehearse with the kids. It was great fun. They would catch me on misspellings or give me a bad time about some piece of dialogue, or come up with something they thought was better. I finally had to kind of show them who was boss and tell them that I was the writer, they were the kids and they had to do what I said.
—Melissa Mathison

LEFT: *The cast of kids and some of their stand-ins. Bottom right is Matthew De Meritt, the boy who is legless and appeared inside the E.T. costume.* BELOW: *The kids spent several hours a day with a teacher attending to their schoolwork.*

                    ELLIOTT
(to Gertie)
You promise?

                    GERTIE
Yes.

                    ELLIOTT
(to Michael) Do you promise?

They move toward E.T. again, kneeling before him.

EXT. OVERLOOK

Keys and his men with Geiger counters.

MARY'S ROOM

She moves into her bedroom and waters a plant in a corner, then moves back near the entrance to water another plant. Gertie comes out of her room in background of Mary. Mary sees her. Gertie is pulling a wagon.

                    MARY
What are you doing, Gert?

                    GERTIE
I'm going to play in Elliott's room.

                    MARY
Okay. Don't let him torture you.

                    GERTIE
I won't, Mary.

Mary moves out of the room.

GERTIE pauses, puts down the handle of her wagon, lifts the very unhappy geranium, and puts it into her wagon. Harvey is wandering around and moves to Elliott's door as Gertie approaches the door, too. She knocks three times.

INT. ELLIOTT'S ROOM – NIGHT

Michael lets Gertie in. Harvey butts his way in behind her. E.T. stands near a table with a huge plate of food before him. He is munching on watermelon and celery at the moment. Elliott across the table from him, looks curiously on.

Michael tries to hurry Gertie along.

                    MICHAEL
Come on. Come on. Hurry up.

                    GERTIE
Don't be so pushy, pushy.

With her wagon, she moves beside Elliott, and starts to unload it. She puts the geranium on the table in front of E.T.

                    GERTIE
A plant for you.

Gertie talks throughout.

                    MICHAEL
(talking over her)
Maybe he's some animal that wasn't supposed to live. You know, like those rabbits we saw that time.

                    ELLIOTT
Don't be lame.

                    GERTIE
(as she puts the Play-Doh on the table)
I brought you some clay. Green, orange, red.

                    MICHAEL
It could be a monkey, or, or an orangutan or something.

                    ELLIOTT
A bald monkey?

                    GERTIE
Is he a pig? He sure eats like one.

SCRIPT NOTES

The shot of Gertie picking up the flower pot was done after the end of principal photography. It was Spielberg's idea to have E.T. make the plant come back to life. He suggested that, perhaps on E.T.'s planet, the creature communicates with plants.

GERTIE
(*to E.T.*) You could make faces, and make them mean and happy, and make them get sharp teeth and bite you.

Michael moves to the nightstand beside Elliott's bed, finds the atlas, and moves next to Elliott with it. Elliott quickly finds a map of the United States. He points.

ELLIOTT
We are here.

GERTIE
And you can make 'em have their head cut off.

ELLIOTT
We're here.

MICHAEL
(*remembering the globe on Elliott's desk*)
No, use this.
(*he hands Elliott the globe*)

Elliott puts the atlas down, sets the globe atop it, and points once again to the United States.

ELLIOTT
Okay, we're here. We are here. Where are you from?

E.T. looks at the globe. He points to the window. Gertie looks under the table at his feet.

GERTIE
I don't like his feet.

ELLIOTT
They're only feet, you little twerp. (*to Michael*) Here. (*to Gertie and Michael*) He's trying to tell us something.

Elliott hands the globe to Michael, and opens the atlas once again. As he rifles through the pages, E.T. extends his hand, stopping him at a page which is a map of the universe.

80

Elliott points to the globe and to the planet Earth in the drawing.

                ELLIOTT
    Earth. Home. Home. Home.

E.T. starts picking up the clay balls Gertie has placed on the table. He starts to roll them, then begins placing them on the solar system. The table begins to shake. Elliott shivers—one of the "cosmic" shivers that run up your spine.

                ELLIOTT
    What's he doing?

                GERTIE
    What's happening?

The balls lift off the book. They rise into the air above the children's heads and they begin to spin, to orbit, really, five of them around the one larger "sun" ball. Harvey looks in amazement at what he sees.

                MICHAEL
    Elliott?

The CHILDREN shock, horror, and realization on their faces.

                ELLIOTT
    Oh no.

As they stare, the balls suddenly fall. Elliott starts. Quickly he moves in the direction of the bedroom window. Michael follows.

Harvey's ears perk up, and he looks in the direction of the window.

Elliott shivers, his face reflecting E.T.'s fear. Michael stands behind him.

                MICHAEL
    Elliott, what is it?

                ELLIOTT
    I don't know. Something scary.

We see E.T.'s hand enter to touch Elliott's shoulder. Elliott just continues to stare out the window.

EXT. BACK YARD

Elliott runs across the backyard, past swings, to brick wall.

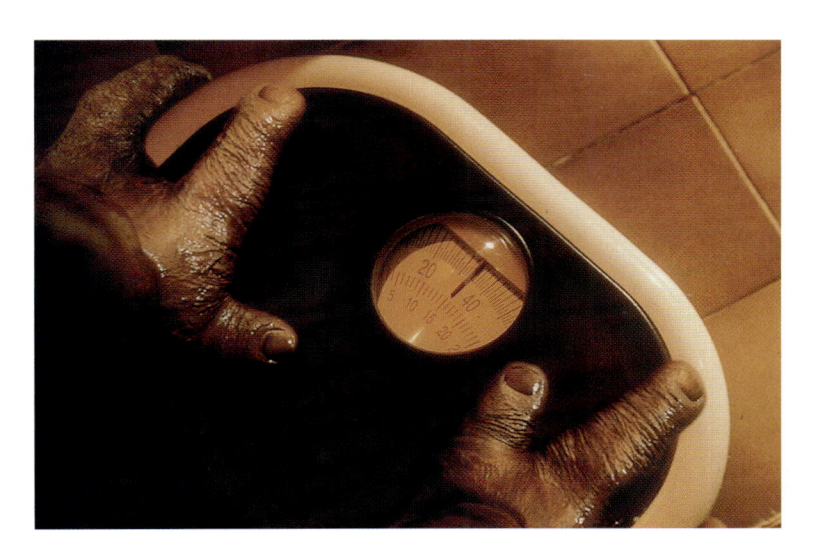

E.T.'s Ugly Feet

Melissa did something that no one's ever done for me on a movie that I directed before or even since. She put every day's work on cards. She put the entire script of that day, not the whole week, on little three by five cards. She included the dialogue and the stage directions. These cards gave me amazing confidence.

Rather than going through the unwieldy script which is full of notes, I had these little cards and I was kind of liberated and unencumbered. I could walk around with these cards in my pocket, pull them out and say, okay, this is what I'm shooting right now. The cards somehow gave me the freedom to go to the kids and say, "We'll do these lines, but let's make it up at the same time. What would you say if this really happened to you?"

I continued to try to get the kids to put their own lines in the movie. For example, when Gertie looks down and says, "I don't like his feet," that's Drew's line.
                —STEVEN SPIELBERG

ABOVE: E.T. steps on the scale.

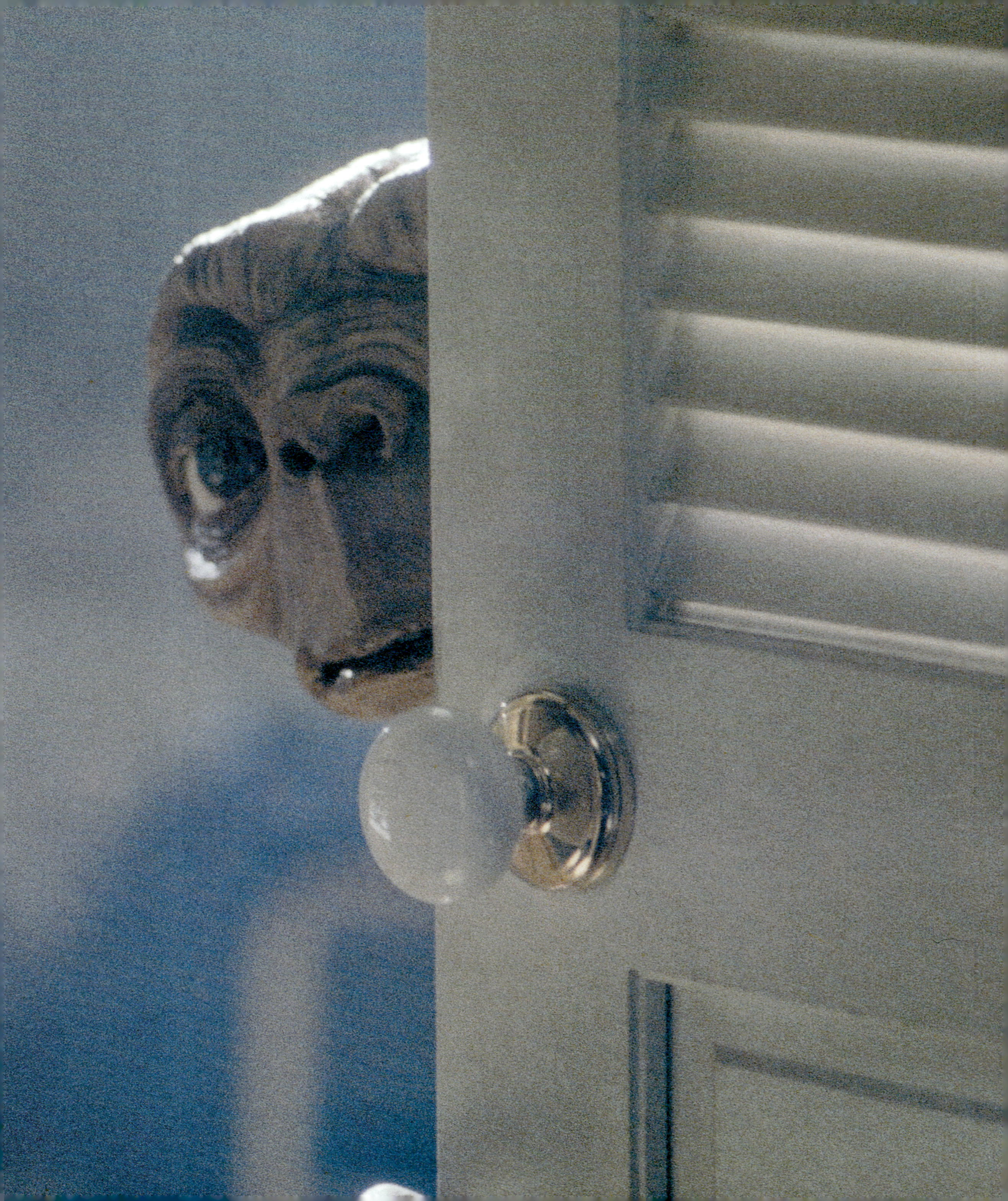

Elliott runs up the steps. The red gate light is on. Hears the sound of keys.

ELLIOTT stands at the gate, illuminated by the red light. He can hear the sound of keys and the steady ticking of a Geiger counter.

INT. THE CLOSET – NIGHT

CAMERA CONTINUING TO MOVE into the closet, past the barricades of toys, etc., and REVEALS E.T. sitting in his living area, looking through one of Gertie's ABC books. He looks up, and his attention is drawn to the geranium, now placed on a box beside him. E.T. stares at the flower.

THE FLOWER

Before our eyes, the flower turns on its stem. As it faces E.T., it straightens. In a burst of life, its tight buds begin to open, suddenly blooming, bursting forth in brilliant flowers. E.T. looks back at his book.

EXT. ELLIOTT'S NEIGHBORHOOD – DAY

Elliott wheels his bicycle along, walking with Michael.

MICHAEL
Did you explain school to him?

ELLIOTT
How do you explain school to higher intelligence?

MICHAEL
Maybe he's not that smart. Maybe he's like a worker bee, who only knows how to push buttons or something.

ELLIOTT
He is, too, smart.

MICHAEL
Okay, I just hope we don't wake up on Mars or somethin', surrounded by millions of little squashy guys.

EXT. STREET CORNER – DAY

They have reached the corner bus stop. Children of all ages are grouped together on four different corners. As Elliott and Michael reach the corner, Tyler yells out.

PRETTY GIRL
Hi, Elliott.

TYLER
Hey, Elliott, where's your goblin?

MICHAEL
Shut up.

STEVE
Did he come back?

GREG
Well, did he?

ELLIOTT
Yeah, he came back. But he's not a goblin. He's a spaceman.

                    GREG, TYLER, & STEVE
Ooooh!

                              STEVE
That's an extraterrestrial.

                              TYLER
Where's he from? Uranus? Get it?
Your anus?

                              GREG
He doesn't get it, Ty.

                              TYLER
Get it? Your anus?

                              GREG
He doesn't get it.

                             ELLIOTT
(*to Tyler*) You're so immature.

                              GREG
And you're such a cintus suprimus.

                             ELLIOTT
Zero charisma.

                              GREG
Cintus suprimus.

                             ELLIOTT
Zero charisma!

The bus has arrived just behind them at this point, and the older boys start to walk to it to enter, but Greg enroute continues with his taunting of Elliott.

                              GREG
Cintus suprimus.

                             ELLIOTT
Shut up, Greg!

                              GREG
Cintus suprimus.

                          PRETTY GIRL
Hi, Elliott.

                             ELLIOTT
(*getting on his bike driving around the bus*)
(*he shouts*)
Zero charisma!

                              GREG
You wimp.

INT. BUS – DAY

Michael sits very concerned, pensive, as the bus moves along.

INT. FRONT DOOR – DAY

Mary comes running down the steps, Gertie stands looking up. She shoos Gertie out the door.

                              MARY
Let's go. Come on, get in the car. We're gonna be late.

Gertie exits; Mary hears an odd sound coming from upstairs. She pauses, then climbs the stairs.

INT. CLOSET – ELLIOTT'S ROOM – DAY

Mary's figure appears through the louvred, doors of the closet. She opens the doors, looks around. E.T. is sitting among the stuffed animals. She does not notice it. She closes the doors again, and we see her exit.

INT. SCIENCE LAB – DAY

> **TEACHER**
> Okay, boys and girls, today we will be doing the actual frog dissection for which we've been preparing, and you will find many similarities.

He steps back as he passes Elliott's desk and looks at the scribbled sheet. Elliott looks on. He turns it over, and replaces it on Elliott's desk.

Elliott looks over his shoulder at a Pretty Girl sitting in the next row behind him, the teacher now at the front of the room and still rambling on and on.

> **TEACHER**
> As you get into the dissection, you will discover that the anatomy...

INT. UPSTAIRS HALLWAY – DAY

E.T. sticks his hand out of Elliott's bedroom door, that now bears the sign reading "DO NOT ENTER." The house is quiet. Only Harvey is home, and he rises from his post outside Elliott's door, moves to E.T., and starts to kiss him.

SCRIPT NOTES

Pat Bilon was in the E.T. suit for the scene where Harvey the dog licks E.T. Bilon was sprayed with liquid beef to motivate the dog but it worked a little too well. The dog got carried away and jumped on E.T.

An early idea for this scene was that E.T. would be made of subatomic particles that can move through solid matters. When he is drunk, he would, for instance, go right through a chair. The concept proved far too complicated and was abandoned.

INT. SCIENCE LAB – DAY

> **TEACHER**
> The scalpel is very sharp. Use discretion when you are cutting. There will be very little blood. There may be a few body fluids.

INT. KITCHEN – DAY

An empty kitchen. E.T. enters from the living room.

E.T. Eats

I made the creature a botanist vegetarian who never eats meat, only junk food, vegetables, and Coors. E.T. comes from a very wet humid planet with probably twice the gravitational pull of the earth.
—STEVEN SPIELBERG

Harvey appears next to him. As E.T. moves into the kitchen, Harvey continually walks in front of him, licking him, etc.

E.T. moves to the refrigerator, and extends his hand to open the door.

The door opens.

He posts himself in front of the opened refrigerator, examining its contents. He takes a carton of potato salad from one of the shelves and manages to get the lid off.

He brings it to his mouth and tastes it with his tongue.

Harvey intermittently barks at him. He tosses the potato salad to Harvey.

Harvey eats the potato salad.

E.T. continues looking in the refrigerator. He spots a can of beer. He takes it out and examines it, finally finds the pop-top and opens it.

He guzzles it down.

INT. SCIENCE LAB – DAY

Suddenly Elliott lets out a burp. The other students look on. The boy sitting behind him afraid that someone will think him guilty, points to Elliott. The children, including the Pretty Girl, look on. Elliott is embarrassed, but recovers quickly.

INT. KITCHEN

E.T. moves over toward the stove and bumps into a cabinet. He turns around and walks once more into a cabinet. He turns around and walks toward the table, but before he reaches it, he topples forward.

INT. CLASSROOM – DAY

Elliott is obviously drunk as he starts to slide down in his seat. Pretty soon he has reached the floor under his desk.

The Pretty Girl who has been looking at the teacher, turns to look at Elliott, as do the other children. They are amazed. One boy mutters "you jerk."

INT. PLAYROOM – DAY

E.T. pops another beer top.

INT. CLASSROOM – DAY

Elliott, with much difficulty, pulls himself back up into his seat.

INT. PLAYROOM – DAY

E.T. pours the contents down the hatch.

INT. CLASSROOM – DAY

Elliott looks at Pretty Girl.

INT. PLAYROOM – DAY

Gertie's Speak & Spell is lying on the coffee table. E.T. presses a button on the toy. The game speaks to him.

          SPEAK & SPELL VOICE
    X-W-V-U-A-F-P

          MALE VOICE (*over toy speaker*)
    That is incorrect. The correct spelling of "nuisance" is N-U-I-S-A-N-C-E.

The T.V. remote control is lying beside the Speak & Spell. E.T., holding a beer in his right hand, picks it up with his left hand and starts pressing buttons.

The T.V. comes on.

INSERT cartoon.

E.T. reacts and screams and throws a beer can at it.

BACK TO E.T.

He presses another button.

INSERT

A spaceship program comes on.

BACK TO E.T.

E.T. watches with interest.

INT. CLASSROOM – DAY

The teacher walks around room dropping cotton balls into jars with frogs in them.

          TEACHER
    Now, class, these are the cotton balls with
    the chloroform. And, as soon as I get
    them all in, be sure and put the lid on
    right away. Now, that's it. That will start
    them going to sleep. And they won't feel

Concept Meeting

One day all the kids go to school and E.T. is totally alone in the house. The house is his for the first time. It will be a whole sequence where he discovers things for the first time.... I would love to see him discovering things that the kids don't see him discover. You hear thump, bump, crash so the mother comes running out and E.T. hides and becomes one of the stuffed animals. The mother looks around and does not see him.

    —STEVEN SPIELBERG, AS QUOTED FROM
    THE TRANSCRIPT OF A CONCEPT MEETING
    WITH MELISSA MATHISON, OCTOBER 28, 1980

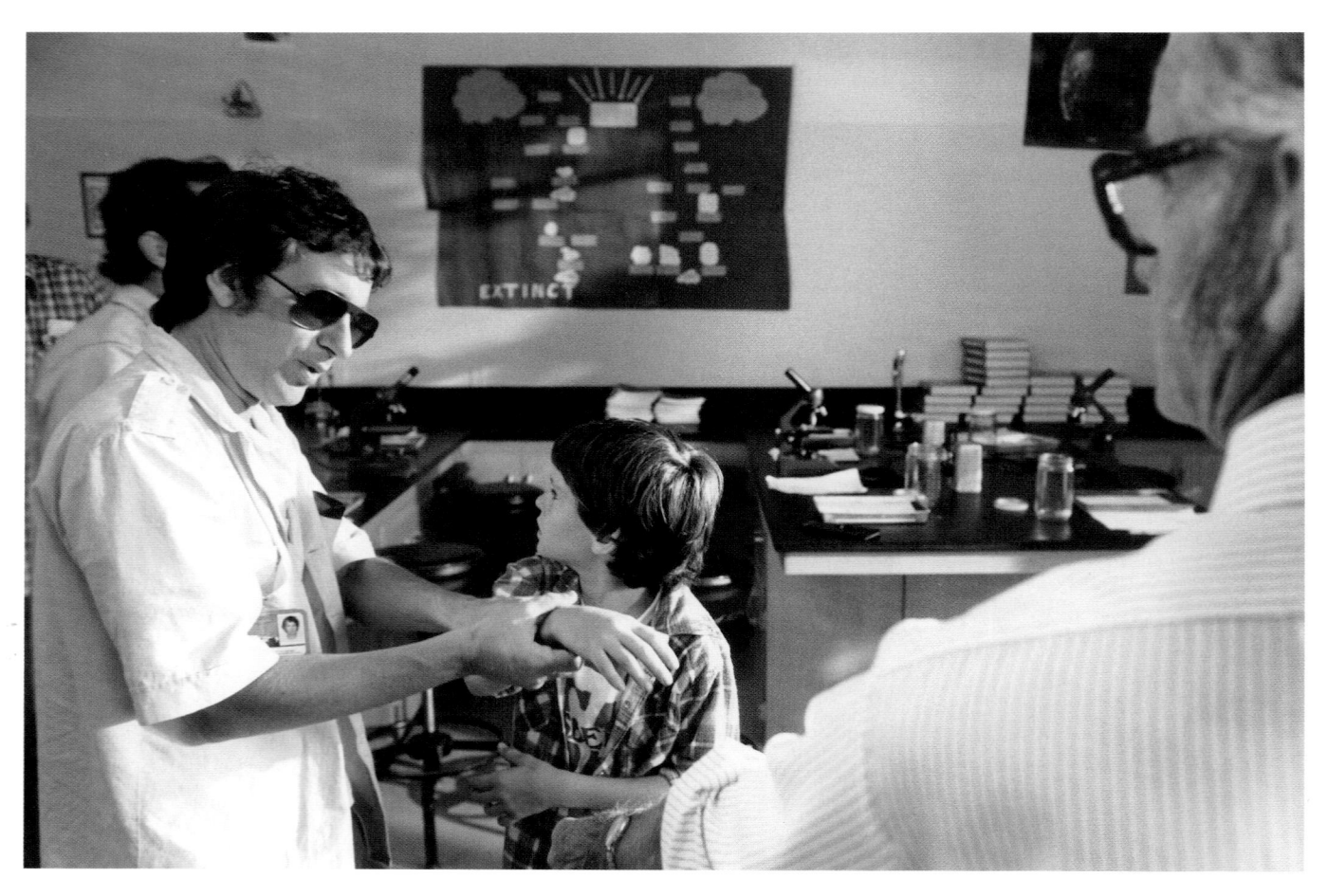

ABOVE: Steven Spielberg rehearses with Henry Thomas for the science class scene where Elliott saves the frogs from dissection.

anything. They won't be hurt. It will take a little while. If you don't want to watch them, you don't have to.

ELLIOTT (*to frogs*)
Say hi. Can you talk? Can you say hi?

INT. KITCHEN

E.T. picks himself up, looking very drunk, to the table.

He spots a newspaper cartoon beside him, and pulls it in front of him. He glances at it.

It is a Buck Rogers cartoon.

This gives him an idea. He looks toward the playroom, spotting things.

INSERT – THE TELEVISION

A telephone commercial is on the T.V. at the moment.

E.T. looks to the Speak & Spell and remote control on the coffee table.

He looks back to the cartoon.

E.T. is on his feet, holding the cartoon. He spins around, spotting items.

INT. CLASSROOM – DAY

ELLIOTT is looking into his jar sympathetically, when suddenly he has the same, clear "thought" that E.T. had.

ELLIOTT (*to himself*)
Save him.

ELLIOTT looks down at the frog, and in an instant, pulls the top from the jar, reaches in, and turns the jar upside down, freeing the frog. The Pretty Girl, next to ELLIOTT, stares at him.

ELLIOTT
Run for your life! Back to the river! Back to the forest! Run!

E.T.'s Makeup

A makeup artist was in charge of spraying E.T. to keep him looking fresh. One day, the artist told E.T. to turn his head and the operator complied, scaring the artist.

ABOVE: E.T. gets a touch-up on set during filming.

The E.T. Family

The chemistry between all of us was so real that we really did feel like a family. We knew we were doing something special and important, but there wasn't any pressure and we made the experience as fun as possible. When the film came out, it seemed it was hitting people the same way it had hit all of us when we were making it. There was a perfect connection between what had happened on the set and what was happening with the audience watching the film. At the time the film came out, I had never been outside California. But when I traveled to the different countries for the foreign releases of *E.T.*, my whole perception of the world changed. I found out how big it was and how different people were. It was really cool to see my character dubbed and speaking all those different languages. But most of all, it seemed everyone was having a profound and heartfelt experience watching the film. I think *E.T.* really taught me that there are no boundaries in friendship. It opened me up as a person, and made me who I am today.
—Drew Barrymore

I didn't have children back in the early eighties and suddenly, on set, I was becoming a father. Every single day, I felt like I was a father to Drew, Henry, and Robert. It felt good. I think I have a big family now because it felt pretty good having three kids back then.
—Steven Spielberg

I had lived in communes for a dozen years before coming to the set of *E.T.* and the set was exactly that: a commune. There were lots of kids running around, everybody was family, everyone knew each other, and everyone was working. I loved the character I played in the film because Steven allowed him to be compassionate and sensitive. He was saying, you can still keep the best part of being a child when you grow up. The 80s were a turbulent time. And I always felt that one of the things that made people love this film was if two or three people as far apart as E.T. and those children could bridge a gap and communicate and love each other, then there was no two people on earth that were that far apart. And it just seems to me that in a time like today that's fraught with cultural misunderstandings and danger and hatred, that this message is being replayed.
—Peter Coyote

Elliott rapidly moves to the Pretty Girl and takes her frog jar, releases the frogs, turns around to the table behind him, jumps over it, and reaching the other side, he again releases the frogs.

ELLIOTT
I want to save you! Let's get outta here!

He moves to the next table and the boy he had made faces at earlier is there, and they struggle as ELLIOTT tries to take his jar to release the frog.

ELLIOTT
Get out! I gotta let him go!

The teacher steps in, pulling ELLIOTT away.

ELLIOTT trying to break away from him, retorts.

ELLIOTT
You've gotta save him!

He pulls away and moves to another table.

INT. KITCHEN

E.T. moves back to the coffee table. He picks up the Speak & Spell, and then something on the television attracts his attention.

INSERT

T.V. cuts to soppy love scene from old movie, *The Quiet Man*.

E.T. watches engrossed.

INT. CLASSROOM – DAY

The class is in total turmoil. One girl stands transfixed in this midst, holding a frog in each hand.

ELLIOTT moves about as if in a daze. He has a thought from E.T.

The Pretty Girl is standing on a chair, as the rest of the class is on their knees trying to pick up frogs freed when the glass cage apparently overturned, which lies on the floor behind them.

> **SCRIPT NOTES**
> The movie playing on the family television is *The Quiet Man*. The same sound from the movie insert is used when Elliott kisses the girl.

INSERT

The hero grabs the heroine, pulls her head back, and kisses her.

INT. CLASSROOM – DAY

A boy is seen crawling along the floor looking for frogs. The Pretty Girl enters and starts for the exit door. Just as she arrives, ELLIOTT grabs her arm and spins her around. The boy ELLIOTT had made the faces at is crawling around on the floor and comes between ELLIOTT and Pretty Girl's feet. ELLIOTT steps up on his back, lowering him to floor, but elevating ELLIOTT up to Pretty Girl's height. ELLIOTT kisses her.

Frogs & Kissing the Girl

I remember sitting down and reading the script for the first time and thinking, "Okay, spaceship, cool. Alien, cool. Kissing a girl? No way. Do I have to do this?"
—HENRY THOMAS

As a kid, I set free about five of the frogs we were supposed to dissect in science class. I let them go and never got caught. So, what the heck, I put it in the movie.
   The toughest thing Henry had to do was kiss the girl on the first day of shooting. He really did not want to do it. In the school scene he stands on top of his classmate to be tall enough to kiss the girl right smack on the lips. He did not want to do this. He didn't want to be a movie actor. At that moment, I saw him giving up his entire career.
—STEVEN SPIELBERG

RIGHT: The "Pretty Girl" Elliott kisses is Erika Eleniak, who eventually starred on Baywatch.

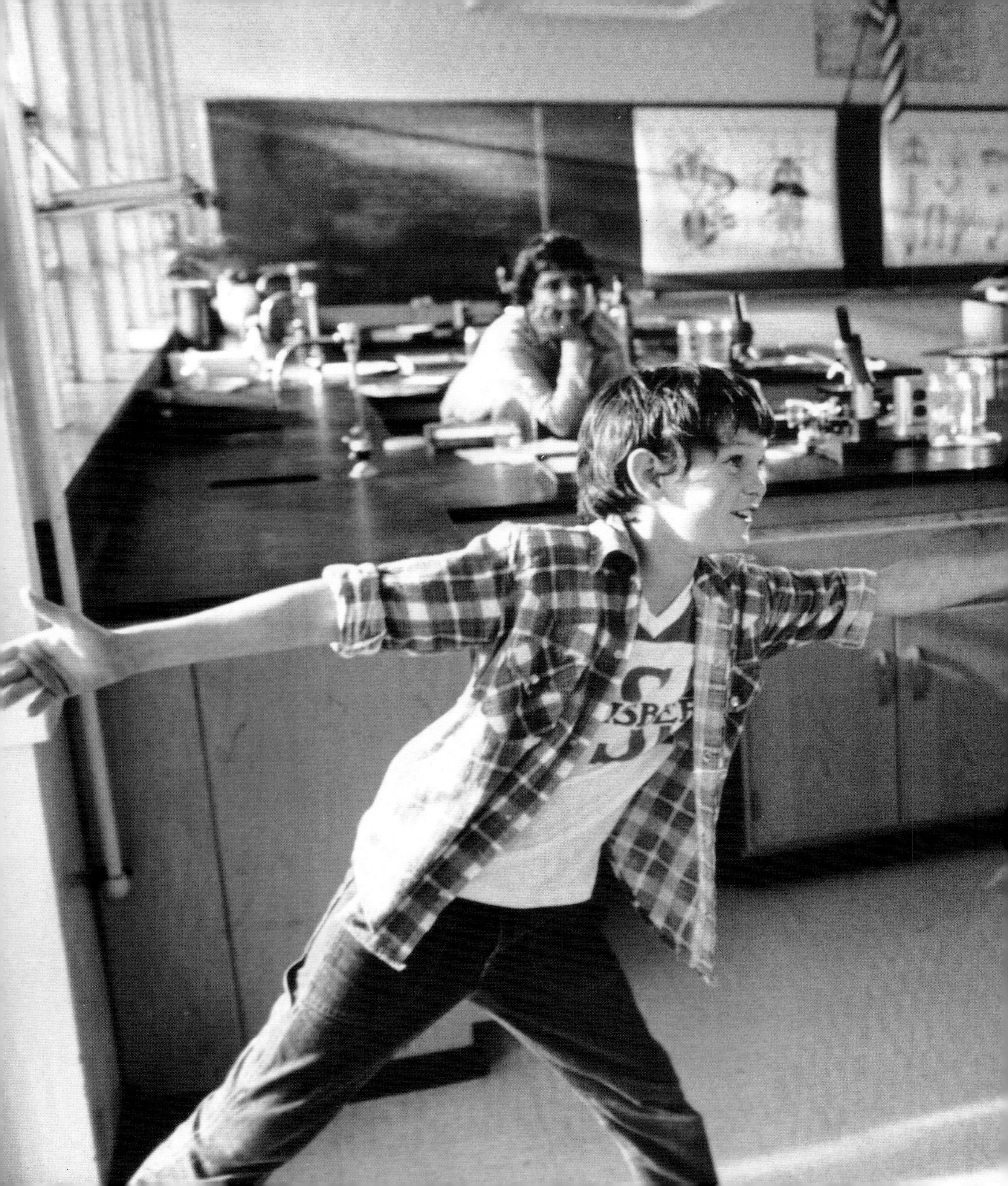

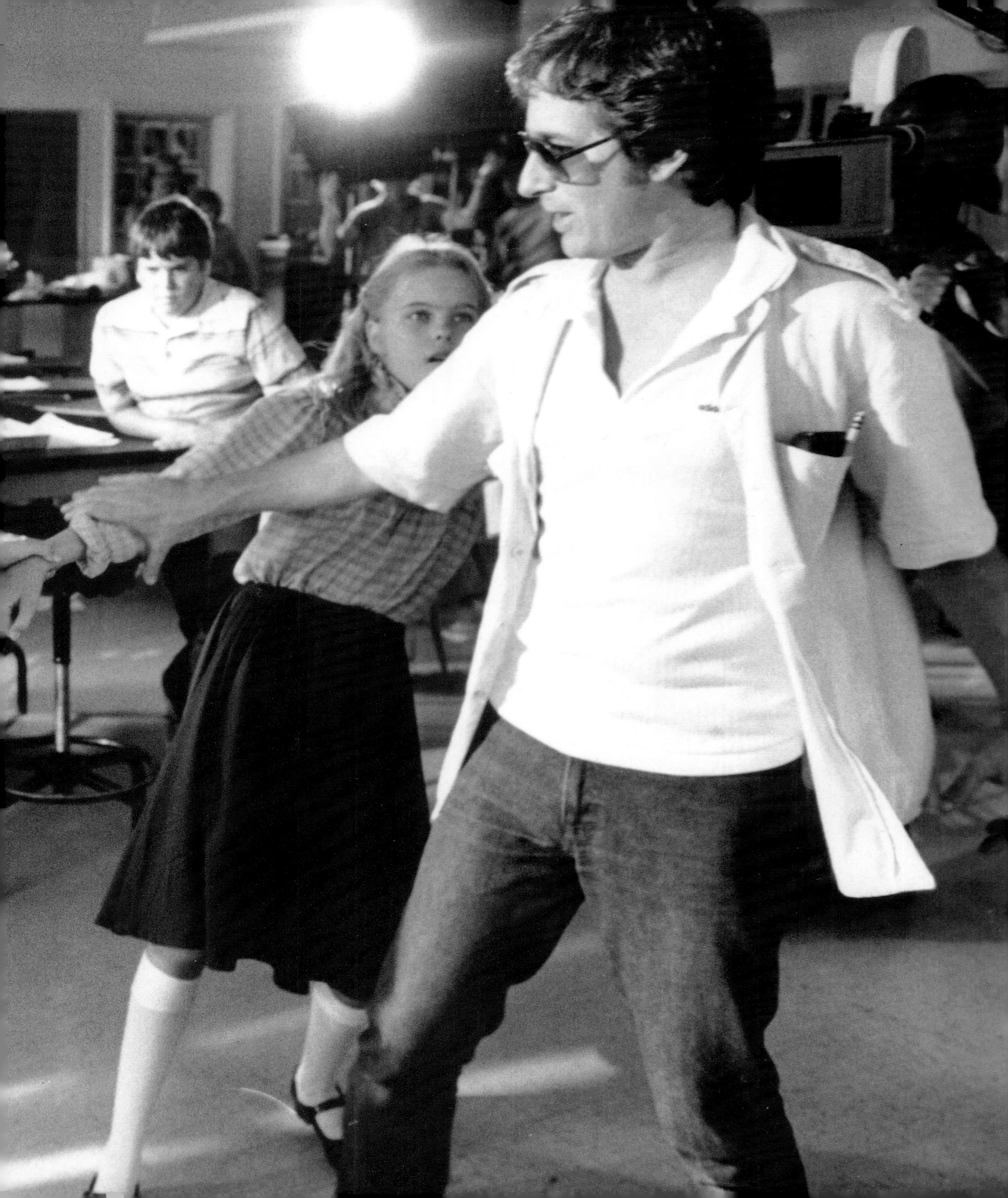

The Nurse

I had this little part in the movie where I'm a nurse. Elliott is acting so berserko in class that they send him down to the school nurse.

They dressed me in this nurse's outfit. I remember there was a big discussion about whether my hair should be flat or sticking out. They chose sticking out.

Luckily, I was only a silhouette. I didn't have to talk but I did have to grab Elliott by the arm. At one point Henry complained that I was grabbing him too hard.

Thank goodness, the scene was cut from the movie.

—Melissa Mathison

Suddenly two arms reach out and grab ELLIOTT by the scruff of the neck. It is the teacher. Pretty Girl looks on in a state of ecstasy, as the teacher holding ELLIOTT's arm marches him away.

EXT. CLASSROOM WINDOWS

We see children move to windows, dropping frogs out.

AREA NEAR TELEVISION

We see a blanket laden with the blender and other items, Speak & Spell, remote, etc., being pulled behind the T.V.

We hear a door opening off camera, and Harvey comes leaping out and disappears.

ANGLE ON MARY as she enters, followed by Gertie. She is loaded down with bags of groceries and dry cleaning. She cannot see E.T. standing between the playroom and the kitchen.

INT. KITCHEN – DAY

Mary puts the dry cleaning down on the table, along with her sweater, and moves to the refrigerator. Gertie has moved just before her, seeing E.T. Mary does not see him.

GERTIE
Here he is.

MARY
Here's who?

She opens the refrigerator door, knocking E.T. down.

GERTIE
The man from the moon, but I think you've killed him already.

Mary has kneeled down, putting the bags on the floor. She picks one up and starts across the room.

MARY
Honey, just as soon as I unload this stuff, okay?

TOP LEFT: Steven Spielberg and Melissa Mathison who is in costume as the school nurse. Her cameo was cut from the film. LEFT: Steven Spielberg and Henry Thomas in a scene where Elliott draws on the walls. This scene was cut from the original release.

Gertie helps E.T. up.

Gertie moves to the other side of the refrigerator, as Mary comes back, putting a carton of tomatoes away. E.T. crosses through the kitchen; Mary does not see him.

GERTIE
I want you to meet somebody.

MARY
Boy, this stuff has gone up so much in one week.

GERTIE
I want you to meet somebody.

MARY
Okay, honey, as soon as I get finished putting all this stuff away. All right?

We see E.T.'s hands pick up a coffee can from the table in the foreground as this conversation takes place. He moves across the room, entering the playroom as Mary moves to the table, not seeing him.

INT. PLAYROOM – DAY

Gertie enters the playroom. E.T. is behind the T.V. set.

GERTIE
B.

INT. KITCHEN – DAY

The phone rings. Mary moves to it and kicks an empty beer can. She bends to pick it up, then answers the phone.

MARY
What's up with this mess in here? Hello?

She moves to the table.

MARY
Hello? Yeah, this is she.

E.T.'s Dialogue in the Movie

p.47	Elliottt. Elliottt.	p.74	(nervously) Ready.
p.54	A	p.75	Thank you.
	B, bee.	p.76	Thank you.
	B. Good. [E.T. laughs]	p.77	Elliottt.
p.55	Home.		E.T. phone home. phone
p.56	Home.		home.
	Be good. Be good.	p.78	Yes. Come.
	Elliottt.	p.81	Ouch.
p.57	Hi.	p.82	Okay.
	Elliottt.	p.89	[E.T. groans]
	E.T.	p.90	Hi. Hey. Good. Okay. For
	E.T.		sure. No. Yes. Please.
p.58	Elliottt, stay.		Thank you. E.T. E.T.
	Hey.		Home…home.
p.59	Elliottt.		[E.T. whimpers]
p.60	E.T.	p.94	[E.T. hiccupping]
	E.T. phone home.	p.96	Thank you Elliottt.
p.61	For sure.	p.107	E.T. phone home. E.T.
	Music.		phone home.
p.62	E.T. phone home.	p.109	Please.
	(softly) Come.	p.120	Yes. Ready.
	More.	p.121	Be good. Thank you.
p.63	Elliottt?		Come? Ouch. I'll be right
	Music?		here. [E.T. smiles]
	Please.		
p.68	Yes, Elliottt?		
	Yes. E.T. stay home.		
	I'll be right here.		
p.72	Okay.		

Page numbers refer to an early draft of the script. This list of E.T.'s dialogue was compiled by producer Kathleen Kennedy.

INT. PLAYROOM – DAY

GERTIE watches T.V.

                GERTIE
Basket. Bandit. Ball. Basket. Bandit. Ball.

            MARY (*off*) (*into telephone*)
What do you mean, acting strangely? He was feeling a little ill yesterday.

                GERTIE
Bugs. Bananas.

INT. KITCHEN – DAY

Mary is still on the phone crossing to the table.

                MARY
Intoxicated?

She picks up the beer can she set down on the table and begins to wonder.

                GERTIE
Bubble. Beetle.

                MARY
You sure you have the right Elliott?

INT. PLAYROOM – DAY

                GERTIE
B. B. Biscuits. Banjo.

E.T. looks at Gertie. Hears the letter "B" (for many things) being repeated on television.

                E.T.
B. B.

                GERTIE
You said B. You said B.

                E.T.
B.

                GERTIE
You said B. Good!

                E.T.
Good.

INT. KITCHEN – DAY

                MARY
Okay, I'll be right down. Thank you.

INT. PLAYROOM – DAY

Mary entering from the kitchen.

                MARY
Gertie? I have to go pick up Elliott. Will you be a good girl and stay—?

                GERTIE
Mommy, he can talk!

                MARY
Of course he can talk. I'll be right back in ten minutes. Stay there.

Mary runs out through the kitchen.

E.T. moves from behind the T.V., and moves to the telephone on the coffee table.

GERTIE

Phone.

E.T.

Phone?

GERTIE

Phone.

E.T.

Phone.

Gertie moves to him.

GERTIE

You wanna call somebody?

INT. STAIRWAY – HALLWAY – SECOND FLOOR – DAY

Elliott runs up the steps and starts toward his bedroom. He hears something in Gertie's room, drops his jacket and bag, and moves to Gertie's room.

MARY (*off*)

I am not paying for frogs. You get yourself a bag and go out in the woods and bag some.

GERTIE

Be good. Be good. Stay here. Stay. And don't tell anybody. No-Nobody. Be good. Be good. Hm.

THROUGH GERTIE'S DOOR – DAY

We see Gertie, wearing her full cowgirl ensemble, struggling to close the closet door.

INT. GERTIE'S ROOM – DAY

Elliott moves into Gertie's room. Gertie looks up and he shoves her out of the way and opens the door.

INT. CLOSET – DAY

E.T. stands there, dressed up as a woman. He stands erect and speaks.

SCRIPT NOTES

Harrison Ford appeared as the principal in some scenes here that were eventually cut from the movie.

Henry Thomas was so excited about meeting his hero from *Star Wars* that he took the day's call sheet to show his friends because he thought they would not believe him.

                    ELLIOTT
Oh, God!

                       E.T.
Eh-eh-eh-eh—Elliott.

                    ELLIOTT
What?!

                    E.T. (*off*)
Elliott. Elliott. El-...

Elliott is amazed.

Gertie moves to E.T.'s side.

                    GERTIE
I taught him how to talk. Now, he can talk now.

Elliott spots the open Speak & Spell and other paraphanelia E.T. has gathered.

                    GERTIE
Look what he brought up here all by himself. What's he need this stuff for?

                    ELLIOTT
E.T. Can you say that?

                    ELLIOTT
Can you say E.T.? E.T.

                       E.T.
E.T. E.T. E.T. Be good.

E.T. turns and moves out of the closet into Elliott's room. Gertie and Elliott follow him.

                    GERTIE
Be good. I taught him that, too.

                    ELLIOTT
You know, you should give him his dignity. This is the most ridiculous thing I've ever seen.

E.T looks back at Elliott. E.T. lifts the Buck Rogers cartoon, and shows it to Elliott.

                    E.T.
　　Phone.

Elliott takes it and looks at it.

                ELLIOTT
　　Phone? He said "phone"? He said "phone"?

                 GERTIE
        (*has seated herself but now rises.*)
　　Can't you understand English? He
　　said "phone."

E.T. quickly moves to the closet. He points.

                    E.T.
　　Home?

Elliott nods.

                ELLIOTT
　　You're right. That's E.T.'s home.

E.T. swiftly moves toward the window. He points again.

                    E.T.
　　Hm? E.T. home phone.

Harrison Ford

Very early on we made several fairly large lifts. We cut the scene where Elliott is taken to the principal's office. The principal was played by Harrison Ford.
　　　　　　　　—Carol Littleton, Editor

Working with Harrison Ford was a very big deal for me. The reason I got involved in film in the first place was because of *Star Wars* which was fantastic to me. *E.T.* came along and there was an alien and a spaceship. I thought, well, it's not *Star Wars* but it's definitely something to do with outer space. And Harrison Ford? Who could ask for anything more?
　　　　　　　　—Henry Thomas

So we have Harrison Ford playing the principal, very strict, in a tweed suit. I didn't show his face that clearly. I just showed the back of his head and his hand tapping. I wasn't showing adults in the movie. I think he did it because he didn't have to really be on camera. He's lecturing Elliott but his back is turned so he's not looking at him, Elliott is sitting in a chair across from the principal.
　　E.T. meanwhile is at home trying to take all these communicator parts and telepathically move them up the stairs. So as E.T. is successful moving this junk heap up the stairs to the bedroom, Elliott starts rising.
　　　　　　　　—Steven Spielberg

Left: E.T. with film editor Carol Littleton. Above: Steven Spielberg and Harrison Ford on location at Elliott's house.

Concept Meeting

I love the image of E.T. not being tall enough to look out the window of the kid's bedroom. He is yearning to look out because he's sort of a prisoner, in a way, and there's life out there. Outside are all the stars and the moon and all you see are his eyes and part of his nose and the childlike yearning to get back home. It reminds the audience that E.T. really belongs home.
—STEVEN SPIELBERG

One of my favorite images in *Heidi*, the only one I remember, is when she went to sleep in this loft. She had a little window and could see the stars. It was a tiny window and she couldn't see any land outside. She would fall asleep just staring out at the stars.
—MELISSA MATHISON, AS QUOTED FROM THE TRANSCRIPT OF A CONCEPT MEETING BETWEEN STEVEN SPIELBERG AND MELISSA MATHISON, OCTOBER 28, 1980

GERTIE
E.T. phone home.

Elliott is momentarily puzzled but quickly realizes.

ELLIOTT
E.T. phone home. E.T. phone home!

GERTIE
He wants to call somebody.

The door opens, and Michael enters. He is amused by E.T.'s attire.

MICHAEL
Wh-Wh-What's all this shit?

E.T.
E.T. phone home.

MICHAEL
Oh, my God. He's talking.

E.T.
Home.

                    ELLIOTT
          E.T. phone home?

                      E.T.
          E.T. phone home.

E.T. points out the window.

                    ELLIOTT
          And they'll come?

                      E.T.
          Come... home. Home.

He pulls off the wig he is wearing.

EXT. ELLIOTT'S HOUSE – NIGHT

A nondescript van moves slowly up the street in front of Elliott's house. On the roof of the van we see electronic equipment, which seems to be honing in on Elliott's house.

                  LITTLE BOY #1
          Come on, I promise, Mom.

                  LITTLE BOY #2
          What book?

                  LITTLE BOY #1
          Any one you want. Spiderman.

                  LITTLE BOY #2
          Football.

                     WIFE #1
          All right, fine. We'll just put a smile on
          our face and try to get through the
          evening. That's all I want to do.

                    HUSBAND #1
          Okay, make some of your garlic bread and
          some carrot cake.

                     WIFE #1
          That's all I want to do.

INT. VAN – NIGHT

We are inside a high-tech, audio "snooper" van. The man operates it, he is wearing headphones.

E.T.'s Voice

In the fall of 1981, I met Pat Welsh, a housewife and amateur photographer, in a camera shop in Marin County. After hearing her voice in the shop, I decided I wanted to record her for either *E.T.* or *Revenge of the Jedi*. She wasn't an actress though she'd briefly pursued ambitions in those directions sometime back in the 1930s or 40s. I explained to her that I was searching for an interesting voice for an alien character and asked if she wanted to audition. We were only a block away from our studio and I took her inside and had her read some of E.T.'s lines like "Phone home."

I had her speak slowly in a rather monotone voice. She spoke Swahili because she and her husband had been in Africa so we recorded a voice test in Swahili, too. She was a very good sport. I recorded her voice and sometimes we did fifty or sixty takes for one line of dialogue. At one point, she recorded without her false teeth. We wanted to create sounds that were unfamiliar to the American public. We made about twenty tapes, each fifteen minutes long. From the five hours of recording, about a minute was used.

I changed it electronically. I lowered the pitch and, to give it an element of the alien character, mixed her voice with the sounds of animals breathing which was sort of non-human. It was that blend I used to envelope the words she spoke. I should mention that there were eighteen different contributors to the voice of E.T. including the animals. Various other people provided a snort or a burp or breath. Pat Welsh's was the most significant single contribution because she spoke the English words but those words were intercut with all kinds of other little noises.

For the scenes where E.T. gets drunk, I used some vocalizations from my old cinema professor at University of Southern California. Why? I guess he played a good drunk alien. Members of the staff at Lucasfilm provided burps and E.T.'s screams are electronically amplified shrieks from an otter. I also recorded other friends of mine breathing and making funny noises and then put all the sounds together.

—BEN BURTT, E.T.'s VOICE DESIGNER

Sounds E.T. Makes in the Movie
- E.T. sucks in his breath.
- E.T. pants.
- E.T. whimpers.
- Tiny sharp teeth are bared as E.T. makes a terrifying noise—an imitative noise—the sound of jet planes and screeching tires.
- E.T. buckles his narrow shoulders and bares his teeth.
- E.T. chews and swallows.
- E.T. pulls his hands to his face and screeches.
- E.T. makes a soft, scared sound with his breath.
- E.T. screams.

We see blinking lights and hear static, and we realize Keys is honing in on the suburban conversations of Elliott's neighborhood.

WIFE #2
I can't ask Kathy to go trick-or-treating in the same old sheet she wore last year.

HUSBAND #2
Can we talk about this some other time?

ELLIOTT
Now I wish I would'a listened in science. Think, Michael.

Keys suddenly stops, adjusts his knobs, and tunes in on this conversation.

INT. GARAGE – NIGHT

Elliott and Michael, each holding a light, are looking around the garage. Elliott holds a pair of shoes, as Michael examines a table full of the usual garage junk. Elliott throws the shoes down, and moves toward Elliott.

MICHAEL
Guess we should just grab anything that looks like he could make a machine out of it.

ELLIOTT
What would make a radar?

MICHAEL
How the hell do I know? You're the genius here. You have absolute power. Remember? "I found him. He belongs to me."

They move toward a table, at which they both kneel.

EXT. ELLIOTT'S HOUSE – NIGHT

A nondescript van moves slowly up the street in front of Elliott's house.

INT. GARAGE – NIGHT

MICHAEL
You know, Elliott...he doesn't look too good anymore.

ELLIOTT
Don't say that! We're fine.

MICHAEL
Huh? What's all this "we" stuff?

EXT. VAN ON STREET

Inside van, Keys is listening to the boy's conversation.

MICHAEL
I mean, you say "we" all the time now. Really, Elliott, I think he might be getting kinda sick.

ELLIOTT
Look, he's fine, Michael!

MICHAEL
Okay, okay! Forget I mentioned it. Grab that Fuzzbuster.

INT. GARAGE – NIGHT

They look at the Fuzzbuster for a moment, then Elliott picks up a shirt and reminiscently continues.

ELLIOTT
Dad's shirt.

MICHAEL
Yeah.

ELLIOTT
Remember when he used to take us out to the ballgames and take us to the movies, and we'd have popcorn fights?

MICHAEL
We'll do that again, Elliott.

ELLIOTT
Sure.

INT. GARAGE – NIGHT

He smells the shirt, then Michael smells the shirt.

MICHAEL
Old Spice.

> ### SCRIPT NOTES
>
> The scene in the garage was improvised. Henry Thomas invented the dialogue about the popcorn fights and his father. Robert Macnaughton also created his own dialogue.
>
> "The conversation between Elliott and his brother, Michael, in the garage at night was photographed in a very contrasty lighting style," according to director of photography, Allen Daviau. "This was done to satisfy our curiosity as to how much detail the film will record in highlight and shadow without regard for the extremely high lighting ratio. Steven had asked me how many stops of overexposure would cause details of the faces to vanish into the brightness from the light being passed between the boys. I told him that I believed that five stops over should do it.
>
> "In the finished scene I am certain that there are moments when the boys' faces reach six stops over and yet details of their eyes and lips are still visible. The Eastman 5247 negative stock was fantastically supple and Steven's staging of these quiet, intimate moments between brothers makes us feel the hope they hold for their divided family."

ELLIOTT
Sea Breeze.

EXT. VAN ON STREET

Inside van, Keys is listening to the boy's conversation.

INT. BEDROOM

Mary and Gertie are cuddling in bed. Mary is reading from a book to Gertie.

MARY
"Peter says, 'The redskins were defeated? Wendy and the boys captured by the pirates? I'll rescue her. I'll rescue her.'"

INT. CLOSET – NIGHT

E.T. is sitting in his nesting area. He opens one of the louvres and listens.

MARY
"He leaps first at his dagger, and then at his grindstone to sharpen it. But Tink alights near the shed and rings out a warning cry. 'Oh, but that is just my medicine.' She says....'Poisoned? Who could have poisoned it?'"

ELLIOTT'S BEDROOM

We can see through the opened louvres that E.T. is still standing, watching, and listening to Mary and Gertie.

MARY
"'I promised Wendy to take it, and I will, as soon as I have sharpened my dagger.' Tink, who sees its red color and remembers the red in the pirate's eye, nobly swallows the draught as Peter's hand is reaching for it. 'Why, Tink, you have drunk my medicine.' She flutters strangely about the room, answering him now in a very faint tinkle."

Elliott moves in and sees E.T. He hurriedly opens the door, puts the box he is carrying down in the closet, and goes to the door where E.T. is. He closes the blind, and turns E.T. around away from it. He moves back to the box of tools he has brought in to help E.T. build his communicator.

He starts to unload it, and in handling a sawblade, cuts his finger.

103

ELLIOTT
Ouch. Ouch.

E.T. looking on.

MARY
"'It was poison and you drank it to save my life? Tink, dear Tink, are you dying?'"

E.T. raises his forefinger, and it slowly takes on a brilliant pink glow. This is new to Elliott, and the boy automatically backs away from E.T.

E.T.
Ouch.

E.T. touches Elliott's wound with his glowing finger. Gently he wipes the finger across Elliott's finger. E.T. pulls his hand away, and the light goes out. Elliott looks down at his hand. The wound is healed.

MARY
"'Her voice is so low I can scarcely tell what she is saying. She says, she says she thinks she could get well again if children believed in fairies. Do you believe in fairies? Say quick that you believe!'"

E.T. moves back to the louvre and opens it, watching and listening once again.

GERTIE
I do, I do, I do!

MARY
"'If you believe, clap your hands.'"

She claps her own hands; Gertie claps hers.

MARY
"Many clap, some don't. A few hiss."

Elliott moves to E.T.'s side. They watch and listen to Mary and Gertie together. Elliott puts a scarf around E.T.'s neck. Elliott puts his arm around E.T.'s shoulder.

> **SCRIPT NOTES**
> In the original script E.T. goes into Mary's room and leaves some Reese's Pieces on her pillow. The scene was shot with Pat Bilon in the E.T. costume. Melissa Mathison wanted to imply, with the scene, that E.T. had a crush on Mary. The scene was cut from the movie.

LEFT: *E.T. and Dee Wallace in a scene that was cut from the movie.*
ABOVE: *Steven Spielberg rehearses with Dee Wallace.*

MARY
"And then perhaps there is a rush of nanas to the nurseries to see what is happening. But Tink is saved. 'Thank you. Oh, thank you, thank you, thank you. And now to rescue Wendy.'"

GERTIE
Will you read it to me again?

MARY
Okay. (reading) "Peter says...."

INT. ELLIOTT'S BEDROOM

Elliott on bed; Michael standing next to him. Both watch E.T. through closet doors.

ELLIOTT
He's putting it together now. I told you he was smart.

MICHAEL
I'm worried, Elliott. He could blow up the whole house.

ELLIOTT
He knows what he's doing.

MICHAEL
Listen to how he's breathing.

INT. CLOSET

E.T. works on building the communicator.

ELLIOTT
It's going to work.

MICHAEL
What's he feeling now?

ELLIOTT
He's feeling everything.

INT. GERANIUMS WILTING

INT. BATHROOM

Elliott puts on makeup as Gertie watches.

ELLIOTT (*in mirror*)
Now, you're going as a ghost. You promised.

GERTIE
I'm only pretending I'm going as a cowgirl.

ELLIOTT
Okay, now, you know the plans by heart, don't you?

ABOVE: As a girl, Melissa Mathison always dressed up as a cowgirl which accounts for why she wrote this into Gertie's character.

GERTIE
Meet you at the lookout. At the lookout.

MARY
(*to Michael*) Listen, buster, you won't get four blocks in this neighborhood dressed like that! Now, I mean it! You are not going as a hippie!

> **SCRIPT NOTES**
> In the movie, Mary's line, "You are not going as a terrorist!" was changed to: "Listen, Buster, you won't get four blocks in this neighborhood dressed like that!"

MICHAEL
But all the guys are!

GERTIE
I'm not stupid, you know.

INT. CLOSET – DAY

Elliott enters the closet, followed by Michael. E.T. is taken aback by Elliott's monster makeup. Michael helps E.T. put the communicator on his back.

ELLIOTT (*to E.T.*)
Ready?

E.T.
Ready.

Elliott moves to E.T. with the ghost sheet.

INT. STAIRCASE – DAY

Three sets of feet move down the steps, among them the cartoon feet E.T. is wearing.

INT. KITCHEN – HALLWAY – LIVING ROOM – DAY

Mary in costume moves through the kitchen, into the hallway, and starts toward the living room.

MICHAEL
No, wait, Mom, don't look.

MARY
Oh, okay.

She stops, turns her back, and dons her mask and ears, completing her costume. In her background, the children enter.

MICHAEL
Okay, Mom, you can look now.

Mary turns and steps into view. She is wearing her leopard dress, an eye mask, frizzed hair, and is carrying a wand with a glittering star on top. She smiles adoringly at her children and laughs.

MARY
Oh, that's great! Stay there!

Halloween

Henry would go from thinking I was his new best friend to thinking I was his school teacher. I would talk to him constantly while the camera was rolling and while Henry was in his dialogue. When Henry first saw *E.T.* at the sneak preview, I turned to him when the movie was over, and asked how he liked it. He said, "It was okay, but you've gotta cut your voice out. Your voice is all the way through the movie." As Henry saw the movie, he kept hearing my voice directing him.

He kept thinking I was his teacher so to surprise him for Halloween, I dressed up as a teacher. But not as a man teacher, I dressed up with a veil and the wig and the lipstick and I became a kind of new kind of me.

—STEVEN SPIELBERG

Halloween was great. He directed the whole day as an old lady.

—HENRY THOMAS

Oh, we had such a good time with Steven dressed up as this old lady and behind the camera with his high heels. It was so brilliant and he looked really great, too.

—DREW BARRYMORE

She runs into the bar and gets the Polaroid camera and moves back to the kids.

REVERSE: THE CHILDREN

Michael is a hobo, in black clothes, a false knife pierces his temple. Elliott is a hunchback, with painted face, and a heavy woolen cape over the communicator on his back. E.T. is supposedly Gertie, disguised as a ghost: white sheet and cartoon feet.

BOYS

E.T. looks up at Michael and notices the knife sticking through the boy's temple.

A white light becomes visible under E.T.'s ghost sheet, and before anyone can stop him, E.T. raises his hand and his healing finger to Michael's artificial wound. Michael seeing the finger, understands but is mortified, pushing the finger down and looking to Elliott for help.

      E.T.
  Ouch. Ouch.

      MICHAEL
  No, it's a fake knife. It's a fake.

      E.T.
  Ouch. Ouch.

Mary has missed all this. She kneels with her camera to snap the photo.

      MARY
  Okay. (*squealing*) Ohhh, you look great!

      MICHAEL
  Thank you.

Debra Winger

My friend Debra Winger came to the set one day when we were shooting the Halloween scene.

  I loved her voice. She had a really low, husky voice and I asked her to read every single E.T. line in the script into a tape recorder. So in the rough cut on the temp track, it's mostly Debra's voice.

        —STEVEN SPIELBERG

      ELLIOTT
  Thank you.

      E.T.
  Thank you.

Luckily Mary snaps the picture just as E.T. speaks so she does not hear him.

FLASH FROM POLAROID

E.T.'s legs buckle and he starts to collapse under the shock of the flash camera. Michael and Elliott grab his arms and pull him back to his feet. Mary has seen none of this; she is busy with the camera. The boys start toward the front door.

EXT. FRONT OF HOUSE – DUSK

Michael, Elliott, and E.T., accompanied by Harvey, move down the driveway in their costumes.

MARY comes out of the house and waves to them, her wand in her hand.

      MARY
  Be back one hour after sundown,
  no later. Bye.

E.T. turns to look back at Mary.

E.T.'s POV

He turns and continues on his way. The boys run to hold his hand, and guide him down the driveway.

      MICHAEL
  Gertie! Come here. Come on.

Mary goes back into the house, showing some concern.

**EXT. FIRE ROAD BELOW LOOKOUT –
TO LOOKOUT – DUSK**

Gertie stands at the lookout waiting. She angrily paces back and forth. She kicks the bike beside her.

EXT. STREETS – DUSK

As we follow Elliott, Michael, E.T., and Harvey down the street we see children, dressed as cats and clowns, etc.

ABOVE and RIGHT: Shooting Halloween as seen through the eyes of E.T. in his ghost costume.

ELLIOTT, E.T., MICHAEL, AND HARVEY move among the throng of "Trick or Treaters."

Among the throng of children, there appears a small YODA approaching them. As he passes, E.T. starts to move toward him.

                      E.T.
    Home. Home. Home. Home. Home.
    Home. Home. Home.

Elliott and Michael quickly overtake him, and they continue on their way. Yoda looks back at them, continuing on his way.

Elliott, Michael, E.T., and Harvey continue on their way into the setting sun.

                      MICHAEL
    Be back one hour after sunset. No later.

                      ELLIOTT
    I'll try as fast as I can, Mike. You gotta
    cover me.

                      ELLIOTT
    (*indicating E.T.*) Well... come on, help me.

                      MICHAEL
    We'll be waiting for you, Elliott. So come
    back, for sure.

They pick him up and start putting him in the basket of the bicycle.

Yoda

For the Halloween scene, I got a Yoda costume and dressed someone as the character. I didn't tell George [Lucas] I was doing this. In the scene, E.T. is covered with a sheet and sees Yoda coming from the other direction. Yoda is oblivious but E.T. recognizes Yoda because, you know, the galaxy is a rather small place among film makers.
—STEVEN SPIELBERG

I hadn't seen the finished movie and when it was completed, we had a screening for ILM which I attended. Steven warned me there was something special in the movie for me.

So we are watching and suddenly Yoda showed up in the film. Everybody in the audience cheered, of course, because it was an ILM screening.

I really loved it. I was amazed and flattered. It was a very funny moment.
—GEORGE LUCAS

I remember George was sitting right next to me during the screening and when Yoda came on the screen, George gave me a little nudge with his arm which, I guess, was his way of saying that was cool.
—STEVEN SPIELBERG

111

EXT. FOREST – DUSK

Elliott is on his bicycle, and E.T. is in the basket, strapped to the handlebars. Elliott guides his bike down a forest path.

EXT. MIDDLE OF THE FOREST – NIGHT

Elliott steers the bicycle toward the really heavy forest. E.T. bounces in his seat.

E.T. with a focused concentration, looks straight ahead.

>ELLIOTT
>It's too bumpy. We'll have to walk from he- e-...

He hardly has time to finish the sentence as the bicycle moves forward, and he almost loses balance, yelling.

E.T. LIFTS THE BICYCLE INTO THE AIR.

>ELLIOTT
>...-e-ere! E.- T.!

EXT. SKY – NIGHT

The bicycle glides five feet over the tall grass and circles the landing site.

>ELLIOTT
>Not so high! Not so high!

E.T. feels Elliott's joy, and in the excitement of his own triumph, E.T. allows the ride to continue. The bicycle rises to the treetops. Elliott rides the bicycle, pedaling as hard as he can, steering through the treetops. He screams, laughing.

EXT. THE SKY – NIGHT

They begin to descend.

>ELLIOTT
>Don't crash, please.

EXT. THE LANDING SITE – NIGHT

The bicycle crashes on impact. Elliott, still laughing, is in a pile with the bicycle and E.T. His feet stick up in the air.

INT. ELLIOTT'S HOUSE/FRONT DOOR – NIGHT

Mary is sitting on the step, twirling her star-wand, obviously angry.

EXT. THE LANDING SITE – NIGHT

>THE COMMUNICATOR has been set upon a rock. The lid is ajar. E.T. opens the lid and connects the hanger with many colored wires attached to it onto a disc-shaped sawblade with teeth around the outer edge.
>
>He picks up a fork nearby which has a tong missing from it, and places it upright on the teeth of the sawblade.
>
>There is a battery beside the record player which E.T. puts a plug into. His hands probe around the other objects, checking their positions.
>
>He places a walkie talkie beside the record player. A Speak & Spell sits beside it.
>
>E.T. leans the Speak & Spell near the record player, and inserts a small microphone into it. His hands check other objects. Then he pauses and folds his hands.
>
>ELLIOTT ties a string to a tree branch. E.T. beside him directing how it should be done.
>
>Elliott moves away from the branch, holding the string in his hand and pulls, testing it.
>
>The wind blows, the tree limb moves, and the string pulls taut.

Over the Moon: Amblin Logo

The shot of the bicycle flying in front of the moon has become the logo for Amblin. When we discussed this shot, it seemed logical that we should shoot this with the real moon. We wanted to get as much realism as possible.

Mike McAlister, effects cameraman, had to scout locations for a place to shoot. We got all these charts out. We wanted to find the trees. I think it took about a week. In the afternoon he'd go out for three or four hours to find the right spot. I think we shot it for two nights and got two or three versions.
—DENNIS MUREN, VISUAL EFFECTS SUPERVISOR

We didn't want a sky with a sliver moon to indicate that this was a great effect shot. We wanted it to look like we'd actually shot that perfect night moon.
—KATHLEEN KENNEDY

ABOVE: The moon, used in the scene of Elliott and E.T. flying, was shot in Nicasio, California, near the ILM studios. The image became the logo for Amblin Entertainment.

EXT. ELLIOTT'S HOUSE – NIGHT

Mary, mumbling to herself, exits the house and heads for the garage. She gets in the car and backs out, holding her wand in her mouth.

> **MARY**
> —that you did this. I really can't believe you did this! I mean, I trusted you. That's the last time you order pizza. Just see who you get to pay for it. Your father's gonna hear about this one! Mexico!

EXT. CAR

Keys and men walk towards Elliott's house.

EXT. NEIGHBORHOOD – NIGHT

A pumpkin is visible with a large flame inside it. As we pull back, we reveal the craziness of teenage Halloween. The innocence of early evening has been replaced by kids in bizarre "punk" outfits roaming the streets. The street is filled with rainbow effects of smoke bombs. It is not a violent sight but one of wild abandon.

Michael holds Gertie by the hand and Harvey by the leash; they move along the scene toward us.

A house is being T.P.'d. The bizarre scene continues.

A group of teenagers are on a corner, surrounding a pumpkin. As they disperse, we see Michael with Gertie and Harvey coming toward us. Mary's car enters from their background to them. The car stops. Mary leans toward them and speaks.

INT. MARY'S CAR – NIGHT

Just as Mary is about to speak, two eggs hit her windshield and the boys run off.

> **MARY**
> Where's Elliott?

The children move to the car. They do not answer.

> **MARY**
> I'm asking you a question.

> **GERTIE**
> Anyways, why would Elliott go to the forest? Why would he do such a thing?

Mary looks to Michael. He looks worried.

> **MARY**
> Get in the car. Get in the car now.

They open the car door.

EXT. LANDING SITE – NIGHT

Elliott is holding the string. He lets go of it and opens the umbrella, which we see is lined with aluminum foil. Attached to its handle is the coffee can holding a UHF receiver.

Elliott moves beside E.T., and they wait for the wind to blow, which will start the action of the communicator.

E.T. and ELLIOTT waiting. Suddenly the wind blows leaves through the air. They look to the direction of the wind and then to the string. It goes taut.

The string pulls the fork, which pulls the sawblade, which activates the Speak & Spell, which is writing once again the strange characters.

Elliott is very excited.

LEFT: *The communicator sends a message into space.* RIGHT: *Behind the scenes during the filming of E.T.'s attempt to rendezvous with his spaceship.*

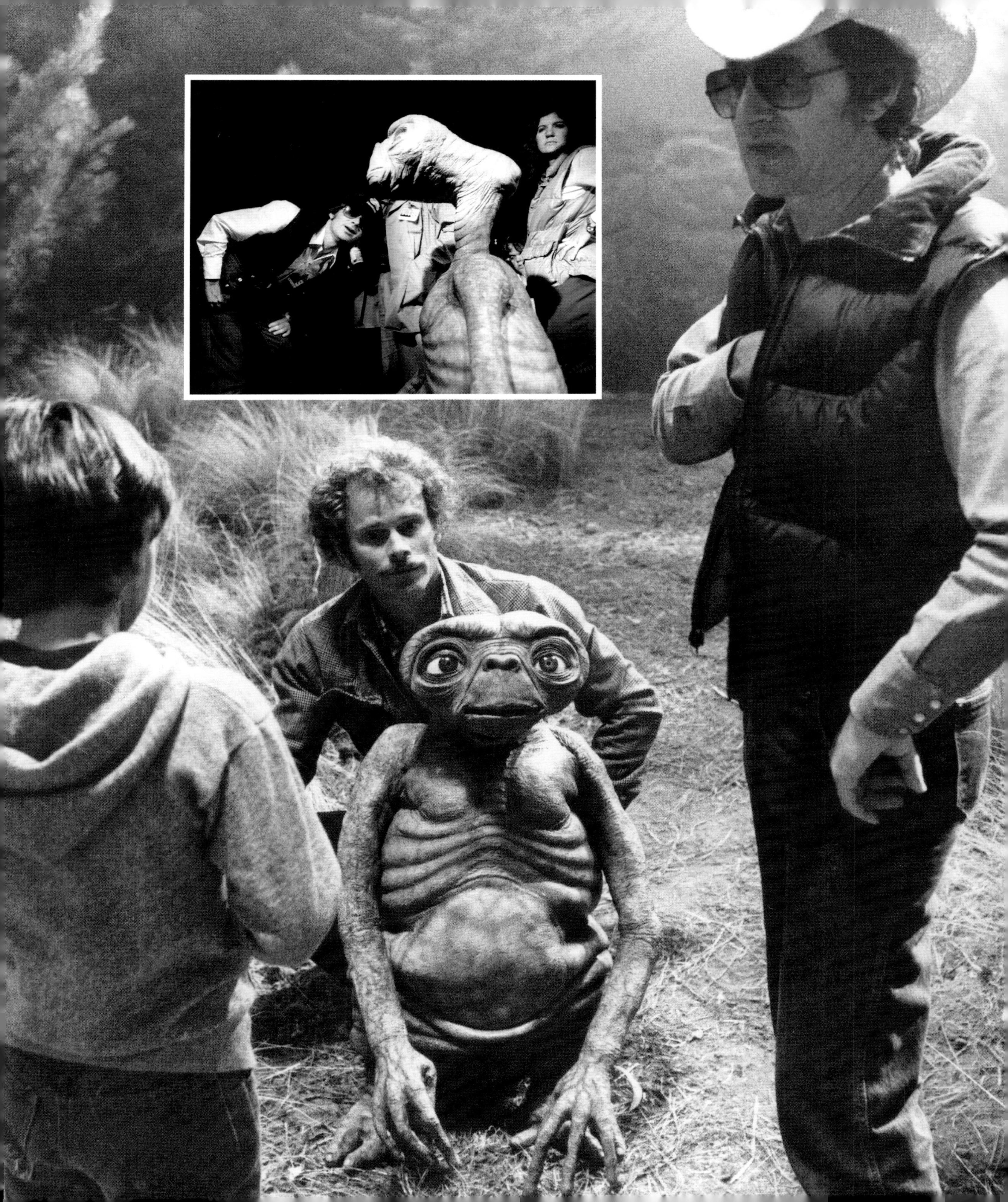

ELLIOTT
E.T., it's working! It's working!

E.T.
Oh! Home.

ELLIOTT
You did it!

E.T.
Home.

ELLIOTT
It's working!

E.T.
Home.

They both look to the sky in anticipation, hoping for some word in return.

ELLIOTT
E.T.! It's working!

INT. HALLWAY – NIGHT

A pumpkin with a lit candle inside sits on a desk top.

Suddenly a wind comes and blows out the candle; we see shadows appear across it. The lights of flashlights now become visible. One light blinds our view.

INT. GERTIE'S ROOM – NIGHT

The dolls sit at tea at a child's toy table and chairs. At the door we begin to see lights flashing across again.

CLOSER ON Raggedy Ann doll. The door opens, and we can see a flashlight pushing it open.

CLOSE ON Indian doll; our view moves to Raggedy Ann and the bookcase behind them. Lights flash across the bookcase and we see: miniwave oven, toy horses, crayons, and various dolls, etc.

INT. SECOND STORY LANDING – NIGHT

We see shadows cast on the wall in the background of the stairs. Our view moves to the hallway leading to Elliott's room. On the floor is a yellow cord coiled on the floor. It begins to move as it is pulled under the door to Elliott's room. Shadows and lights from flashlights flash across the louvred door. The end of the cord pulls taut, moving a chair back against the wall.

EXT. LANDING SITE – NIGHT

Elliott stands at the top of the slope near the landing site marked by a gate. Elliott moves down the slope. E.T. stands near the machine looking off at the sky. Elliott standing nearby begins toward him.

> **ELLIOTT**
> We have to go now, E.T. We're so late already.

E.T. just stares at the sky.

> **ELLIOTT**
> *(now in front of E.T.)*
> We have to go home now, E.T.

No response.

> **ELLIOTT**
> *(he moves beside E.T. looking in the direction of the sky too)*
> You should give 'em some time.

E.T. looks at Elliott. He is crying...he puts his hand to his chest and whispers.

> **E.T.**
> Ouch.

> **ELLIOTT**
> *(moves in front of him once more.)*
> You could be happy here. I could take care of you. I wouldn't let anybody hurt you. We could grow up together, E.T.

E.T. looks up at the sky. He refuses to budge. Elliott slides down beside the rock, looking up at E.T. He is crying. E.T. extends his hand and touches Elliott's face and smiles.

> **E.T.**
> Home.

SCRIPT NOTES

During the filming of the scene where the neighborhood houses get covered in toilet paper, Steven Spielberg played Wagner's "Charge of Valkyrie" in the background, the same music Francis Ford Coppola used in *Apocalypse Now*. Originally cut from the 1982 release, a very small portion of the scene has been restored to the movie.

Was E.T. Real?

The kids believed that E.T. was real despite seeing the technical operators, the special effects technician, and all the levers and wires. All of them believed in him.
—STEVEN SPIELBERG

There were a lot of different elements but for some reason, no matter what, E.T. was always very real to me.
—DREW BARRYMORE

It was amazing. Once everything was set to go, the cameras were rolling and you were in the scene, everything was incredibly real.
—HENRY THOMAS

EXT. LANDING SITE – DAWN

Elliott is wrapped in his woolen cape asleep.

His goblin makeup has smeared and run, and he looks terrible. Elliott wakes up with a shudder. He looks around him.

E.T. is gone. He rises and moves to the communicator and tests it.

He starts moving around and looking for E.T. He moves up the slope.

ELLIOTT
E.T.? E.T.?!

INT. KITCHEN – DAWN

Mary moves toward the refrigerator. A uniformed man stands nearby. (We never see the policeman's face)

POLICEMAN
Uh, how was he dressed when last seen?

She opens the door of the refrigerator and puts a quart of milk away. She stands looking for something in the refrigerator.

MARY
He was dressed as a...hunchback.

POLICEMAN
Hunchback.

Michael and Gertie are seated nearby.

POLICEMAN
Is there anything to indicate that he, he might have run away? Any family problems or recent arguments?

MARY
Um, my husband and I just separated recently, and...it hasn't been easy on the children. But....

Mary looks to him.

GERTIE
My father's in Mexico.

MARY
But run away? I— Where would he have gone?

Mary closes the refrigerator door, revealing Elliott standing behind it.

MICHAEL (*overlapping*)
Elliott!

MARY
Elliott.

Michael, Gertie, and Mary all run to Elliott. Mary is down on her knees hugging him.

MARY
Oh, Elliott! Don't ever do this again, Elliott! Oh, oh, my— You're so hot.

Elliott looks terrible. His makeup has run and is smeared all over his face, and he is definitely ill. His cape is around him; he is shivering.

MARY
(*to Gertie*)
Run up and draw him a bath. Quick, Gert.
(*Gertie goes out.*)

                    MARY
          (to Elliott)
     Sorry I yelled at you.

She moves him to a seat, then remembers the policeman. She rises to him.

                    MARY
     Um...thanks very much for all your
     trouble.

She backs him out of the room.

Elliott looks to Michael.

                    ELLIOTT
     Is he here?

Michael shakes his head no.

                    ELLIOTT
     You gotta find him, Mike.

                    MICHAEL
     Where is he?

                    ELLIOTT
     In the forest. The bald spot. You gotta
     find him.

EXT. ELLIOTT'S HOUSE – DAY

Michael gets on the bicycle in the garage and goes careening down the driveway on Elliott's bicycle.

EXT. STREET – DAY

A car pulls out and follows Michael. We can see the forms of three men sitting in the car.

ANGLE FROM INSIDE THE CAR

The men follow Michael down the street. He makes a left turn.

SIDE ANGLE

We are on a suburban street as Michael comes by and the car is still following. Michael looks over his shoulder and sees the blue car.

Michael still driving along a neighborhood street, once more looks over his shoulder. He is sure he is being followed. He turns around a corner.

He is pumping the bike up a hill with the blue car still on his trail. He frantically looks about for some way out. He makes a turn into a driveway of a house.

We are in an alleyway overlooking the backyard of a house. We see Michael frantically driving around the house, across the grass, through the gate, up the alley. The blue car has found an opening into the alley. They almost meet, but Michael continues on. He must find a way out. He skids and barrels up an incline leading to

Facts and Figures: The Character of E.T.

- Steven Spielberg averaged fifteen takes on E.T. and three on the human actors.

- E.T.'s legs were sculpted by artist Lauron Marems. Steven Spielberg sent Marems to the parking lot to look at the rubber housing on his car's stick shift which was how he wanted E.T.'s legs to look.

- Construction of the creature began in March of 1981, seven months before the film began shooting.

- E.T. is forty-eight inches high with the neck at rest and fifty-six inches tall when the neck is extended. The head is twenty inches long and the eyes are three inches in diameter.

- A pair of gloves were made out of latex that were finer than surgical gloves. The gloves had zippers and tubes that allowed for the infusion of air to simulate a pulse. Caprice Rothe auditioned with six other mimes and won the part of E.T.'s hands.

- As a prop, E.T. was insured for $1,200,000.

ABOVE: Carlo Rambaldi and his staff work on E.T.

a pathway. He has stopped them; they cannot climb the incline; and he continues on his way.

EXT. FIRE ROAD – DAY

Michael huffs and puffs the bicycle up the dirt road.

EXT. FOREST – DAY

Michael moves through the forest on Elliott's bike. He arrives at the slope of the landing site and descends it. He gets off his bike and moves around frantically, looking for and calling E.T.

MICHAEL
E.T.! E.T.! E.T.!

He moves to the communicator.

He looks around at E.T.'s effort, then spots something at the top of the slope. He moves toward it.

AT THE TOP OF THE SLOPE

Michael moves up the slope to find E.T.'s ghost sheet hanging on the gate there. He holds it in his hand and looks around some more.

MICHAEL moves across a bridge over a creek, his eyes everywhere.

EXT. CREEK – DAY

Michael sees something at the creek. He stops his bike, and quickly moves down the hill to the creek carrying E.T.'s ghost sheet in his hand.

WHAT HE SEES: Lying in the creek, his head twisted at a grotesque angle, is E.T.

MICHAEL
No! No!

BACK TO MICHAEL

Michael stoops down. The spaceman is breathing heavily. His inclination is to touch him but somehow he momentarily can't.

A HELICOPTER is heard over head. Michael looks up and immediately reacts, covering E.T. with the sheet, hiding him from view.

EXT. HOUSE – DAY

Establishing shot, then Keys enters (shadow).

INT. HALLWAY – MARY'S BEDROOM – DAY

Mary moves up the steps, and Michael moves to meet her.

ABOVE: The crew sets up a scene where E.T. is found in the creek bed.

MICHAEL
Mom? Would you come with me?

MARY
What is it?

She moves up the stairs to him, and into the bedroom.

MICHAEL
Mary, just come with me.

MARY
Michael, what?

They move to the bathroom door in Mary's room.

MICHAEL
Mom, remember the goblin?

MARY
Michael, what are you talking about?

They are at the door.

MICHAEL
Just swear the most excellent promise you can make.

MARY
Michael.

Mary impatiently looks at him. Michael musters his courage, opens the door, and moves in beside the tub to kneel.

INT. BATHROOM

In the bathroom, Elliott and E.T. are both on the floor, sick. Gertie sits on top of the sink, looking sadly on.

Mary's first impression is that it is one of their toys. She is going to go along with the joke.

MARY
That's terrific.

E.T. turns his head to her and extends his arm. The sight for Mary is repulsive.

E.T.
Mom.

She is out of control. Her hand relaxes, spilling the coffee in the cup she is carrying to the floor.

ELLIOTT
We're sick. I think we're dying.

She speaks to Michael without taking her eyes off E.T.

MARY
Michael. Go downstairs.

Michael hesitates.

MICHAEL
Mom, it's okay.

Mary frightened, nauseated.

GERTIE
He's not gonna hurt you, Mom.

MICHAEL
He's not gonna hurt you.

MARY
(*she reaches to Michael*)
Michael, get her downstairs!

GERTIE
He's the man from the moon. The man from the moon!

Michael moves to Gertie, picks her up off the sink, and moves out of the bathroom with her.

Mary reaches in and picks Elliott up off the floor and runs out of the bathroom. Elliott weakly protests.

ELLIOTT
You don't know him! You don't know him!

E.T.
Mom!

E.T. is alone. He reaches his arms out to her.

ELLIOTT
We can't leave him alone!

Mary continues on her way, paying no heed.

INT. STAIRWAY – DAY

Michael enters carrying Gertie piggyback, and runs down steps. Mary enters, carrying Elliott in front of her. Elliott protests as Mary starts down the steps.

INT. FRONT DOOR – DAY

Michael runs down the steps with Gertie riding piggyback with him.

He opens the front door and is shocked. He moves back.

Mary comes running down steps carrying Elliott. She starts to move back, and a man dressed in a huge, cumbersome, Apollo-type space suit enters toward her.

She runs toward the hallway, and another of the similarly dressed men moves to her. She backs away.

Mary, with Elliott, runs through the kitchen followed by Michael with Gertie. They run through the playroom and toward the sliding glass leading to the back patio. Another Apollo-type enters.

She and the children all back up to the window on the other side of the room.

An Apollo–type starts to enter.

Mary screams.

MARY
This is my home!

EXT. NIGHT

A line of astronauts rises up out of the dusky street.

INT. BATHROOM – DAY

E.T. still lies on the floor, skin discolored and very sick.

AT THE DOOR

An astronaut appears. He sees E.T. E.T. reaches out to him for help.

E.T.
Home. Home.

EXT. ELLIOTT'S HOUSE – NIGHT

Establishing shot: We witness the results of an incredible metamorphosis.

The entire house has been draped in a heavy, transparent vinyl. Huge air hoses climb up over the roof, and others are being carried in. Bright lights are everywhere illuminating the house. On either side, we see huge scaffolding. The cul-de-sac has been cordoned off, and the driveway is blocked by trucks, trailers, and government cars. The eerie picture is completed by the comings and goings of men in blue jumpsuits. A huge air hose is on the front driveway and men in space suits move through this.

HEAR THE SOUND OF KEYS.

INT. TRAILER – NIGHT

Keys, seen from the waist down, pulls on a space suit. As Keys pulls on the helmet, we see his entire body, and then he exits.

EXT. TRAILER LEADING INTO HUGE AIR HOSE IN DRIVEWAY

Keys exits the trailer, and steps right into the oversized air hose and moves along inside it up to a zippered door.

INT. AIR HOSE – NIGHT

Keys has reached the zipper door (the pneumatic seal), goes through it, and enters STAGE ONE of this quarantined house — the living room.

INT. LIVING ROOM – NIGHT

Elliott's house has been invaded, by "the best and the brightest": scientists and doctors, military experts, geologists, psychologists, and biologists. All have come to probe the mystery that has lived within this house. It will become apparent that they have found, to their surprise, that their job now includes saving two lives: Elliott's and E.T.'s. Keys moves past Mary and Gertie.

Mary and Gertie sit in the disheveled room, as doctors and nurses run a battery of superficial tests on them.

Mary's panic has given way to disbelieving calm. Behind her is a video monitor recording activity in the playroom. On the monitor, we see Elliott and E.T. lying on hospital beds. Mary looks up at her questioners.

MARY
I don't know!

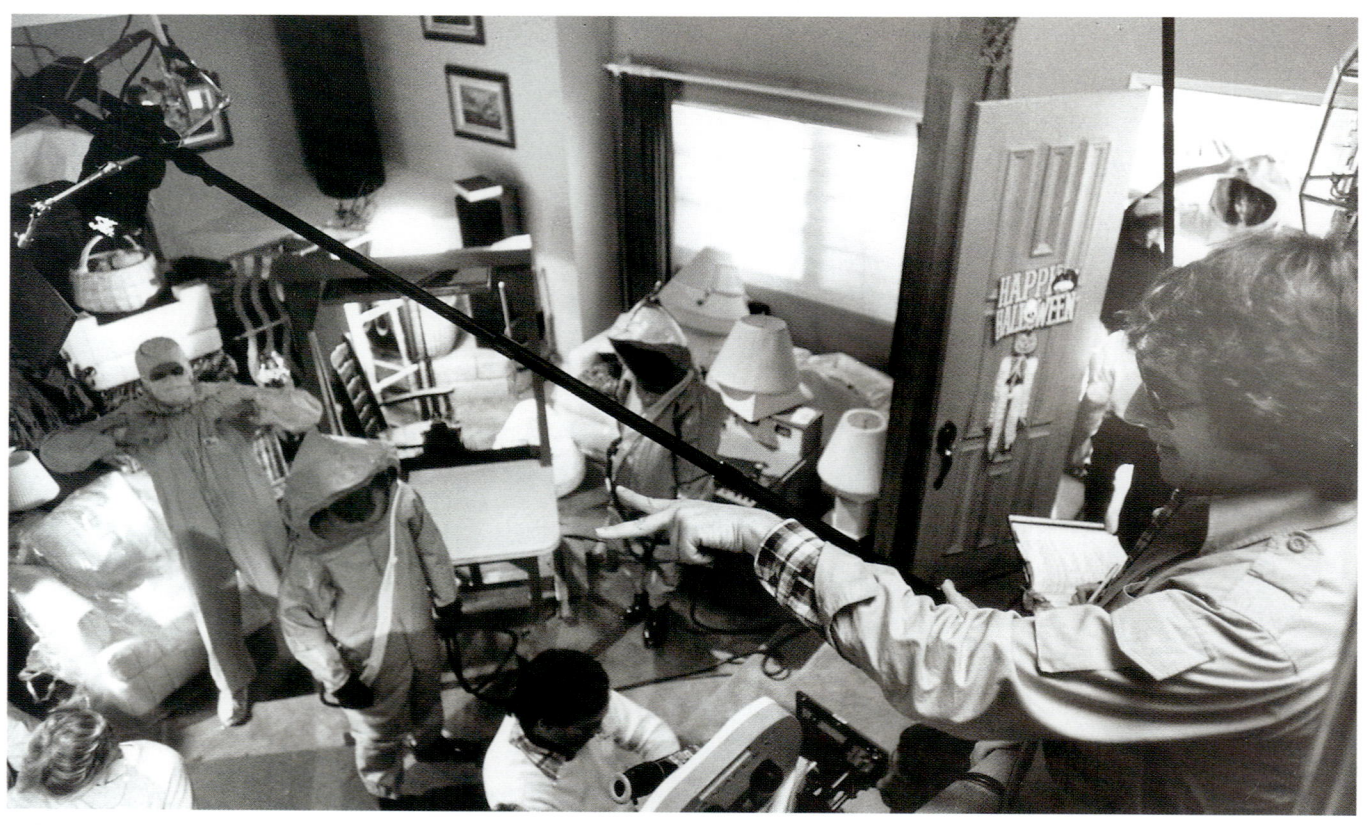

RIGHT: *Steven Spielberg directing the action during the scene where the government sets up shop in the family's house.*

EMERGENCY DOCTOR #1
(off) (overlapping)
Does he sleep at night? Has it gotten any smaller?

MARY
(who has been answering briefly with "I don't know" at this point, flares)
I don't know! What's the matter with Elliott?

A nurse snips hair samples from their heads.

EMERGENCY DOCTOR ONE
Has it taken any food, or water?

ANOTHER DOCTOR
Has it changed at all since you first saw it?

EMERGENCY DOCTOR #2
Have you noticed any surface sweating?

> **PRODUCTION NOTES**
> The house that was rented for the film was wrapped in a piece of clear plastic that measured 80 x 150 feet and cost $18,000. The weather was quite warm when these scenes were shot, over 100 degrees, so the temperature under the plastic was even hotter. Also, the style of lighting was drastically changed from warm and cozy to harsh and glaring.

MARY
No.

EMERGENCY DOCTOR #2
Has it lost any hair?

GERTIE
He never had any hair.

EMERGENCY DOCTOR #1
Are the children all right?

124

                    MARY
Yes.

Not far from them, Michael is being interrogated by a psychiatrist.

                    PSYCHIATRIST
Did it ever build anything, or write anything down?

                    MICHAEL
Uh... no.

                    PSYCHIATRIST
But you say it, it has the ability to manipulate its own environment?

Behind Michael and the psychiatrist, we can see Elliott and E.T. on another monitor.

                    MICHAEL
He's smart. He communicates through Elliott.

                    PSYCHIATRIST
Elliott thinks its thoughts?

                    MICHAEL
No, Elliott... Elliott feels his feelings.

CLOSE ON KEYS IN THE AIR SHOWER.

We see and hear the heavy stream of air purging Keys of contamination as he starts to take off his blue outfit and put on the white one necessary to enter the isolation area in the kitchen/playroom.

> PRODUCTION NOTES
>
> Remembering a visit to one of the space launches, Steven Spielberg asked Kathleen Kennedy to call NASA to inquire about obtaining space suits for this scene. NASA referred Kennedy to Space Gear, a company that makes suits for NASA promotion. The film company rented three of their suits.

The following dialogue is fast and furious, with test results being shouted from corners of the room and questions being tossed in on top of answers. Many test results will be accompanied by inserts of the appropriate machinery and readouts.

                    FEMALE TECH #1
We've identified his primary carrier protein by electrophoresis. It's definitely not albumin.

                    ELLIOTT DOCTOR
Cerebellar testing shows no deficits on F.N.F. and H.T.S. testing.

WE SEE E.T.'s and Elliott's EEG machines. The readouts are identical.

                    MALE TECH #1
The E.E.G. analysis shows complete coherence and synchronization of brainwave activities between both subjects.

INT. KITCHEN/PLAYROOM – NIGHT

Keys enters from the air shower, now completely dressed in the "clean room" suit.

It might have been assumed that the visual shock of the house quarantine had reached its peak, but the look of the kitchen/playroom is terrifying. The entire area is draped in plastic, crammed full of machines, monitors, and people wearing the anonymous, masked "clean room" suits.

Keys moves from the kitchen to the playroom where Elliott and E.T. lie on gurneys inside an isolation booth.

FEMALE DOCTOR #2
Skin biopsy reveals nine millimeters of organized, cross-linked extra-cellular material.

FEMALE DOCTOR #3
We're working on his buccal scraping, hoping to get a karyotype.

MALE DOCTOR #3
That'll be with I.V. and oral contrast. If there's no response to twenty per kilo, let's move to hypertonic saline.

FEMALE DOCTOR #2
Let's try for a muscle biopsy next. I want that sent for frozen section and electron microscopy.

FEMALE DOCTOR #4
We have hetastarch available.

FEMALE DOCTOR #3
Add bilirubin, S.G.O.T., S.G.P.T., alk phos, and L.D.H. to his chemistries.

MALE DOCTOR #3
Prep five per kilo.

FEMALE DOCTOR #4
A C.V.P. line could help.

MALE DOCTOR #3
I think you'll get more information with a Swan-Ganz.

FEMALE DOCTOR #4
Fine, but let's do it under fluoroscopy.

FEMALE DOCTOR #2
And a set of cardiac enzymes. Maybe he had an M.I.

ELLIOTT
You have no right to do this.

MALE TECH #1
Oxygen saturation is 82 percent on room air.

ELLIOTT
You're scaring him!

FEMALE TECH #2
Any hemoglobin present?

MALE TECH #1
None detected. I've isolated non-nucleated cells from the blood stream.

MALE DOCTOR #4
B.P. one hundred over seventy.

ELLIOTT
You're scaring him!

MALE DOCTOR #4
Respiratory rate twelve.

DOCTOR
Good air entry but decreased tidal volume on the boy. Put him on O-two, five liters by nasal cannula, and draw a blood gas in ten minutes.

MALE DOCTOR #3
Temperature has dropped from twenty to seventeen degrees centigrade.

FEMALE DOCTOR #2
Get a hypothermia blanket and some warm lamps.

ELLIOTT
Leave him alone.

FEMALE DOCTOR #2
S-PEP shows an absence of spike in the gamma globulin range.

FEMALE DOCTOR #3
He's got a very different immune system.

ELLIOTT
Just leave him alone. I can take care of him.

ELLIOTT and E.T. lie side by side, tubed, taped, and needled. Keys is outside near where E.T. lies.

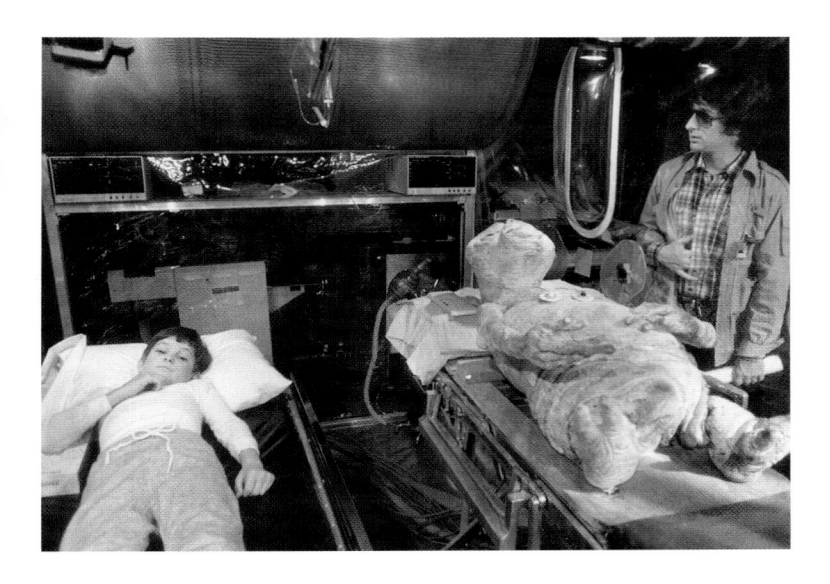

The Hospital

In the earliest scripts, E.T. and Elliott were taken to a hospital when they got sick towards the end of the film. Then Michael and his friends rescue them from there.

I remember scouting hospital after hospital but we couldn't find one we really liked that would be available to us on a scale that we needed.

—Allen Daviau

Steven flew into Los Angeles International Airport and, at the time, they were building the Bradley Terminal. They had erected a temporary pneumatic structure for international flights.

Well, Steven had this absolutely brilliant idea to re-create that kind of structure in the family house. It was psychologically so appropriate to the story to take this warm, comfortable environment where the kids are growing up and turn it into a nightmare.

—James D. Bissell, Production Designer

It made a lot of sense to me that the house would be the place the government would seal up. They would shut down the surrounding neighborhood and do their work there.

—Steven Spielberg

Top and Right: Behind the scenes during the filming of the doctors treating E.T. and Elliott.

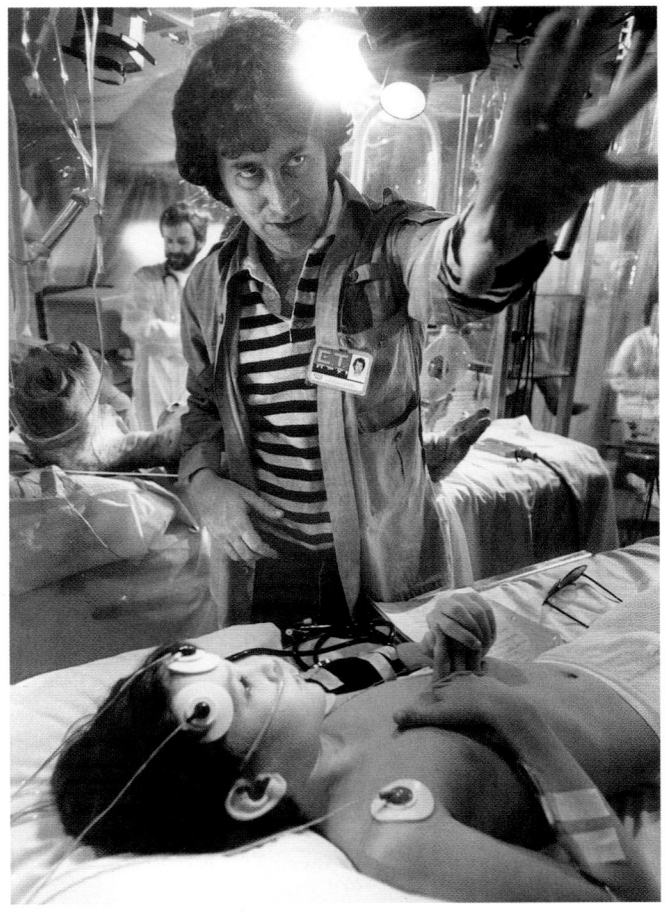

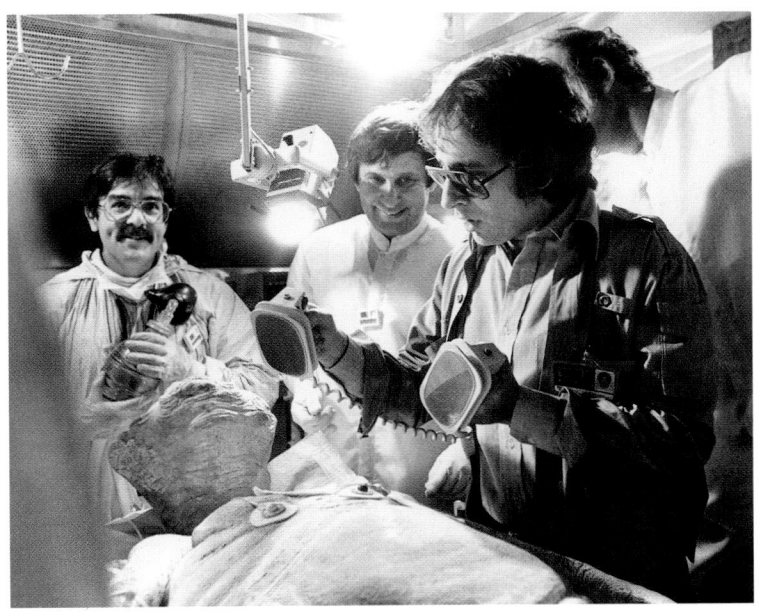

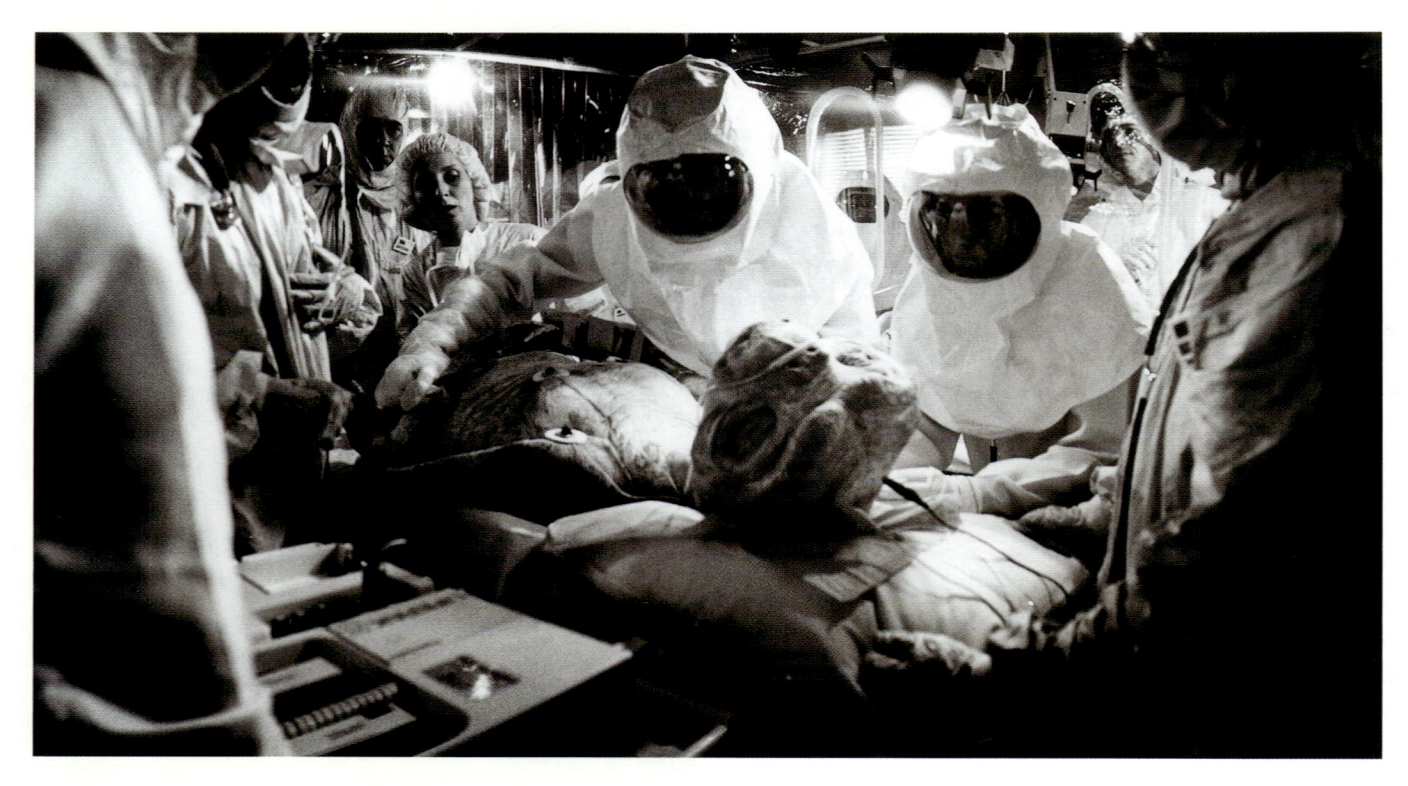

MALE DOCTOR #5
Get a Doppler scope in here and set me up for a two-D cardiac echo.

FEMALE DOCTOR #2
Skin is cool and diaphoretic.

FEMALE DOCTOR #3
We have to consider all shock-tiologies.

MALE DOCTOR #5
No, he's not perfusing at all. He needs inotropic support. P.H. is down to seven-point-oh-three. He's got a metabolic acidosis.

MALE DOCTOR #3
It could be sepsis.

FEMALE DOCTOR #1
We've drawn two sets of blood cultures.

MALE DOCTOR #5
He needs broad-spectrum coverage. How about Amp, Gent, and Flagyl?

> **PRODUCTION NOTES**
> Many real doctors were hired for these scenes including Dr. Stein (Steven Spielberg's personal physician at the time), Rhoda Makoff whose friend jogged with casting director Mike Fenton, and Alex Lamponi whose job was to treat E.T. as a real person.

FEMALE TECH #1
Cardiac output one-point-nine liters per meter squared body surface area per minute. Ejection fraction is 20 percent.

Keys has reached the side of the isolation booth that Elliott is on. He raps on the plastic separating them three times.

KEYS
Elliott.

Elliott looks to Keys.

KEYS
I've been to the forest.

MILITARY DOCTOR
He shouldn't talk now.

KEYS
Well, he has to talk now, Major.

KEYS
Elliott, that machine, what does it do?

ELLIOTT
The communicator? Is it still working?

KEYS
It's doing something. What?

ELLIOTT
I really shouldn't tell.

ELLIOTT
He came to me. He came to me.

KEYS
Elliott, he came to me, too. I've been wishing for this since I was ten years old. I don't want him to die. What can we do that we're not already doing?

ELLIOTT
He needs to go home. He's calling his people. And I don't know where they are. He needs to go home.

KEYS
Elliott, I don't think that he was left here intentionally. But his being here is a miracle, Elliott. It's a miracle. And you did the best that anybody could do. I'm glad he met you first.

Keys rises. Elliott looks after him. He raises up a little.

D.N.A. DOCTOR
He's got D.N.A.

FEMALE TECH #1
Incredible.

D.N.A. DOCTOR
He's got D.N.A.! He doesn't have four nucleotides, like we do. He has six.

MALE TECH #1
I've got de-synchronization of the two brain-wave activities.

MALE DOCTOR #6
What are they?

D.N.A. DOCTOR
One is inosine, and there's a pyrimidine we can't identify.

FEMALE DOCTOR #1
That's a thousand times more genetic diversity.

ELLIOTT
E.T.!

FEMALE NURSE #1
The boy's condition is stabilizing. His blood pressure is coming back up.

FEMALE DOCTOR #2
He's making proteins we've never even heard of.

FEMALE DOCTOR #3
Two hundred and sixteen codons compared to our sixty-four.

ELLIOTT
E.T.

E.T.
Elliott.

PRODUCTION NOTES

For this sequence, Kathleen Kennedy and Melissa Mathison spent time in a local L.A. hospital to research the procedures for treating a patient with E.T.'s condition. Mathison didn't like working on these scenes because they had to be so technically accurate.

There is a sudden hush, then a rush of excitement.

FEMALE DOCTOR #1
He's speaking!

FEMALE NURSE #1
He's talking.

ELLIOTT
E.T., stay with me. Please.

E.T.
Stay.

ELLIOTT
Together.

ELLIOTT
I'll be right here. I'll be right here.

E.T.
Stay, Elliott. Stay. Stay. Stay. Stay.

FEMALE NURSE #1
The creature's pressure is bottoming out. His complexes are slow and widening.

FEMALE DOCTOR #1
How's the boy?

FEMALE NURSE #1
He's converting back to normal sinus rhythm.

MALE DOCTOR #3
They're separating.

FEMALE NURSE #1
Yes.

MALE DOCTOR #3
Boy and creature are separating.

FEMALE NURSE #1
Definitely separating.

KEYS
What does that mean?

FEMALE DOCTOR #1
The boy is coming back. We're losing E.T.

ELLIOTT
E.T., answer me, please.

FEMALE DOCTOR #2
Everything's going to be fine, Elliott.

ELLIOTT
Please!

FEMALE DOCTOR #2
Just relax.

INT. ELLIOTT'S ROOM – NIGHT

Michael enters Elliott's room. Michael looks around, then enters the closet.

INT. CLOSET – NIGHT

E.T.'s closet. All of his things are there. There is still a crease where his body once sat. Michael sits in that spot. He falls asleep.

INT. CLOSET – DAY

It is morning. The sun shines in on Michael's eyes. He opens them, rubs them, and looks around. He sees the geranium.

Before our eyes, the plant sinks on its stem. Its branches droop. Whatever flowers are left fall off. The plant dies.

CLOSE ON MICHAEL

Slow realization. He screams.

MICHAEL
No.

INT. PLAYROOM – DAY

ELLIOTT
(*screaming*)
E.T., don't go!

A nurse checks her monitor.

NURSE
No blood pressure!

SAVE HIM DOCTOR
He's got no pulse or respiration! We can't get a pulse or blood pressure on the creature!

FEMALE NURSE #1
It doesn't look like he's breathing.

EMERGENCY DOCTOR #1
We gotta get in there!

There is pandemonium. The emergency doctors and their assistants run to the isolation room.

MILITARY DOCTOR
Hey, you can't break the, you can't break the sterile field like that!

The emergency doctors ignore him. They pull down the plastic wall separating them from E.T. They immediately start working on E.T.

EMERGENCY DOCTOR
Get him back. Get him back.

ELLIOTT
Leave him alone!

EMERGENCY DOCTOR #2
How's he doing? How's the child doing?

ELLIOTT
You're killing him! Leave him alone!

EMERGENCY DOCTOR #2
Unhook him, and get him outta here.

SAVE HIM DOCTOR
Let's move it!

EMERGENCY DOCTOR #2
Okay, let's get the boy out of here!

EMERGENCY DOCTOR #1
He's not breathing.

EMERGENCY DOCTOR #2
Get him moving! Get him moving!

SAVE HIM DOCTOR
The child—get him outta here.

They wheel Elliott out quickly and move E.T.'s bed over as Elliott screams.

ELLIOTT
Stop it! You're killing him! You're killing him!

There is really pandemonium here. The doctors all keep talking. (Many, many ad-libs here).

SAVE HIM DOCTOR
Let's get him moving! Come on!

EMERGENCY DOCTOR #1
Let's go. Move that gurney over here!

ELLIOTT
You're killing him! You're killing him!

EMERGENCY DOCTOR #1
Let's go! Start C.P.R.

Once again the clammer and din of background opinions ensue.

One of the doctors reenters, having helped wheel Elliott out, and pulls down the other plastic wall. Some of the doctors start ripping off masks and hats.

ELLIOTT
You're killing him! He came to me!

EMERGENCY DOCTOR #1
Begin C.P.R.!

SAVE HIM DOCTOR
Come on! He'll be fine. Do we have a pulse?

EMERGENCY DOCTOR #2
Come on, let's ventilate him. Any pulses?

MALE DOCTOR #4
No femoral pulse.

EMERGENCY DOCTOR #2
Any pulses?

ANGLE ON ELLIOTT

He is still screaming and pulling off his IV and monitoring devices.

ELLIOTT
He came to me!

ANGLE ON EMERGENCY DOCTORS WITH E.T.

          EMERGENCY DOCTOR #2
Okay, let's do C.P.R. Come on, let's go!

          FEMALE NURSE #2
How many compressions?

          SAVE HIM DOCTOR
Go on, let's go, let's start.

          FEMALE NURSE #1
No breath sounds.

          EMERGENCY DOCTOR #2
Sixty per minute, please. Come on.

          FEMALE NURSE #1
Minimal breath sounds.

          MALE DOCTOR #4
Ventilation isn't good.

          DEFIBRILLATOR DOCTOR
One and two and three and four.

          SAVE HIM DOCTOR
Calm down! Calm down!

          EMERGENCY DOCTOR #2
Let's try some bretyllium. Can I have some bretyllium, please?

          EMERGENCY DOCTOR #2
Let's go, bretyllium.

          EMERGENCY DOCTOR #1
Getting a pulse?

          EMERGENCY DOCTOR #2
Bretyllium, five milligrams.

          FEMALE DOCTOR #1
Compressed air. Can we have compressed air, please.

          EMERGENCY DOCTOR #2
Can we have the saline, please?

          EMERGENCY DOCTOR #2
Thank you.

Drew's Tears

I don't think tears have ever been that readily available to me in my entire life.
—DREW BARRYMORE

Drew was meant to be in this movie. She got the part, and became my best friend on the film.
—STEVEN SPIELBERG

MALE DOCTOR #4

All IV push.

An IV bag and tubing is passed to the nurse, and the IV is connected to the indwelling hepa-cath in E.T.'s arm.

EMERGENCY DOCTOR #1

He's not ventilating!

EMERGENCY DOCTOR #1

His pupils are fixed and dilated.

FEMALE DOCTOR #1

Give him some more drugs.

MALE DOCTOR #4

Let's go!

EMERGENCY DOCTOR #2

Quiet! Quiet!

MILITARY DOCTOR

Defibrillate him!

MALE DOCTOR #4

Let's go!

EMERGENCY DOCTOR #1

We're losing him. We're losing him.

EMERGENCY DOCTOR #2

Go!

DEFIBRILLATOR DOCTOR

Everybody stand clear.

EMERGENCY DOCTOR #1

Clear.

ANGLE ON GERTIE

She jumps, reacting to the jolt given to E.T.

> **PRODUCTION NOTES**
> Steve Townsend, E.T.'s technical supervisor, was lying under the gurney while E.T. was given shock treatments and he poked the gurney with a stick with each "shock."

EMERGENCY DOCTOR #1

We're losing him.

FEMALE DOCTOR #1

One more time, let's do it.

EMERGENCY DOCTOR #2

Quiet!

EMERGENCY DOCTOR #2

Quiet!

EMERGENCY DOCTOR #2

It's still V. fib.

EMERGENCY DOCTOR #1

Okay, let's try it. Okay, let's go.

FEMALE NURSE #2

All right.

EMERGENCY DOCTOR #2

Okay, let's go.

EMERGENCY DOCTOR #2

Quiet!

ANGLE ON ELLIOTT

In his background, Mary and Gertie enter from the air shower in the hallway. They move to Elliott. Mary touches Elliott's arm. He turns to see his mother.

MARY

Elliott?

> **ELLIOTT**
> Mom!

They embrace. They all cry. Gertie looks on and cries too.

ANGLE ON ELLIOTT, MARY, AND GERTIE.

Michael enters in their background. He moves near the kitchen area and looks on sadly.

> **EMERGENCY DOCTOR #2**
> Let's continue C.P.R., please.

EXT. HOUSE – DAY

There is a sudden flurry of activity around the house. Men in blue jumpsuits are breaking apart the air tubes and carrying equipment in all directions.

EXT. CUL-DE-SAC – DAY

The boys, Tyler, Steve and Greg, are behind the sawhorses which cordon off the circular end of the street. There is quite a crowd of people behind them: neighbors, newsmen, the curious. The boys are straddling bicycles.

> **STEVE**
> Something's happening.
>
> **GREG**
> Ooooh. They're gonna die.
>
> **TYLER**
> Shut up, Greg.
>
> **STEVE**
> Something is definitely happening.

INT. PLAYROOM – DAY

About two hours later. The ER doctors are still working on E.T. We see Elliott standing near the window, a blanket wrapped around him. He just looks on numbly.

> **EMERGENCY DOCTOR #2**
> Does anybody have any ideas?
>
> **SAVE HIM DOCTOR**
> E.E.G.'s flat. E.K.G.'s flat.
>
> **MILITARY DOCTOR**
> Okay, I'm gonna call it.

> **PRODUCTION NOTES**
> It was easier for Henry Thomas to cry than to laugh. He said that, to bring on tears, all he had to do was think about his dog, Oso, who was killed when Henry was seven years old.

> **EMERGENCY DOCTOR #1**
> Oh, I, I don't know.
>
> **EMERGENCY DOCTOR #2**
> I think he's dead.
>
> **MILITARY DOCTOR**
> All right, I'm calling it. What time do you have?
>
> **FEMALE NURSE #1**
> Fifteen thirty-six.
>
> **MILITARY DOCTOR**
> Okay, fifteen hours, thirty-six minutes. Okay. Let's pack him in ice. Let's leave.

The doctors start putting out the lights, shut off monitors, and leave the isolation room; Elliott remains. Keys, still outside the booth, now moves into the room.

CLOSE

Keys bends to E.T. Keys closes E.T.'s eyes.

BACK TO MARY AND GERTIE

> **GERTIE**
> Is he dead, Mama?
>
> **MARY**
> I think so, sweetheart.
>
> **GERTIE**
> Can we wish for him to come back?
>
> **MARY**
> Yeah.
>
> **GERTIE**
> I wish.

                    MARY

I wish, too.

ANGLE IN KITCHEN

Several men wheel a lead box, a small coffin, toward the isolation booth. Michael looks on.

They pass in foreground of Mary and Gertie. Mary, realizing this is too much for Gertie to watch, picks her up and moves toward the hallway leading to the living room.

                    MARY

Come on, Gert. We'll wait for Elliott in the front room.

TIME LAPSE HERE

ISOLATION ROOM – SOME TIME LATER

                EMERGENCY DOCTOR #1

Cardiac arrest was terminated at fifteen hundred hours and thirty-six minutes. He received intravenous Lidocaine, intravenous epinephrine, a Lidocaine drip...two-point-seven percent sodium-chloride dilution, catheters from the A-line and the, uh... intravenous line should be sent for culture. He was monitored with an...E.E.G. and an E.K.G. to be interpolated with.

Elliott stands just outside the isolation room, Keys nearby him. Keys moves to Elliott.

                    KEYS

They're gonna have to take him away now.

                    ELLIOTT

They're just gonna cut him all up.

                    KEYS

Would you just like to spend some time alone with him?

ANGLE ON ELLIOTT

Elliott does not answer. Keys moves him toward the room. Elliott goes to one side of the lead box, while Keys goes to the other. Keys whispers to the doctors making their report. They look around and exit.

                    DOCTOR

Could, uh, we all step out for a minute, please?

In the kitchen Michael moves out with everyone else through the air shower leading to the dining room. Once in the dining room, he looks on.

Keys opens the lid of the lead box and leaves. Elliott is alone with E.T. Through the glass in the open lid, he looks at his friend who is encased in a plastic bag zippered closed.

ELLIOTT, a tear in his eye, begins to talk to his friend.

                    ELLIOTT

Look at what they've done to you. I'm so sorry. You must be dead...because I... don't know how to feel. I can't feel anything anymore. You're going someplace else now. I'll believe in you all my life. Every day. E.T., I love you.

Elliott closes the lid, but before it closes, the heart light comes on. Elliott, so bereaved, doesn't notice it. He moves toward the kitchen.

The geranium Michael placed on the counter between the kitchen and playroom is still there. As Elliott passes it, something catches his eye. He stops and looks at the geranium. It is beginning to blossom again. A momentary hesitation, then realization.

                    ELLIOTT
Oh, my God.

Swiftly, he moves back toward the lead box and throws the lid open. The heart light is on. Momentarily stunned, he touches it, then quickly begins to unzipper the plastic bag which encases E.T.

He looks at E.T.'s face. E.T.'s head turns toward him, his eyes open — he speaks.

                    E.T.
E.T. phone home.

                    ELLIOTT
          (*running his fingers through his hair*)
HA HA ———

Elliott looks around to be sure no one has heard his outburst.

                    E.T.
Home. Phone home. Phone home.

                    ELLIOTT
Does this mean they're coming?

                    E.T.
Yes.

                    ELLIOTT
God.

                    E.T.
E.T. phone home.

                    E.T.
E.T. phone home.

Elliott puts his hand over E.T.'s mouth.

                    ELLIOTT
Stay.

                    E.T.
E.T. phone home.

                    ELLIOTT
Shhh. Shut up.

                    E.T.
Phone. Phone home.

                    ELLIOTT
Quiet!

                    E.T.
Phone, phone, phone. E.T. phone home.

Keys and other men begin to reenter the room. Elliott sees this and panics.

                    ELLIOTT
Would you shut up?

                    E.T.
Phone home. E.T. phone home. E.T. phone home. E.T. phone home. E.T. phone home. Phone home. Home. Home.

He quickly grabs the blanket from the floor that has fallen from his shoulders and covers E.T.'s heart light. He begins to close the lid, then quickly opens it, momentarily.

                    E.T.
Elliott. Elliott. Elliott. Stay. Stay.

He closes the lid and throws himself across the box, pretending to sob loudly.

Keys approaches him and takes him away from the box.

                    KEYS
Elliott, why don't you come with me?

                    ELLIOTT
No.

                    KEYS
Elliott, why don't you come with me?

                    ELLIOTT
          (*hanging on to the box*)
No. No. No.

                    ELLIOTT
No!

                    KEYS
It's all right.

                    ELLIOTT
No!

                    KEYS
It's all right.

Keys moves him toward the kitchen; the geranium is still coming alive again. Keys sees Elliott looking at it and:

                    KEYS
Uh, would you like the flowers?

Elliott, quickly diverting Keys' attention, begins once more to bellow.

The men at the lead box seal the box closed.

Keys leads Elliott through the air shower where Michael stands talking to a man. Elliott throws his arms around his brother and Keys leaves them alone, moving on.

Elliott quickly pulls Michael into the air shower which turns on. Elliott is shouting over the sound of the air pumping in.

                    ELLIOTT
He's alive!

                    MICHAEL
What?

                    ELLIOTT
He's alive!

                    MICHAEL
All right!

Michael jumps up, hitting his head on the ceiling of the air shower, then starts to exit toward E.T. Elliott quickly stops him.

                    ELLIOTT
It's glowing. It's glowing right here. Hey!

> **PRODUCTION NOTES**
>
> Melissa Mathison never meant for anyone to know what was in this note Elliott hands to Mary. She told Henry to write a note as Elliott, and this is what he wrote: "Dear Mom, E.T. is alive. We are going to the forest. Don't try and stop us."

In the kitchen we can see the geranium is now fully blossomed.

INT. LIVING ROOM – DAY

Gertie, carrying the geranium, moves toward Keys and Mary, who stand talking.

                    GERTIE
Are they gone, Mama?

                    MARY
Who's gone, honey?

Mary answers, but turns to her conversation with Keys.

                    KEYS
You'll be detained, honestly, eight days to two weeks.

Gertie perseveres.

                    GERTIE
The boys.

                    MARY
What boys? (*to Keys*) Well, I just need—

Mary, paying little attention, continues with her conversation with Keys.

                    GERTIE
I'm supposed to give you this note when they're gone.

She is waving a note before Mary. This peaks Mary's interest. She grabs for the note.

                    MARY
Give it to me now, Gertie.

She moves off by herself to read it, Gertie and Keys look on.

                    MARY
(*reading the note*)
Oh, my God!

INT. AIR HOSE

Elliott enters the tube as the two men carrying the lead box have finished and are exiting it.

He moves over to the curtain, which separates the front of the van from the back, and pulls it back, frightening Michael who screams.

ELLIOTT
Where's your mask?

MICHAEL
Uh, it's back here.

ELLIOTT
Well, get it on!

MICHAEL
I'm trying!

EXT. HOUSE – DAY

A man in a brown suit walks around the side of the van still attached to the house by the air tube and starts toward the back. He pauses and walks back to the window of driver's side of the cab and looks in. We see Michael, dressed in a blue jumpsuit.

AGENT #1
Hey, who are you?

MICHAEL
I'm driving.

AGENT #1
Open the door, son.

INT. VAN

MICHAEL (*to Elliott in rear of van*)
There's a guy out here. What do I do?!

ELLIOTT
Well, what are you waiting for? Let's go!

ELLIOTT
Well, let's get out of here, Michael!

MICHAEL
I've never driven forward before!

EXT. HOUSE – DAY

The van pulls away from the front of the house. As it zigzags down the driveway, it rips the air tube away from the front door. The pneumatic seal is broken. Before our eyes, the plastic curtain, draping the house, collapses. The van skids to the bottom of the driveway, pulling twenty feet of air hose behind it like the flailing tail of a dragon.

EXT. TOP OF CUL-DE-SAC – DAY

Michael leans on the horn. Policemen scurry to move the sawhorses. The crowd parts to let the van through. The boys are still in the crowd. The van slows down long enough for the barriers to be removed and long enough for the boys to look in the front seat and see Michael as he pulls his hood off.

TYLER
Michael?

STEVE
Michael!

GREG
Mike?

MICHAEL
Get the bikes.

TYLER
Are you all right?

MICHAEL
Meet us at the playground at the top of the hill.

TYLER
Let's do it!

ELLIOTT
Go, Michael! Go come on!

Michael steps on the gas and zigzags down the hill, pulling its tail behind it.

EXT. CUL-DE-SAC

The boys put on their head gear — masks.

EXT. VAN – DAY

The van careens down the street, the men in the air tube the van is dragging.

They are trying to gain some balance as it bounces along the street.

INT. VAN – THROUGH WINDSHIELD

Michael is driving, almost talking to himself.

MICHAEL
We're all gonna die, and they're never gonna give me my license.

INT. REAR OF VAN

Elliott is struggling to understand how to loosen the tube, which is attached to the van by latches.

He studies and tugs.

INT. VAN – FRONT SEAT/REAR OF VAN

MICHAEL
Where's the playground?

ELLIOTT
It's near the preschool.

MICHAEL
Where's that?!

ELLIOTT
I don't know streets! Mom always drives me!

MICHAEL
Son of a bitch.

Elliott finally gets one latch loose, looks at it, smiles, and then goes to work one by one, pulling the many latches loose.

REVERSE – IN THE TUBE

The men are still coming, struggling, falling. But coming closer.

BACK TO ELLIOTT

He is having trouble with one of the latches; the men are still coming. He finally gets it out.

EXT. ELLIOTT'S HOUSE – EXT./INT. CAR

Mary moves the car out of the garage through the plastic. Gertie is on the seat beside her, holding the geranium.

Keys enters from under the plastic and runs to the car.

KEYS
Where are you going?

Gertie moves across in front of Mary to the window near Keys, holding her geranium.

GERTIE
To the spaceship.

MARY
Shh.

KEYS
Spaceship?

GERTIE
To the spaceship to the moon.

Mary unhappily pulls Gertie away from the window, muttering.

MARY
(*to Gertie*) Be quiet.

KEYS
Oh, my God.

INT. BACK OF THE VAN – DAY

Elliott is just pulling on the last several latches. Throws one to man in tube.

EXT. STREET – DAY

The van comes down a hill and rounds a corner when the tube is freed. It falls to the ground.

The two men struggle for a moment, then rise, unhurt but angry, shaking fists after the vehicle moving on furiously.

EXT. STREET – DAY

The van comes around a bend headed toward the playground.

EXT. PLAYGROUND – DAY

There are the boys, standing in formation, straddling their bikes. Michael's and Elliott's bicycles are ready to be mounted.

The van screeches to a halt, smoke from the dried ice pouring out of it. The boys move to the van. They see Elliott and E.T. standing in the rear of the van. E.T.'s heart light is really flashing now. The boys freeze when they see who is standing next to Elliott. Elliott smiles at the boys.

>   ELLIOTT
> Okay, he's a man from outer space, and we're taking him to his spaceship.
>
>   GREG
> (*dumbfounded*)
> Well, can't he just beam up?
>
>   ELLIOTT
> This is reality, Greg.

EXT. STREET – DAY

The official cars come around a bend, and all park beside the playground. Car doors open and men begin running into the park. Among them is Mary. Keys begins running.

EXT. PLAYGROUND – DAY

>   AGENT #3
> Keep her back!
>
>   MARY
> No!
>
>   AGENT #3
> Hold her back!

Mary arrives at the van.

The van is empty.

>   MARY
> No! No! No! No!
>
>   AGENT #3
> Where are they?
>
>   AGENT #1
> There's nobody here!

She moves off looking desperately about trying to see where they might have gone.

EXT. STREETS – DAY

Michael, Steve, Tyler, and Greg are speeding along on their bicycles. They flank Elliott's with E.T. in it. They move down the street. As they near a corner, two cars enter to block their way. They round the corner. The cars cannot follow, screeching to a halt. One man from one of the cars, gets out and pursues them on foot, as they head toward a hill.

>   GREG
> Where are we going?
>
>   ELLIOTT
> To the forest!

The boys move up the hill. A car suddenly appears, once more pursuing them, and they pedal frantically in front of the car. More cars appear out of nowhere as they near an intersection, converge, then the boys peel off in another direction.

>   ELLIOTT
> Follow me!

EXT. LOT – DAY

The boys ride into a lot through which the cars cannot enter. The boys are really riding now, jumping hills, etc. Elliott is in the lead, but the boys surround him, protecting him and E.T. They are headed toward a hill.

Guns

I really regret two cuts in the movie. I regret that a gun was used as a threat to stop children on bicycles in that last shot before E.T. opens his eyes and the bikes take off. The gun was not pointing at the kid but brandished in a kind of at-ready position. Also, there was a quick cut of a gun in the cop's hand when they find the abandoned Econoline van. Dry ice is pouring out of the back of the van, and E.T. is gone.

I really regret having any guns in the movie and in the reissue the picture I'll use the miracle of CGI to remove the guns from the cops' hands. I'll simply delete the shot of the cop holding the gun right before E.T. flies.

—STEVEN SPIELBERG IN 1995

ABOVE: In this scene in the original release, the policemen held guns in their hands. In these two photos from the 2002 release, the guns were digitally deleted and replaced with walkie talkies.

ABOVE: The kids outpace the police in the climatic chase scene. *BELOW LEFT:* Filming the flight of the bikes. *BELOW RIGHT:* Steven Spielberg and stuntman Ted Grossman who has worked on many of Spielberg's films, including Jaws *and* Raiders of the Lost Ark.

DRIVER
We've got 'em at the bottom of the hill.

Lead pursuit car stops at bottom of hill. Driver talks into the car microphone, as the passenger gets out of the car and heads up a hill.

DRIVER
This is unit three-oh-two. We've cut the kids off at the bottom of the hill. Send backup units. Over and out.

As the man nears the top of the hill, the boys appear and jump the hill, missing the man beneath them.

They continue to the bottom of the hill and turn toward a construction site. Several cars appear to continue their pursuit. The boys disappear into the construction site.

They are riding down a path in the rear end of the construction site.

STEVE (*reacting to car pursuing them*)
Let's split up!

MICHAEL
Okay!

Tyler reacts. Steve and Tyler peel off down a steep slope.

Michael, Elliott, and E.T. continue with Greg.

ELLIOTT
Hang on!

We find the boys moving along a tree lined street. They think they have eluded their pursuers. Steve is the last in line.

TYLER
We made it! (*removing his mask*)

Suddenly men appear from out of nowhere on foot, grabbing for Steve.

TYLER
Oh, shit!

As he continues behind all the others.

They drive on furiously, and in their path, they see cars entering from every corner and driveway as they approach an intersection.

It appears they will crash right into the cars, but they don't. Instead, they rise above the cars.

E.T. has regained his strength. The five bicycles lift into the air flying over the cars, over the streets, over the houses.

STEVE
Whoa!

TYLER
Whoa!

GREG
Tell me when it's over!

EXT. LANDING SITE – DUSK

The bicycles land in the tall grass. The other boys stop there.

Elliott and E.T. make an incredible jump, onto the landing site.

EXT. LANDING SITE – DUSK

Elliott moves to the communicator. The wind is blowing and leaves have covered over the communicator. He starts to clear the leaves off when a light attracts his attention. He looks up. His reactions are of awe, appreciation, and sadness.

EXT. TALL GRASS – DUSK

The boys move to the foreground, as they look off at the miraculous sight in the sky.

Music in the Sky

One of the experiences in my work with Steven Spielberg on *E.T.* that's most clear in my mind had to do with the end of the movie. I'm referring to the sequence that includes the bicycle chase where the boys are trying to escape from the authorities and bring E.T. back to his mothership. The sequence involved a lot of specific musical cues. An accent for each speed bump of the bicycles; a very dramatic accent for the police cars; a special lift for the bikes taking-off; sentimental music for the good-bye scene between E.T. and Elliott; and finally, when the spaceship takes off, the orchestra swells up and hits an accent when the spaceship whooshes away. So you can imagine in the space of that 15 minutes of film how many precise musical accents are needed and how each one has to be exactly in the right place. I wrote the music mathematically to configure with each of those occurrences and worked it all out.

Then when the orchestra assembled, and I had the film in front of me, I made attempt after attempt to record the music to exactly all of those arithmetic parameters. But I was never able to get a perfect recording that felt right musically and emotionally. I kept trying over and over again and finally, I said to Steven, "I don't think I can get this right. Maybe I need to do something else." And he said, "Why don't you take the movie off. Don't look at it. Forget the movie and conduct the orchestra the way you would want to conduct it in a concert so that the performance is just completely uninhibited by any considerations of mathematics and measurement." And I did that, and all of us agreed the music felt better. Then Steven re-edited slightly the last part of the film to configure with the musical performance that I felt was more powerful emotionally. And I think the result is that the end of the film has this kind of musical experience where it sweeps you away.

—JOHN WILLIAMS

EXT. LANDING SITE – DUSK

    E.T. looking off at the sky. Elliott is behind him near the rock with the communicator. A lavender light shines on E.T. Elliott, looking at the sky, moves to E.T.'s side.

    Elliott looks to E.T., his emotions are mixed. E.T. looks to Elliott; they both look back to the sky.

ANGLE – THE SPACESHIP

    The spaceship descends.

ANGLE ON BOYS

ANGLE ON E.T.

                     E.T.
    Home.

ANGLE ON ELLIOTT

ANGLE ON E.T.

    Heart light beats as spaceship lands.

My Favorite E.T.

I always felt that E.T. had twelve hearts, and each heart belonged to one of the operators. Each one had a separate function to move his cheek, create a smile, create a blink, create a pulsing of blood through veins in the neck, etc. But they were all E.T.'s fathers, or I used to call them, E.T.'s hearts.

    My favorite E.T. is the one that touches his heart, and he looks up when he sees the spaceship descending through the trees to come to get him at the end of the movie.

    That was an E.T. completely operated by wires that moved armatures that stretched the latex and of the skin and gave E.T. his look of wonder. That was my favorite all-time E.T.

—STEVEN SPIELBERG

ANGLE – THE SPACESHIP

The spaceship lands.

EXT. TALL GRASS – DUSK

The area is illuminated with a brilliant, pastel light.

EXT. FIRE ROAD – DUSK

Mary pulls her car to a stop on the forest road.

>   **GERTIE**
> Stop the car, Mama! They're over there! They're over there!

EXT. LANDING SITE – DUSK

At this moment, the door of the spaceship opens.

Gertie has reached the top of the rocky incline. Near the spaceship we see Michael running to her as she approaches Elliott and E.T.

As she and Michael approach Elliott, moves away allowing them a moment with E.T.

Gertie and Michael beside E.T.

>   **GERTIE**
> (*handing E.T. the geranium*)
> I just wanted to say good-bye.

>   **MICHAEL**
> He doesn't know good-bye.

>   **E.T.**
> Be good.

>   **GERTIE**
> Yes.

As she steps back, Michael moves in. He touches E.T.'s forehead, and E.T. pulls back, then relaxes.

>   **E.T.**
> Thank you.

Good-bye E.T. Scene

I think it was good to shoot the movie somewhat in continuity because you can't explain to a kid that we're shooting the last scene first and the first scene last. It doesn't make sense to them. I wanted the kids to be caught up as themselves and as their characters so that, by the time they say goodbye to E.T., their emotions are genuine. So we shot the movie in sequence, and it worked. Every single shot you see of Elliott crying and hugging E.T. in the good-bye scene was all on take one.

—STEVEN SPIELBERG

The hardest scene for me was the good-bye scene. I had worked so much with the E.T. character, and it had become very tangible to me. I could just draw on what was going on in the scene.

—HENRY THOMAS

                    MICHAEL
You're welcome.

Michael smiles and takes Gertie's hand moving away from E.T. as Elliott comes back for his last moments with E.T. E.T. puts the geranium down on the ground.

They stand looking at each other. In the background, we see Mary and Keys arrive and stand beside the boys.

                       E.T.
Come.

                     ELLIOTT
Stay.

E.T.'s heart light is on, illuminating Elliott's face. E.T. touches his heart and brings his hand to his mouth.

                       E.T.
Ouch.

Elliott presses his own chest and mouth and repeats:

                     ELLIOTT
Ouch.

The two friends stare at one another for a moment. Then together they reach their arms out and embrace. In the background, Mary kneels near the landing pad of the spaceship. It is a tender moment. Mary apprehensive; E.T. and Elliott very saddened. They pull apart.

E.T. moves his hand to Elliott's head, touches his finger lightly to the boy's forehead, and speaks, his finger lit up as in the healing situations.

                       E.T.
I'll be right here.

                     ELLIOTT
Bye.

147

E.T. picks up the geranium he had set down, and turns toward the spaceship. He moves toward it.

E.T. moves up the ramp.

E.T. enters, and Elliott moves a little closer. Harvey comes running in and starts up the spaceship gangplank. Elliott calls to him and finally retrieves him. They both stand looking at the ship as the door closes.

Mary, Keys, and the boys look on, as do Gertie and Michael.

They all watch the spaceship.

EXT. SKY – DUSK INTO NIGHT

The spaceship lifts into the air moving into the darkening sky to become smaller and smaller until it is only a speck of white light: the first star of the evening.

THE END

Ending

There was a final scene we shot where Elliott and the boys are playing *Dungeons and Dragons* again, echoing the beginning. However, now Elliott is the ringmaster rather then the annoying little brother. He's grown. He has confidence. He's the master of his own destiny.

The camera rises, and you see that the communicator is on the roof. You can only assume that one day they'll be in touch again. It was a nice ending, but we didn't use it.

Henry was so emotional in that final scene that it was hard to go anywhere else. Ultimately, it didn't really matter whether they were going to see each other again. That was not the point anymore.

—MELISSA MATHISON

RIGHT: A big cake was only part of the celebration for the child actors at the conclusion of filming E.T.

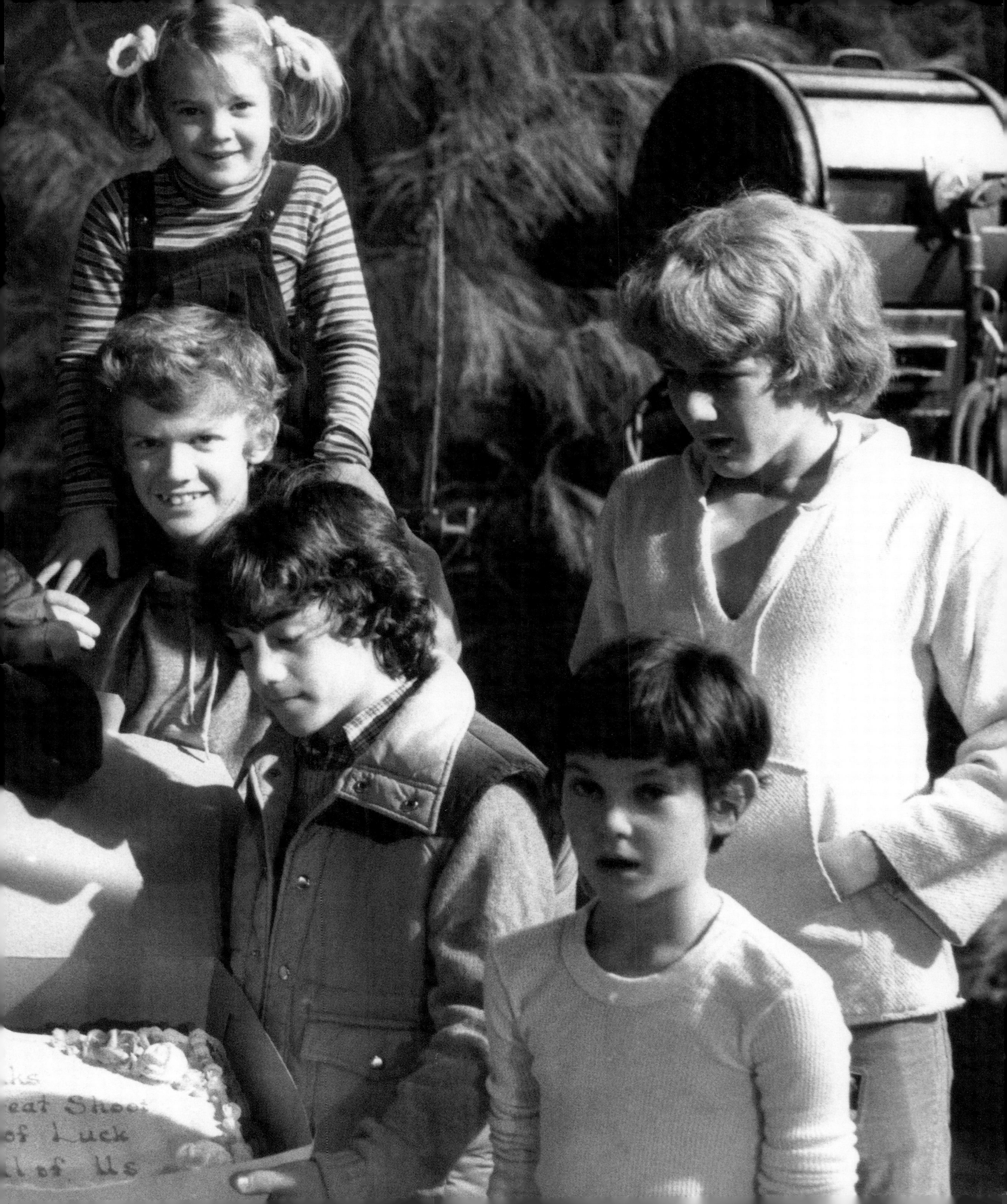
of Luck

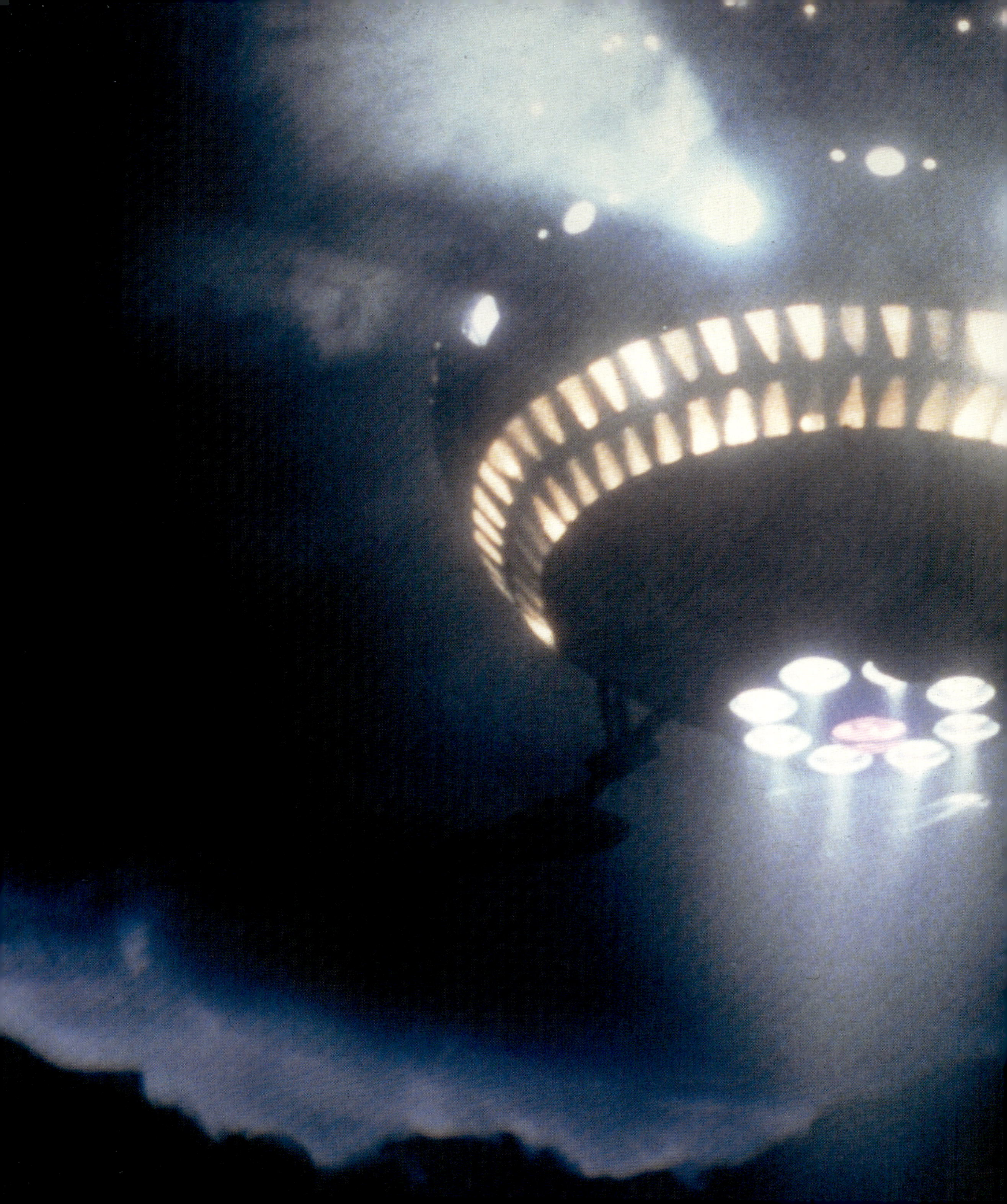

PART THREE:
POSTPRODUCTION AND BEYOND

BIKES and BOYS

LEFT: *Effects cameraman Mike McAlister.* ABOVE: *(from left to right) Mike McAlister; Steven Spielberg; Pat Sweeney, VFX camera assistant; Kenneth F. Smith, optical photography supervisor; Michael Fulmer, chief model maker; Kathleen Kennedy; Warren Franklin, VFX production coordinator; and Dennis Muren, VFX Supervisor.*

ILM: Industrial Light and Magic

Industrial Light and Magic began working on *E.T.* in May of 1981 under the supervision of Dennis Muren.

- To create the flying bike scenes, miniatures were built of all the bikes and the boys. The bikes were fully functional, with working wheels and brakes.

- The Elliott puppet was fifteen-and-one-half inches high, the smallest of all the puppets. Others were eighteen to twenty-two inches. Five different heads were built and clothes were made for the puppets.

- The scenes of the kids flying on their bikes were shot in front of a blue screen with the bike attached to a special rotating head. The final shots are a combination of miniature bikes and this live action in front of a blue screen. The riders passing through beams of sunlight and darkness were optically enhanced at a later date.

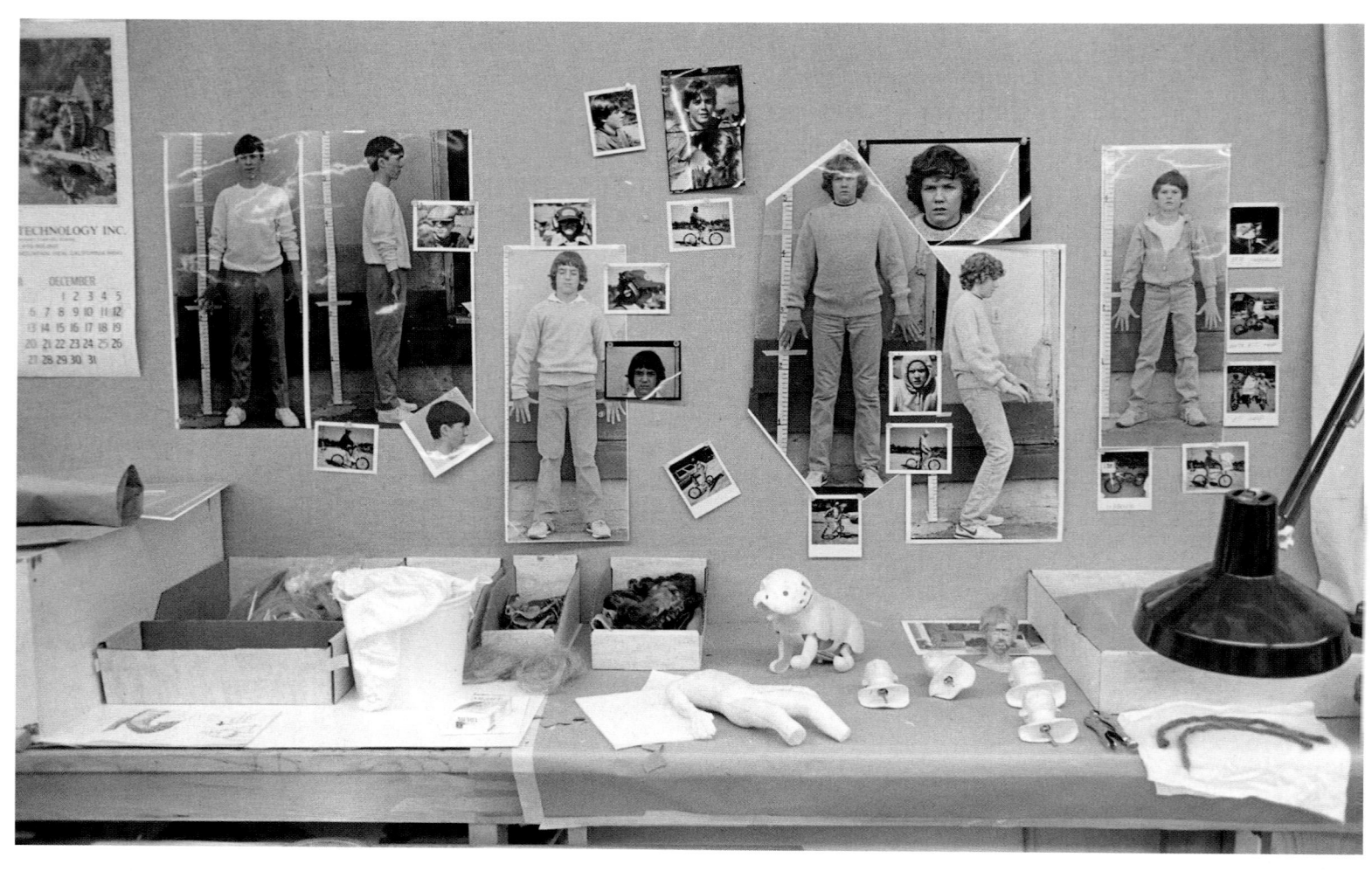

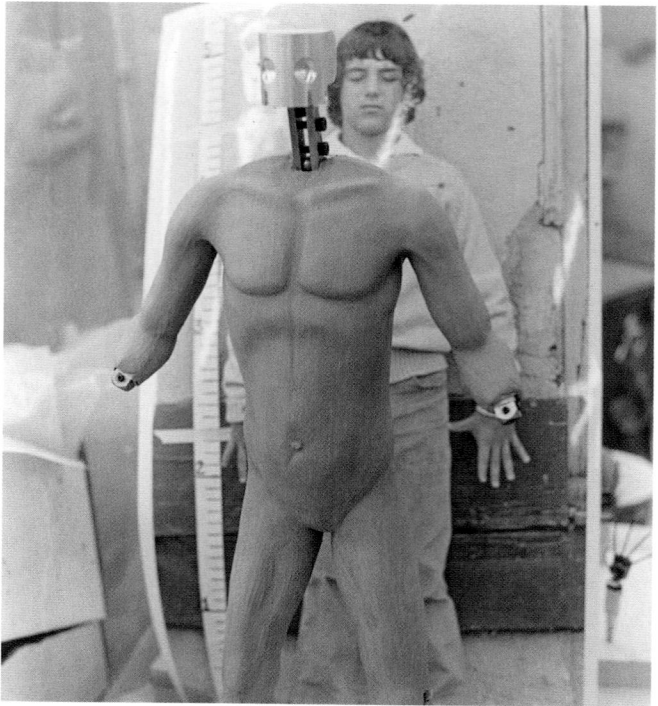

For the flying sequences, models of the bikes and each of the kids were created. BELOW RIGHT: *The sequences were realized by Michael Fulmer and Tom St. Amand.* OPPOSITE PAGE: *The actors pose with their miniature doubles, each of which was dressed in matching costumes.*

154

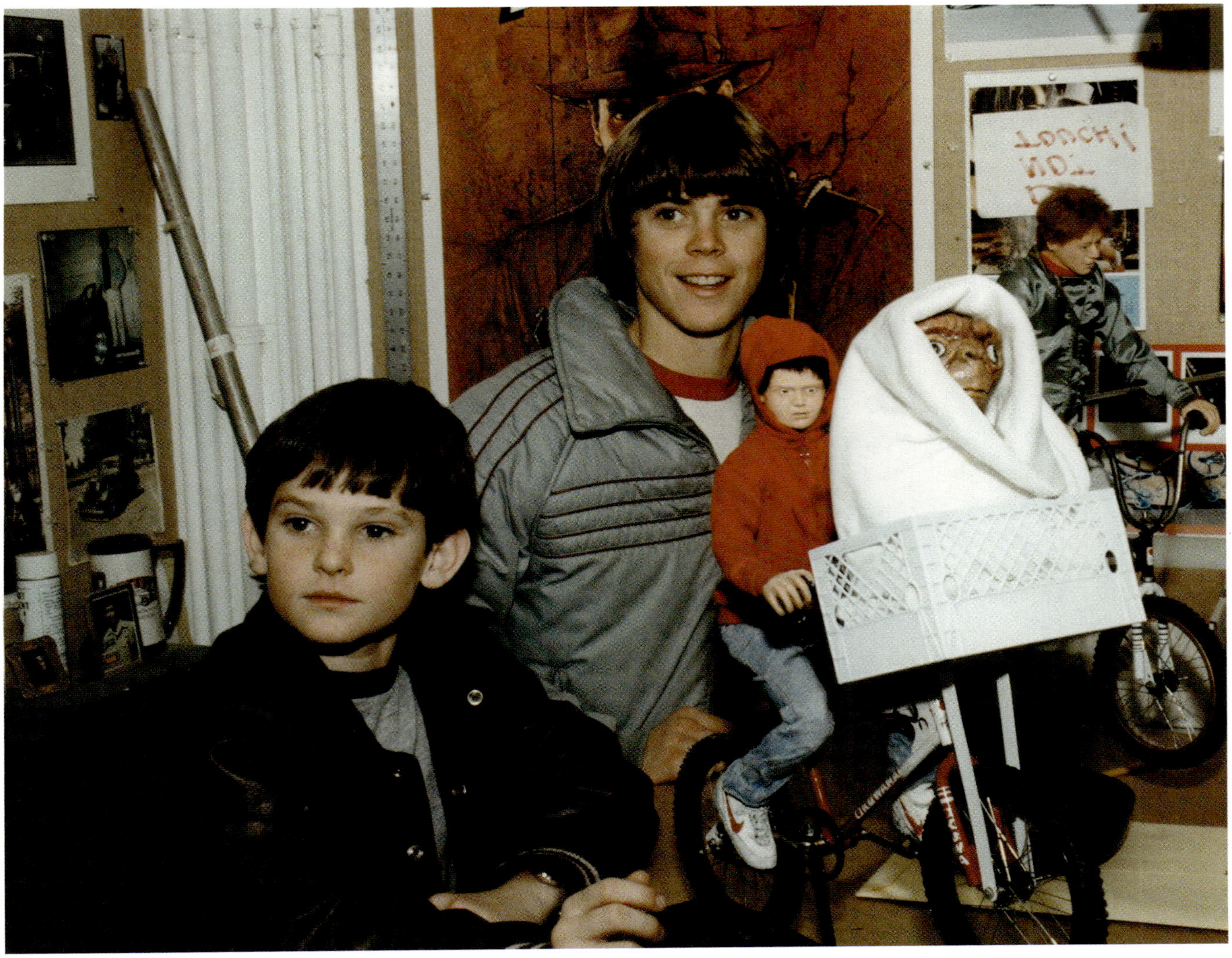

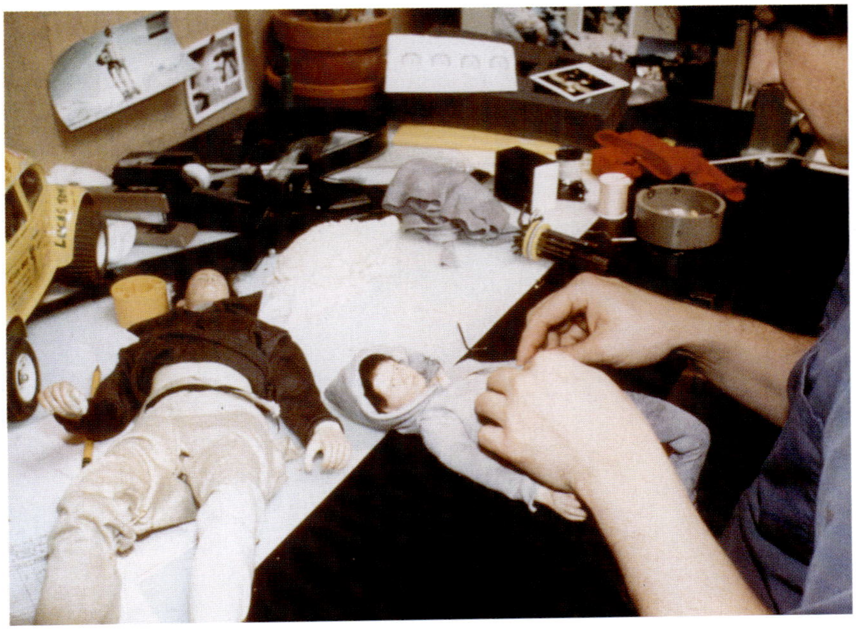

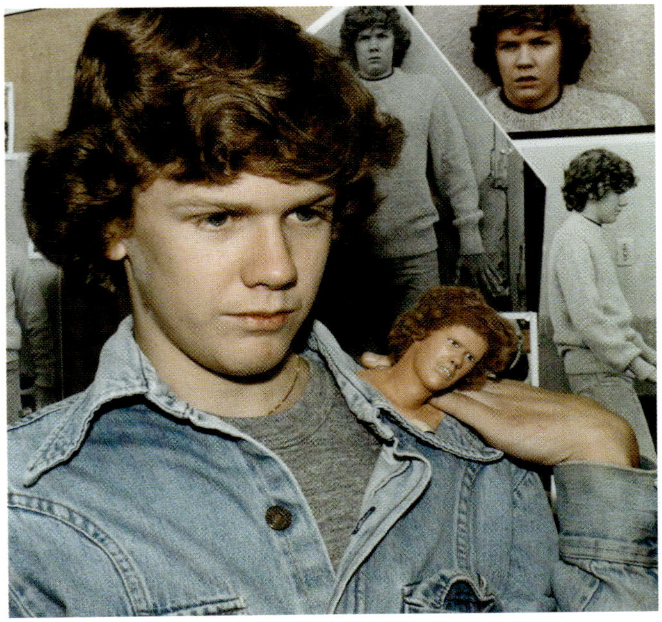

ABOVE: Dennis Muren working on the miniature set of the San Fernando Valley used in the original release. LEFT: *Dennis Muren (at camera) and Lorne Peterson (rear) setting up another miniature of the field landing area and painted backdrop.* OPPOSITE PAGE: *Top: Matte painting that was used to create reflections on the dome top of the miniature space ship. Below: Mike McAlister filming one of the miniature figures for the flying sequence.*

Matte Paintings and Miniatures

▪ *E.T.* was the first film to feature a new ILM process called "Latent Image Matte Painting" which was used in the scenes of Elliott in the garden at night.

▪ A second miniature set was created for the background when Elliott's bike lifts off the ground. The model incorporated trees, an escarpment, and a small canyon.

▪ The largest miniature set was thirteen by fourteen feet and re-created the section of the forest where Elliott and his friends land towards the end of the movie. Real leaves from juniper trees were used on the set.

▪ Twelve matte paintings were designed for *E.T.*

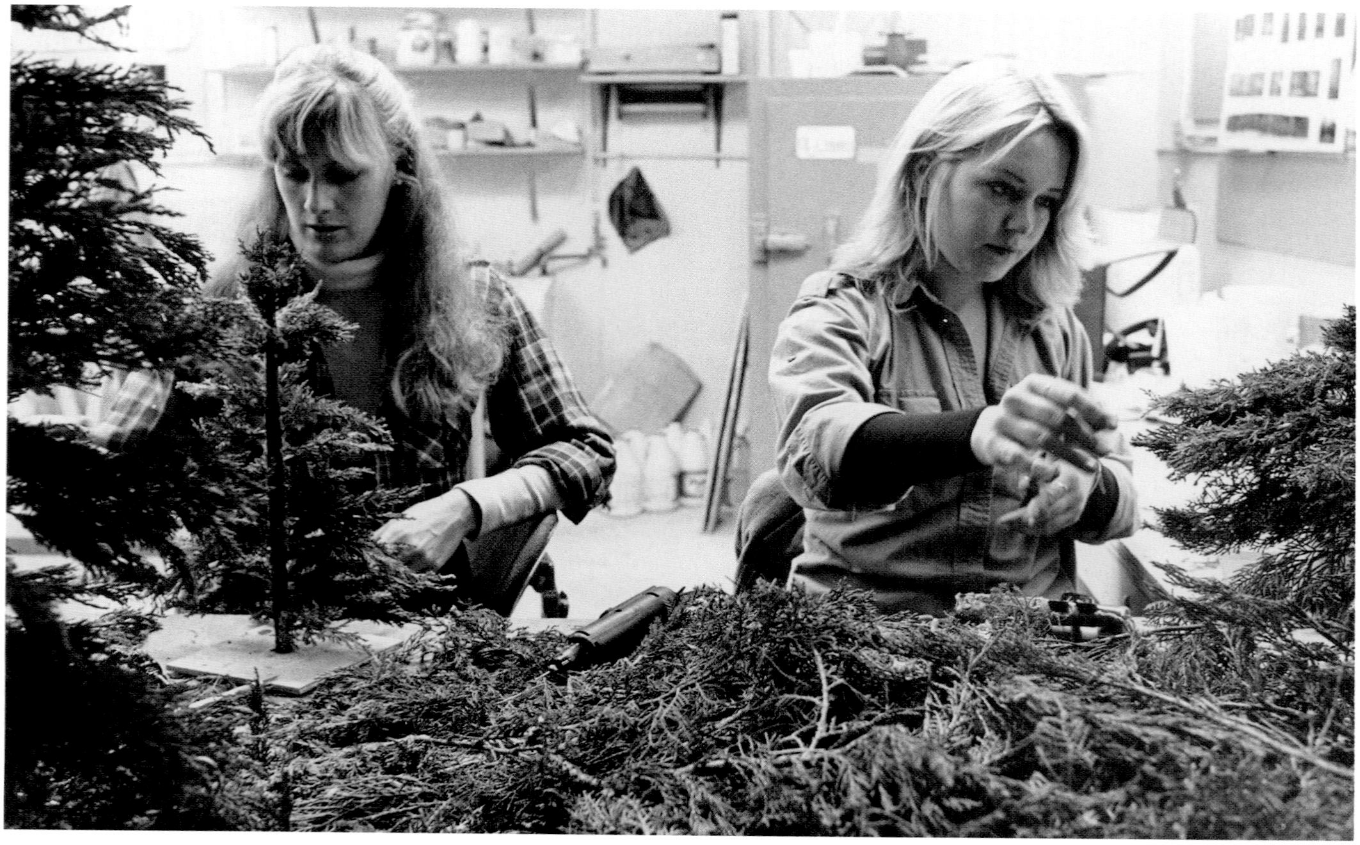

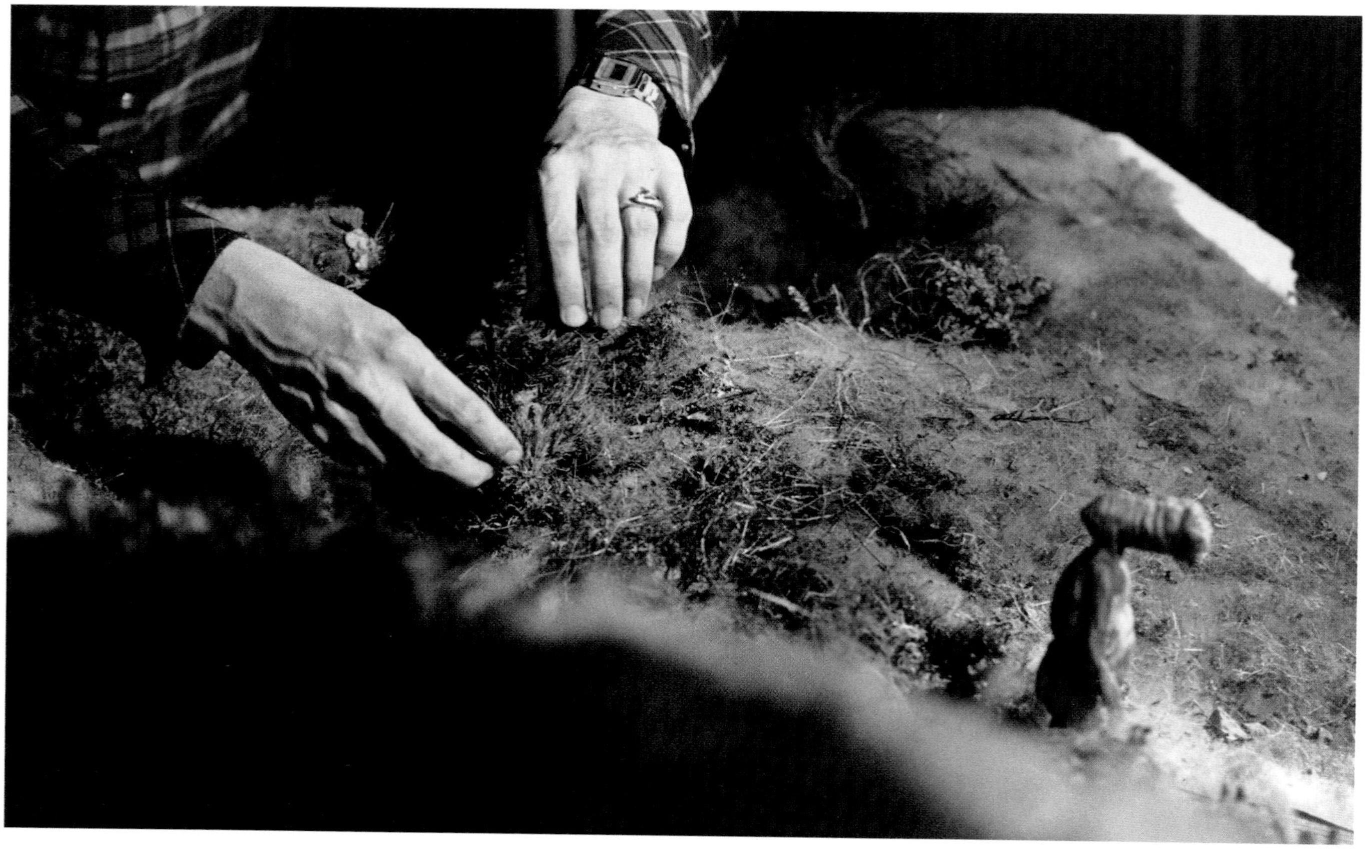

To create the scene where E.T. discovers the San Fernando Valley, a miniature E.T., only six inches high, was created and set on a miniature landscape of the valley. The background valley measured four by eight feet and was created by artist Chris Evans. Humorous details such as the McDonald's Golden Arches, neon signs for Taco Bell, KFC, and a movie marquee featuring *Star Wars* were added for realism. The E.T. puppet was created and manipulated by Tom St. Amand.

Both these pages show photos of the ILM staff at work on the miniature sets of both the forest scene and the San Fernando Valley. LEFT ABOVE: Model makers Suzanne Pastor and Jessie Boberg. LEFT BOTTOM: Dennis Muren setting up the six-inch-tall rod puppet for the field-landing scene. ABOVE: Neil Krepela, shooting the matte painting. RIGHT: Dennis Muren in a photo that demonstrates the scale of the set.

The SPACESHIP

Building the Ship

The first idea was to create a flat, saucer-shaped ship, but designer Ralph McQuarrie ultimately created a ship in the shape of a diving bell. This shape was used because, according to Spielberg, the aliens originated from an extremely moist and humid planet. The bottom of the ship was encrusted with tiny barnacles and crustaceans.

It took three months to build the ship. Everything on board moved, at the insistence of Steven Spielberg.

LEFT: This composite image was created as a possible poster for the release of the movie in 1982. ABOVE: This is a cloud tank that the model makers used for E.T. They filled the bottom of the tank with cold salt water, laid a sheet of plastic over that, and then added warm fresh water to the top. They then pulled the sheet out and the two types of water stayed separate. Tempera powder was released through the pipes, which stayed afloat in the water and created nice thick clouds. RIGHT: Steven Spielberg and Tom Smith discussing the filming of the miniature space ship.

161

162

Steven Spielberg also had the notion that E.T.'s world was divisible by three. Consequently, the ship was designed with three landing gears and nine light pods. The dome of the ship reflected the sky and landscape.

A number of different ships were built before the final one was approved. Two ships were built by model maker Charles Bailey. One model was two feet in diameter, fully detailed and controlled by a joy stick and computer. The second model was three feet wide and meant to be used for its shape and lights.

Building and filming the spaceship at ILM. FAR LEFT: Marty Brenneis and Mike Mackenzie. TOP LEFT: Sean Casey. CENTER LEFT: Bess Wiley and Charlie Bailey. BOTTOM LEFT: Charlie Bailey. ABOVE: The model makers created a dome out of plywood that had a forest scene painted on the interior surface. The surface of the spaceship was like a chrome mirror, so the dome of the ship reflected the matte painting. Pictured here is Selwyn Eddy, visual effects camera assistant. RIGHT: Matte painter Chris Evans is painting clouds on the inside of a bowl shaped dome. This dome was then placed in-between the stage lights and the spaceship. The light shone through the dome and reflected the clouds onto the ship.

163

Music

ABOVE: *John Williams, composer, at work with his orchestra.*

The composer doesn't have the benefit of all the beautiful visuals and the dissolves that are added later. The first time I saw E.T., it was without the scene with the bicycle riding over the moon because that was a special effect shot added later in post-production.

We knew we had a creature that could fly. Though E.T. is not of our own species, he is part of our spiritual oneness. Going over the moon is a fantastic idea and it needed great sweep and a feeling of freedom in the music. Here we lose gravity, we're in space and the composer and the orchestra have to emphasize the feeling that we are finally free.

—JOHN WILLAMS

I've always felt that Johnny was my musical re-write artist. He'd come in, see my movie and musically re-write the whole thing. He makes it much better. He can take a moment and uplift it. He can take a tear that's just forming in your eye and make it fall.

—STEVEN SPIELBERG

Testing the Title

Five different titles were tested for the film. These included:

The Extra Terrestrial   *E.T. and Me*

Upon A Star   *The Landing*   *E.T.*

The following were the results of the test, as revealed in a Universal memo entitled: "Title Treatment Test: Interest-in-Seeing Scores."

Conclusion:

1) *Extra Terrestrial* and *Upon a Star* generated the best response, followed by *The Landing* and *E.T.*

2) *E.T. and Me* had the lowest level of interest.

3) "Not one person polled defined *E.T.* as an abbreviation for extraterrestrial."

As a result of this test, Universal decided to call the movie *E.T.: The Extra-Terrestrial* which would define the abbreviation, just in case people didn't understand the meaning of E.T. Today, the abbreviation is part of our common vocabulary.

LEFT: Photo of Drew Barrymore and E.T. used on a promotional button when the film was still called E.T. & Me. RIGHT: The original art used for the first-release poster. Steven Spielberg designed the campaign for E.T. by taking a photograph on an insert stage, positioning a young boy's hand and E.T.'s hand. The ad art later became a winner of one of *The Hollywood Reporter's Key Art Awards*.

E.T.

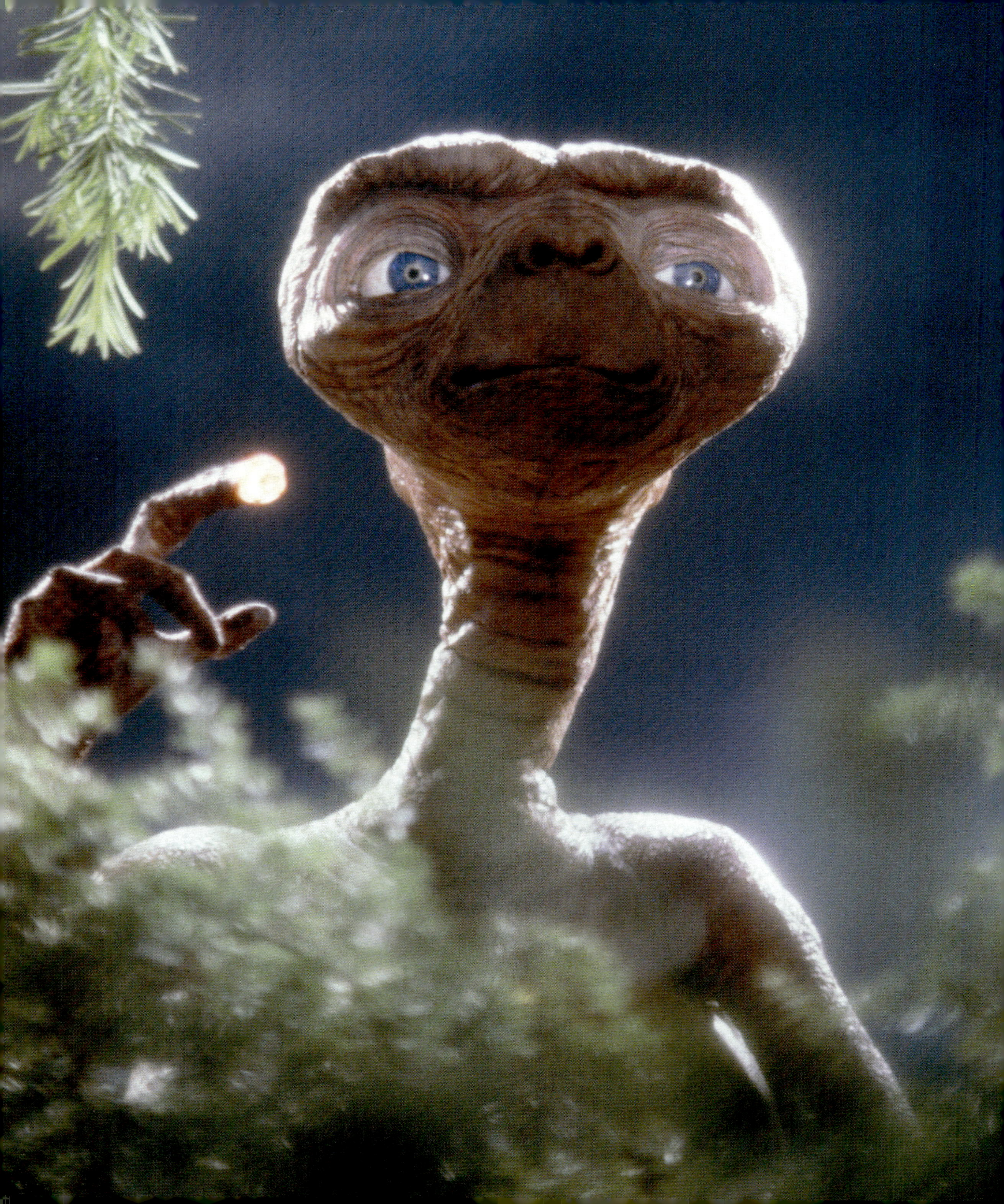

Sneak Preview

I took the film to my good luck theatre, the Medallion Theatre in Dallas, Texas, where I had also previewed Jaws and Close Encounters very successfully. I also had my first very bad preview of 1941 in that same theatre, but I still wanted to take E.T. to Texas. And I remember there was a terrible omen. As we got off the airplane, we walked to the baggage claim area. And a bird had gotten trapped. It kept trying to get out and somebody said, "That's a bad sign." Just when I heard that, our film came down the ramp, spooling out of the cans! And I thought, this is a bad dress rehearsal for what's about to happen tonight. This is not good. But don't believe in superstition or any of these signs, because sometimes they don't mean much.

You never know what you got until you show your movie to an audience for the first time. I didn't pretend that E.T. was anything other then a kid's movie about kids, so I didn't know what to expect.

The sneak preview of E.T. was almost a religious experience.

Everybody paid complete attention and there was a real feeling of identification. You could just slice the atmosphere. It was emotional, loving, and generous on the audience's part. It was a wonderful, tender experience that I'll never forget.

—STEVEN SPIELBERG

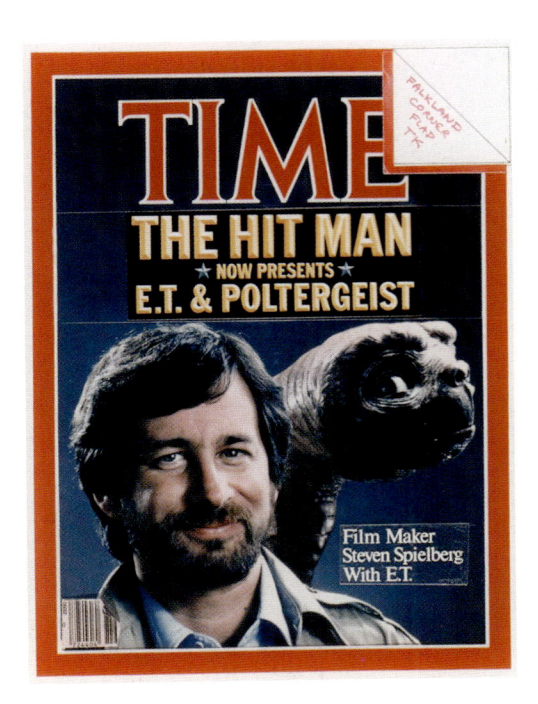

Left: A mock-up of a proposed cover of Time *magazine which was redesigned due to the outbreak of the Falkland war.*

Cannes Film Festival

I remember Steven sitting next to me at the sneak preview, and he kept pounding on my leg. In fact I had black and blue marks because he kept squeezing and pounding my leg. He kept saying, "They're laughing, they're laughing. They like it, they like it."

It was overwhelming to see the reaction of all those kids. At the end of the movie, everybody stood up and clapped which is a reaction you just never see.

I think that's when we had a little hint that this might be kind of big.

—MELISSA MATHISON

We showed the movie on the last night at Cannes. About fifteen minutes before the end, people started to clap and stomp their feet. We thought, "What is this?"

At first, I thought, "Oh my god, they don't like the movie." Then we realized it was just the opposite. They loved the movie.

—KATHLEEN KENNEDY

I'd never been to the Cannes Film Festival and what a way to go for the first time!

At the end of the festival we had a standing ovation. I remember I kept standing up and sitting down but they kept clapping. I was getting embarrassed. I turned to Melissa and made her get up. Everybody around me took a bow. We were all getting up and sitting down. It was an amazing experience for all of us.

I looked down at one person who wasn't clapping. He was standing there holding up a little lighter and I could see this little flame. It was Jerry Lewis holding the lighter and smiling, a truly wonderful thing to see.

I got this telegram from [French filmmaker] François Truffaut [who starred as scientist Claude Lacombe in *Close Encounters*] which meant so much to me. It said, "You belong here more then me," echoing one of his lines from *Close Encounters of the Third Kind*. It just broke me up.

That will never be equaled.

—STEVEN SPIELBERG

167

Box Office and Reviews

E.T. would have been a success if Universal had gotten their investment back. I just wanted to make the film. I had to see that picture come to fruition. So, everything else was icing on the cake.
—STEVEN SPIELBERG

Box Office

E.T. opened on June 11, 1982, and grossed $11.8 million on the first weekend. The grosses only increased in the following weeks: $12.4 million the next week, $12.8 million the third week and $13.7 million on the fourth. The original domestic release went on to gross more than $359 million. The re-release earned approximately $40 million worldwide. Internationally, E.T. has earned $303 million. To date, E.T. has grossed more than $700 million.

The following are excerpts from some of the original reviews that appeared in the press after the movie was released in March of 1982.

Watching this vibrantly comic, boundlessly touching fantasy, you feel that Spielberg has, for the first time, put his breathtaking technical skills at the service of his deepest feelings.
—MICHAEL SRAGOW, ROLLING STONE

A triumph almost beyond imagining.
—KENNETH TURAN, CALIFORNIA

A dream of a movie, a bliss-out . . . Genuinely entrancing movies are almost as rare as extra-terrestrial visitors.
—PAULINE KAEL, NEW YORKER

The best Disney movie Walt Disney never made.
—VARIETY

E.T. is as contemporary as laser beam technology but it's full of the timeless longings expressed in children's literature of all eras.
—VINCENT CANBY, THE NEW YORK TIMES

A fabulous masterpiece that leaves all who see it with a warm and radiant glow of optimism and joy.
—REX REED, NEW YORK DAILY NEWS

One of the most beautiful fantasy adventures ever made. The millions who see it will stay rooted in their seats, astonished at what movies can do.
—DAVID DENBY, NEW YORK MAGAZINE

A miracle movie and one that confirms Spielberg as a master storyteller of his medium. . . A perfectly poised mixture of sweet comedy and ten-speed melodrama, of death and resurrection, of a friendship so pure and powerful it seems like an idealized love.
—RICHARD CORLISS, TIME

1982 Awards

ACADEMY AWARD NOMINATIONS
　　Best Picture, Best Director, Best Original Screenplay, Best Cinematography, Best Editing

ACADEMY AWARDS WINNER
　　Best Sound (Robert Knudson, Robert Glass, Don Digirolamo, Gene Cantamessa)
　　Best Visual Effects (Carlo Rambaldi, Dennis Muren, Kenneth F. Smith)
　　Best Sound Effects Editing (Charles L. Campbell, Ben Burtt)
　　Best Original Score (John Williams)

BAFTA NOMINATIONS
　　Best Film, Director, Screenplay, Outstanding Newcomer (Henry Thomas, Drew Barrymore), Cinematography, Music, Film Editing, Make-Up Artist, Production Design/Art Direction, Sound and Visual Effects.
The only winner was John Williams for the Best Music.

GRAMMY AWARD—John Williams

GOLDEN GLOBE—John Williams

| FILMS | VIDEO | CABLE | MUSIC | TALENT | STAGE |

VARIETY

PRICE $1.25
NEWS...

Published Weekly at 154 West 46th Street, New York, N.Y. 10036, by Variety, Inc. Annual subscription, $60. Single copies $1.25.
Second Class Postage Paid at New York, N.Y. and at Additional Mailing Offices
©COPYRIGHT, 1982, BY VARIETY, INC. ALL RIGHTS RESERVED

Vol. 307 No. 4   USPS 656-960   New York, Wednesday, July 7, 1982

THE SPACEMAN THAT SAVED H'WOOD

WILL SUCCESS SPOIL THE E.T.?!

Grownup Pix Sick; Kid Stuff Socko

Sydney, May 25

The E.T. PHENOMENON

E.T. Mania

After the initial success of E.T., MCA/Universal licensed more than two hundred spin-offs of the characters. E.T. appeared on lunch boxes, cereal boxes, dolls, ice cream (vanilla flavored but colored green), clothing and much more.

171

Part of the celebration of the *E.T.* phenomenon is the E.T. Adventure ride at Universal Studios theme parks. Since the opening of the first attraction in 1990, tens of millions of visitors have flown with E.T. on a starbound bike to help save him and his home planet in a thrill-filled adventure. Universal Studios theme parks are located in Hollywood, California; Orlando, Florida; and Osaka, Japan.

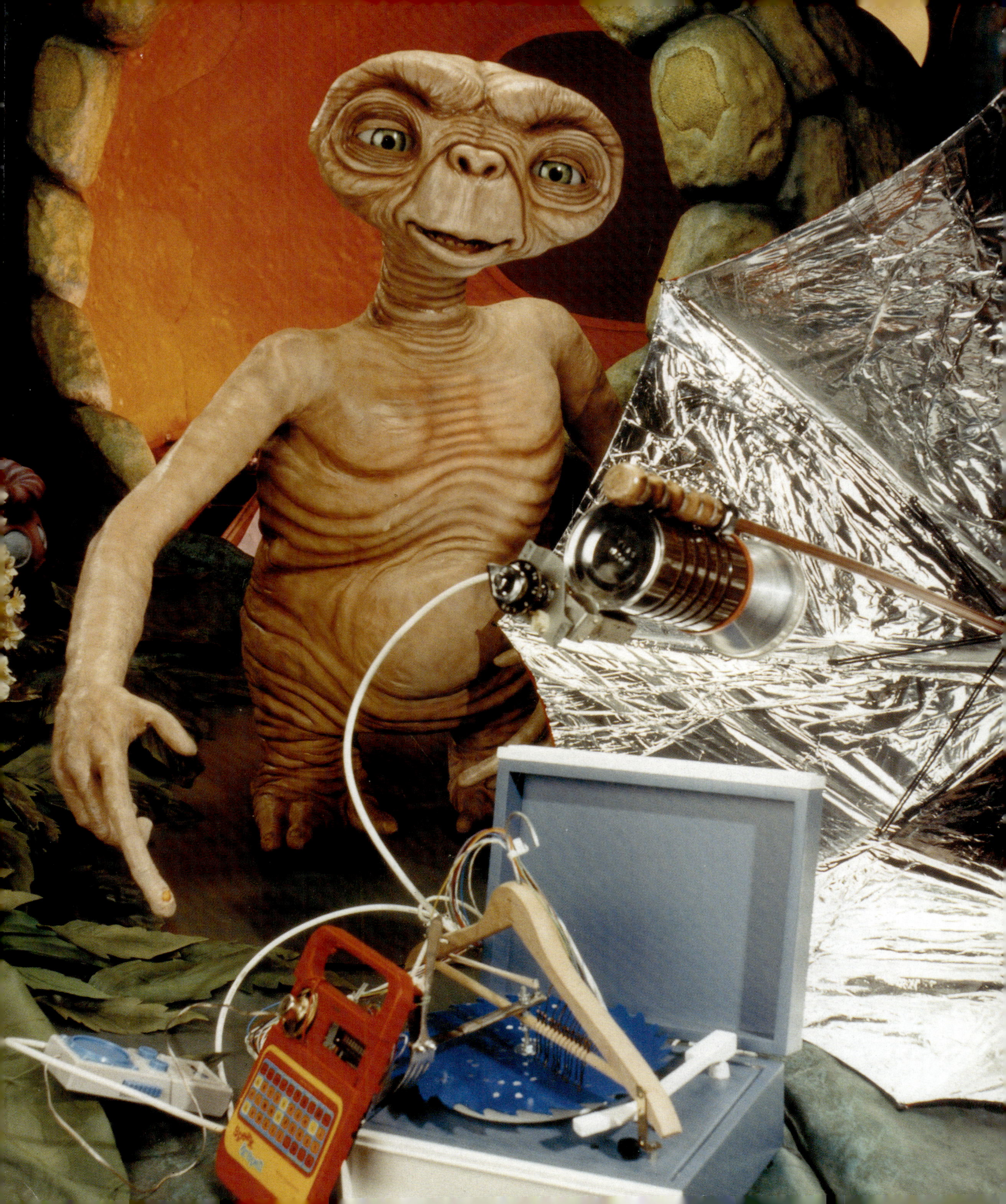

The RESTORATION

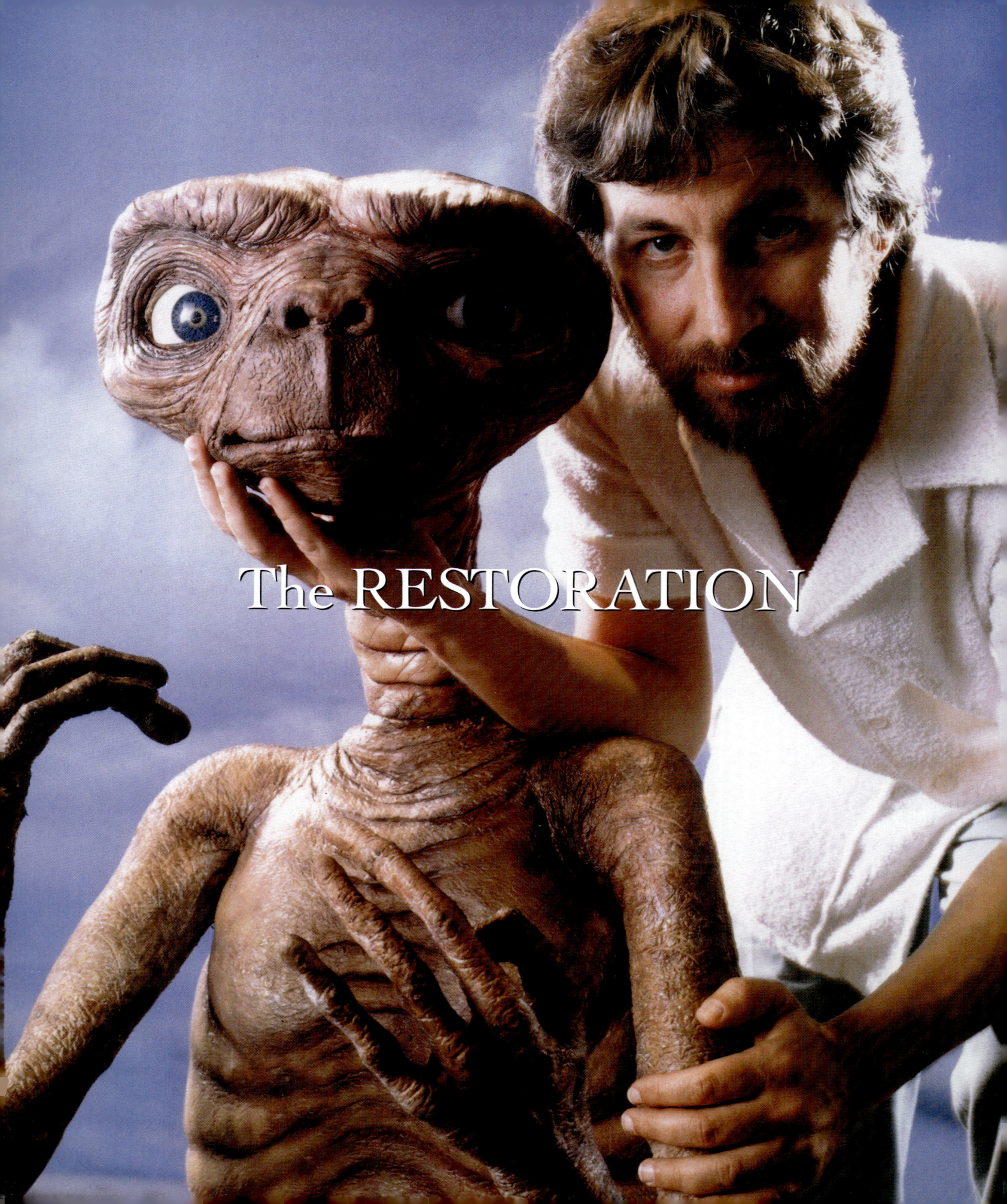

An E.T. for 2002

This is a movie that crosses over so many generations, and there's a whole new generation that's never experienced it in the theater.

I have two kids of my own now, a five-year-old and a three-year-old, and Steven Spielberg has seven children. We took all of our children to a small theater and watched the movie together. It was so incredible to watch the movie play with a room full of kids that were our own, especially because his youngest and my youngest had never seen it. It played to them with the same enthusiasm as it did to young kids twenty years ago.

So my guess is that there are a lot of parents out there with small children who remember this movie as a genuine personal experience of their childhood and now they get to share it with their own kids. I think that's quite extraordinary. There are also a number of kids who grew up seeing or knowing about this movie; they are now college age, and they are going to have a completely different experience watching this movie as adults in a movie theater. As much as we appreciate the world of videos and DVDs, certain kinds of movies simply play differently in a packed movie theater and that's what I think is going to be fun about the reissue of E.T.

Another reason to think about reissuing the movie was the fact that we're now sitting here with a new tool in computer graphics which meant we could go back and make some subtle adjustments to certain things we wanted to fix while, of course, maintaining what we loved about E.T. Steven made clear that he didn't want any change that would call attention to itself. He wanted the changes to really assimilate into what people remember about this movie.

In the original version, E.T. was an animatronic figure; he was not blue-screened into a shot. On the set, he was lit by real lights. He moved his head and opened his mouth on film. There was a quality about him that came across because of how he was created so that made altering him much more challenging. We were trying to stay with the E.T. that we had created and not turn him into something that would be like an animated character, for instance. The last thing we wanted to do was change

ABOVE: Eunice Kennedy Shriver and some of the athletes who participate in Special Olympics.

E.T. and Special Olympics

Eunice Kennedy Shriver saw in E.T. a symbol of acceptance, friendship, and hope for people who appeared different, neglected, or misunderstood...a shining light able to shatter the barriers of indifference, ignorance, and negativity and overcome enormous odds to win his freedom. This magical creature who touched so many, moved the founder of Special Olympics to write at once to producer/director Steven Spielberg about his pioneering movie. Spielberg liked the idea of making E.T. a "special friend" of Special Olympics, and in partnership with Universal Studios, pushed ahead with the E.T. promotion in a number of ways: developing a special costume so that E.T. could appear at a Special Olympics State Games, allowing a special showing of *E.T. The Extra-Terrestrial* at the 1983 Special Olympics World Winter Games in Park City, Utah, and re-releasing the movie itself. But of various efforts, none would reach the public more directly than a sixty-second television spot featuring E.T. that told an unparalleled story of a Special Olympics athlete's heroism and spirit. Now, twenty years later, the message of *E.T.* still captures the essence of Special Olympics—that differences are to be celebrated and that acceptance, understanding, and friendship can transcend barriers and surmount obstacles. This unlikely hero, E.T., with whom Mrs. Shriver and the world became enamored, spread his message of friendship and understanding—just as more than one million Special Olympics athletes in more than 150 countries change the world every day with their courage and inspiration and messages of hope and possibility.

175

E.T., but we felt that a little bit of futzing here and there was not necessarily a bad thing.

Over the years, we just get technically better and better at recreating reality. So, it's very seductive when you're in a situation where you can improve a movie that is laden with relatively primitive effects, even though those effetcts were very well done in their time and lend a certain kind of charm to the experience.

I am a strong proponent of looking at the world of computer graphics as simply one more tool available to filmmakers. I don't think it is necessarily a replacement of live action movies for characters. Looking back at *Jurassic Park* and the way we constructed that, I think the believability and the reality in those dinosaurs comes from the combination of both the live action and computer graphics. When you can literally put something in a real environment and have it be lit by the same components as everything else in that environment, it becomes grounded in reality. If we were to do *E.T.* again, we would probably do some combination of computer graphics and an animatronics character.

The minute we decided to do the reissue, we looked at the chase scenes where the police are after the boys. For a long time, Steven realized it would be highly unlikely that the police would be chasing a group of kids on bicycles and draw their guns. I suppose there could be an argument made that, well, it's okay because it's only a movie, but I think on many levels, Steven regretted that he had used guns in the original film. So we changed the guns to walkie talkies which was probably more realistic anyway.

We put back two scenes. One was a wonderful scene in the bathroom and the other was sort of a side scene to what's become a fairly symbolic Halloween moment in the movie. Then we went in and literally on a shot-by-shot basis looked at E.T. and identified areas of performance we thought could be slightly improved. We did quite a bit in that area although I emphasize the word "subtle" because most of it was really quite modest.

We adjusted some of the flying sequences in the movie, mainly because we now have the opportunity to add a bit more realistic behavior in the flying. It's not that we went in and changed anything about the flying sequence, per se; we just made it slightly more believable. The bicycles dip a little bit more, rather than just going in a straight line so they look more realistic.

I think *E.T.* is enormously relevant because, much like the other movies that Steven has created, here he really began exploring themes of tolerance. This is an issue that is extremely important to the world today. In its own way, the story of E.T. is about understanding and the ultimate acceptance of this alien character.

I believe *E.T.* is a movie that defines Steven Spielberg. On many levels this was a deeply personal film for him, and I think that there are aspects of *E.T.* that have informed a lot of what he's done since then. He was exploring a transition for himself of acceptance and acknowledging a lot of things that had happened in his personal life, such as his feelings of abandonment when his parents divorced. I think the way that translates to kids is that there's also a kind of child-like empowerment in the movie. Elliott represents a child that feels disconnected and abandoned and then is empowered in the process of befriending E.T. So it becomes a coming of age story where the child is able to do a very adult thing; say good-bye to someone he loves. In a sense Elliott is handing off his childhood and becoming an adult, which is something we can all look back on and identify with.

—KATHLEEN KENNEDY, PRODUCER

ABOVE: Clockwise from top left: Robert Macnaughton, Dee Wallace Stone, Kathleen Kennedy, Peter Coyote, Drew Barrymore, Steven Spielberg, Henry Thomas reunited for the twentieth anniversary of E.T.

Updating the Charm

I started at ILM twenty years ago and my very first project was to build the prototype for E.T.'s space ship. I absolutely loved the film and was very excited to be involved in the restoration, although I wondered how we should restore a film that was already perfect.

Initially, Steven Spielberg went through the entire film with us and noted each shot he wanted to change or re-do, including all the original effects. In addition, there were about 60 shots of the E.T. puppet that Steven asked us to remove digitally and replace with a computer graphics puppet so that we could hone the performance. Ultimately, it broke down into those two basic groups: the original effects and new character work.

Even though the puppet was brilliant, the technology was limited in 1982. Steven and his crew were very adept at hiding those limitations. The movie was very dark and smoky and E.T. was usually covered or you only saw his hand or his head come around the corner. It was very stylish but a lot was left to the imagination. If this film was shot today, chances are E.T. would be an all CG character. You would see him head to toe in broad daylight.

One of my personal goals on the project was to make sure that the effects were seamless and with all the charm of the original film. I didn't want it to be obvious that we went in and added some scenes or updated some of the shots. I think we succeeded and that when people see the film, they're not going to notice our work.

—BILL GEORGE, VISUAL EFFECTS SUPERVISOR

ABOVE: Model maker Mark Siegel rebuilds the E.T. puppet from scratch for the ILM restoration of the film in 2002.

Running

In the original film, the puppet E.T. was put on tracks and driven along. It works but it looks a little odd, like he's driving a car. Our challenge was to figure out how E.T. would move quickly. He never runs in the film, he kind of shuffles. He's got these little teeny feet. So the idea of him shuffling along really fast was not going to work.

We started to analyze how his body was constructed and decided the creature he most resembled was a gorilla. He's got these very, very long arms and these very short legs. So Colin [Brady] and I developed a run that was very gorilla-like, where he actually uses his front legs to help him move along. We did a test animation that Steven saw and loved right off the bat.

—Bill George, Visual Effects Supervisor

Above: The scene of E.T. running at the opening of the film was enhanced by ILM.

One of our other challenges was that we didn't want to make E.T. too smooth or fluid in his motion, which is usually an artifact of computer animation. There was a beautiful warmth in the way the original E.T. moved. Sometimes we would describe him as a baby crossed with an old man. He had the innocence of a baby but he also had this kind of jittery quality. So even though we had the opportunity to make E.T. move perfectly smooth, we decided to add these little bumps and jitters.

We also would think of him as an animal. Sometimes he was very catlike. Sometimes he was like a bunny. Other times he was like a turtle. But we found any time we moved him into the direction of a monkey, it seemed wrong, especially around his nose area. So we always had to pull it back towards this kind of turtle character, which also seemed appropriate because he had the ability to bring his head down into his body like a turtle. Quite often, we were actually mixing our computer-generated head with the puppet body and I think that actually gave the best results.

—Colin Brady, Animation Supervisor

Home Alone

The home alone sequence is when E.T. is exploring the refrigerator. E.T. is wearing a bathrobe and reaching into the refrigerator. All we replaced was the head and the neck. The hands are from the original puppet. We added additional animation to the head where he sticks his tongue into the potato salad. We tried to make his facial expression more curious.

—Bill George, Visual Effects Supervisor

Bathtub

Initially, E.T. was wearing a robe in the bathtub sequence which I think was to hide the fact that he was either operated by cables or by a little person in a costume. The first thing we asked Steven was if we could disrobe E.T. and show more of his body. It was more interesting to see how he's walking. Steven agreed.

We wanted the animation to be the best, so we ended up replacing a lot more than we originally thought we would. The only shots where you see a full body E.T. is when he's falling back into the bathtub. There's the first reveal of E.T.'s long neck that was kind of a funny shot. From the neck up, it's our computer E.T., and from the robe down, it's the original. That's the only shot where we kept the robe. The shot was simply about learning that E.T.'s neck can extend to such a length. It's a very playful sequence, so we brought his chin up a little bit, as he stretches his head and looks around in a somewhat of a playful manner. He looks back towards Elliott, and you can see he's showing off a little bit.

—Colin Brady, Animation Supervisor

LEFT: *Scenes that were digitally-enhanced for the 2002 release.*

Beer Drinking

When his neck is elongated he resembles an elderly person. How could we make him even more like a human? In this scene where he is drinking beer, we replaced his head with a computer animated head which provided more freedom in moving the individual cheekbones and the musculature on the face.

The original model had this beer just spilling off his stiff neck. We replaced it with computer graphic animation. In the new footage, you can actually see his Adam's apple kind of gulping as he drinks the beer. The interesting thing for me, as a visual effects editor, was how much we added to the animation.

—David Tanaka, Supervising Visual Effects Editor

E.T. Dresses Up

At first, I was a bit hesitant to work on the re-release of *E.T.*, one of my favorite films, especially as a kid. I always thought every frame was perfect. It was almost as if someone asked me to paint over the Mona Lisa to make it a better painting. But here we were working with Steven Spielberg, so I couldn't refuse.

One of the big challenges with E.T. is that he's more than just a special effect. He's more than just a creature or even an alien. He's not a cartoon character either. We had to think of him as a living, breathing actor and so we approached him much in the same way you would direct an actor's performance. We shot a lot of video reference of ourselves and really tried to get into his head. We focused on the eyes quite a bit.

For example, we were really challenged in the scene where E.T. wears the dress and the wig. Here was a classic shot, and I remember trying to pull a direction out of Steven. What is E.T. thinking? Is he embarrassed? Is he angry? Is he having fun? Steven finally said, "He's insulted."

So we discussed what someone does when they're insulted and decided he would be trying to divert attention anywhere else in the room but towards himself. So we had E.T.'s eyes dart around the room as he sighs. The first time we showed it to Steven, he laughed out loud, and we knew we nailed it. —COLIN BRADY, ANIMATION SUPERVISOR

ABOVE: E.T. in 2002 and in 1982 (right).

Phone Home

The phone home sequence was very challenging for us. We called it the powdered donut look. E.T.'s got this white crust all over him because he has just died and been resurrected. We had to digitally recreate that effect which is not a solid surface but a lot of different layers. Also he's lying down in this bag filled with smoke. So what you see in the final shot is a combination of the old puppet up to where the zipper happens, then our CG puppet takes over. We added a lot of layering of smoke and other elements to recreate the original look.

—Bill George, Visual Effects Supervisor

BOTH PAGES: *These images are from the bluescreen shoot at ILM. For E.T. 2002, ILM opted to use actors for the kids flying on the bikes sequence. In the 1982 original, miniatures were used.* BELOW: *Model maker Mark Buck.*

Flying

Luckily, the negative from the movie and the ILM effects were archived which allowed us to use the original backgrounds for the sequence where the kids are flying on the bikes. Originally [in 1982], the decision was made to shoot the kids as puppets. I screened that footage and although the animation and the lighting were amazing, there were still a lot of technical limitations. For example, the spokes on the wheels fell through. Steven also wanted to get more dynamic movement on the bikes. For this restoration, we used new kids on full sized bikes against blue screen to replace the puppets. Steven wanted the kids to put their legs out to the side when they landed, almost like landing gear.

In reviewing the original effects of Elliott flying across the moon, I was able to pinpoint the things I wanted to change. One was Elliott's cape. He's wearing this kind of hunchback cape because it's Halloween but the cape on the puppet was static. I wanted to see that cape moving in the wind. So when we shot the effect, we used wires and put a big fan on the kid.

—BILL GEORGE, VISUAL EFFECTS SUPERVISOR

Since we're dealing with a film that was created twenty years ago, we couldn't get the original cast of boys who are all adults now. So we poured through photos of kids and had a huge casting call to find someone who could play Henry Thomas. Height and perspective and many other parts of their appearance were considered when we cast these boys for the blue screen footage.

In the flying bike scene, we have the original footage of Henry looking at his surroundings. Since we can't replace Henry Thomas, how do we enhance that? How do we make the flight more magical?

In the close-ups we literally photographed a blue screen cape to partially put behind the actor as a fresh new digital composite. Adding these tiny little nuances gives more of a subconscious feeling that this kid is actually in flight and you're riding with him. Another example of that is we actually brought in pine trees and photographed them moving against blue screen to also composite behind Henry.

—DAVID TANAKA, SUPERVISING VISUAL EFFECTS EDITOR

Credits

UNIVERSAL PICTURES

E.T.
THE EXTRA-TERRESTRIAL

DEE WALLACE
PETER COYOTE
ROBERT MACNAUGHTON
DREW BARRYMORE
and HENRY THOMAS as Elliott

MUSIC BY JOHN WILLIAMS

EDITED BY CAROL LITTLETON

PRODUCTION DESIGNER JAMES D. BISSELL

DIRECTOR OF PHOTOGRAPHY ALLEN DAVIAU

WRITTEN BY MELISSA MATHISON

PRODUCED BY
STEVEN SPIELBERG & KATHLEEN KENNEDY

DIRECTED BY STEVEN SPIELBERG

Production Supervisor	FRANK MARSHALL
Associate Producer	MELISSA MATHISON
Production Manager	WALLACE WORSLEY
First Assistant Director	KATY EMDE
Second Assistant Director	DANIEL ATTIAS
E.T. Created by	CARLO RAMBALDI
Visual Effect Supervisor	DENNIS MUREN

Casting by MIKE FENTON & JANE FEINBERG Marci Liroff

Set Decorator	JACKIE CARR
2nd Unit Director	GLENN RANDALL
DGA Trainee	JOHN FLYNN
Production Coordinator	SUE DWIGGINS
Script Supervisor	ESTHER VIVANTE
Location Services	DICK VANE
Assistant to Mr. Spielberg	JANICE POBER
Assistant to Ms. Kennedy	DENISE DURHAM
Assistant to Mr. Marshall	PATTY RUMPH
Production Associates	MICHAEL BURMEISTER
	LANCE YOUNG
Production Accountant	BONNE RADFORD
Assistant Accountant	JANE GOE
Cine Guarantors II Representative	PATRICIA ROEDIG
Camera Operators	JOHN FLECKENSTEIN
	JOHN CONNOR
First Assistant Cameraman	STEVEN SHAW
Second Assistant Cameraman	RICHARD FEE
Still Photographer	BRUCE McBROOM
Sound Mixer	GENE CANTAMESSA
Boom Man	RAUL BRUCE
Sound Technician	CHARLES PAYNE
Gaffer	JAMES PLANNETTE
Lighting Best Boy	JOSEPH CAPSHAW
Key Grip	GENE KEARNEY
Grip Best Boy	BOB MUNOZ
Dolly Grip	DONALD HARTLEY
Construction Coordinator	ERNEST DEPEW
Set Designer	WILLIAM TEEGARDEN
Production Illustrator	ED VERREAUX
Propmaker Foremen	EERO HAUTANEN
	JACK JENNINGS
	JOHN VILLARINO
Labor Foreman	CLARK SHINDEL
Paint Foreman	JAMES MOSS
Greensman	LESLIE BUTCHER

Rendez-vous

Rendez-vous is the end sequence. There is a shot at the end of the film where the boys and E.T. are waiting off to the side as the ship comes down and lands next to them. Originally, the entire background was shot as a miniature. The boys were shot against a blue screen and then composited into the shot. The miniature ship came down and landed on a miniature landscape but the problem was that the landscape didn't move. In that situation, a lot of wind would be created by the ship landing. In the updated version we re-created the landing site as a full-sized set. This time the kids (our stand-ins) were shot in the set with wind and light effects.
—Bill George, Visual Effects Supervisor

Above and Right: ILM enhanced the scenes of the spaceship landing for the 2002 release.

E.T.'s Healing Powers

Steven asked us to replace the shot of E.T.'s finger lighting up and touching Elliott's head. We had to paint out the old hand over Elliott's face. Now painting a refrigerator door is one thing, painting a character's face is another. It was very difficult, but Steven wanted E.T. to point with the other hand. If you look at the original, the hand is a little crumpled and awkward even though the shot worked well. But we had to change hands. In our new shot, even though we could make the hand move smoothly, we wanted the animation to be filled with many beautiful imperfections. These imperfections keep the movement from looking too sterile and computer-generated, and retain the human touch that the original puppet had. Steven also wanted us to enhance the shots where E.T. says good-bye. Here was an opportunity to really focus on emotion and, in many ways, I'm the most happy with these shots.

—COLIN BRADY, ANIMATION SUPERVISOR

ABOVE: E.T.'s good-bye was revisited by the ILM crew and greatly enhanced for the new version of the film. BELOW: E.T. and Elliott in the final good-bye scene. The inset is from the 1982 release and the larger image from the 2002 re-release.

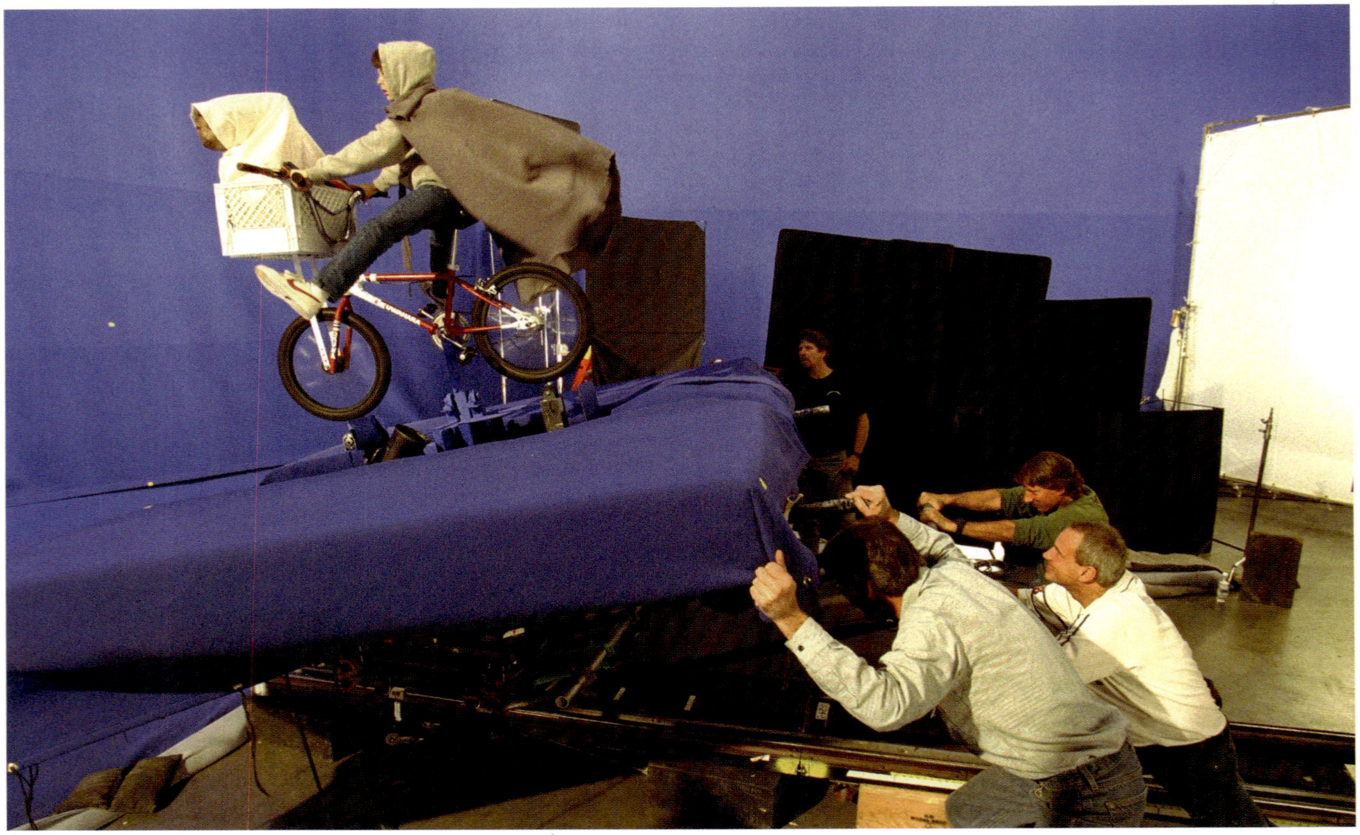

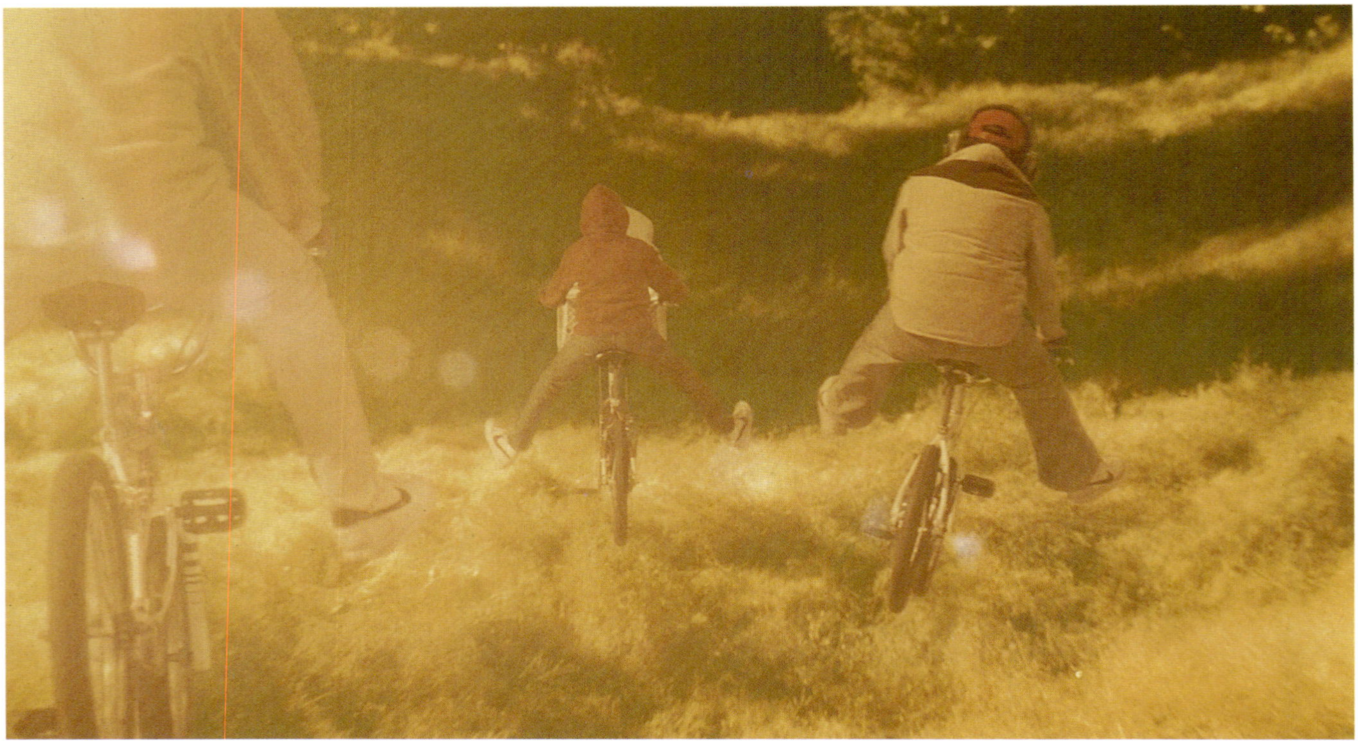

Credits

Set Dressing Leadwoman	SANDRA RENFROE
Prop Master	RUSSELL GOBLE
Assistant Propertymen	KEN WALKER
	MICHAEL DUNN
Costumer	DEBORAH SCOTT
Assistant Costumer	DANIEL MOORE
Hairstylist	LOLA 'SKIP' McNALLEY
Makeup	ROBERT SIDELL, S.M.A.
Transportation Coordinator	EUGENE SCHWARTZ
Transportation Captain	JOHN FEINBLATT
Location Production Vehicle	PRODUCERS LOCATION VEHICLE
Location Security	LOCATION SECURITY SERVICE
Craft Service	RAMON PAHOYO
First Aid	PHYLLIS LEVIN
Teacher	ADRIA LICKLIDER
Unit Publicist	LYLA FOGGIA
Animal Talent	DENNIS GRISCO'S ANIMAL TALENT
Harvey's Owner & Trainer	RICHARD L. CALKINS
Extra Casting	JUDI'S CASTING SERVICE
First Assistant Editor	KATHLEEN KORTH
Second Assistant Editor	BRUCE CANNON
Supervising Sound Editor	CHARLES L. CAMPBELL
Sound Effects Editors	DAVID A. PETTIJOHN
	LOUIS L. EDEMANN
	RICHARD C. FRANKLIN, JR.
	SAMUEL C. CRUTCHER
Post Production Dialogue	NORMAN B. SCHWARTZ for lipSSync inc.
ADR Editors	HANK SALERNO
	NICHOLAS KORDA
Assistant Sound Editor	CHUCK NEELY
Foley by	JOHN ROESCH
	JOAN ROWE
E.T.'s Voice Design	BEN BURTT
Music Editor	KENNETH HALL
Orchestrations	HERBERT W. SPENCER
Re-Recording Mixers	BUZZ KNUDSON
	ROBERT GLASS
	DON DIGIROLAMO
Negative Cutters	DONAH BASSETT
	DENNIS E. BROOKINS
Color Timer	ROBERT RARING
Titles	PACIFIC TITLE & ART STUDIO
E.T. Technical Supervisor	STEVE TOWNSEND
Optical Effects Coordinator	MITCHELL SUSKIN
Additional E.T. Effects	ROBERT SHORT
Special Artistic Consultant	CRAIG REARDON
Communicator Design	HENRY FEINBERG
E.T. Eyes Design	BEVERLY HOFFMAN
Medical Unit Consultants	DAVID CARLBERG, Ph.D.
	ROBERT W. SCHOLLER
Special Effects Coordinator	DALE MARTIN
Special Effects Assistants	GARY CRAWFORD
	ANDREW MILLER
	ROBERT WORTHINGTON
E.T. Movement Coordinator	CAPRICE ROTHE
E.T. Operators	ROBERT AVILA
	EUGENE CRUM
	FRANK SCHEPLER
	BOB TOWNSEND
	STEVE WILLIS
	RICHARD ZARRO
	RONALD ZARRO
Special E.T. Movement	PAT BILON
	TAMARA DE TREAUX
	MATTHEW DE MERITT
	TINA PALMER
	NANCY MACLEAN
	PAM YBARRA

Special Visual Effects Produced at INDUSTRIAL LIGHT & MAGIC, a division of Lucasfilm, Ltd., Marin County, California

Effects Cameraman	MIKE McALISTER
Camera Operators	ROBERT ELSWIT
	DON DOW
Camera Assistants	PAT SWEENY
	KARL HERRMANN
	SELWYN EDDY III
	MIKE OWENS
Optical Photography Supervisor	KENNETH F. SMITH
Optical Printer Operator	DAVID BERRY
Optical Line-up	RALPH GORDON
Optical Technicians	DUNCAN MYERS

Credits

Optical Technicians	TIM GEIDEMAN
	BOB CHRISOULIS
Go-Motion™ Figures	TOM ST. AMAND
Model Shop Supervisor	LORNE PETERSON
Chief Model Makers	CHARLIE BAILEY
	MIKE FULMER
Model Makers	SCOTT MARSHALL
	EASE OWYEUNG
	MIKE COCHRAIN
	SUZANNE PASTOR
	MICHAEL STEFFE
	JESSIE BOBERG
	RANDY OTTENBERG
Space Ship Design	RALPH McQUARRIE
Matte Painting Supervisor	MICHAEL PANGRAZIO
Matte Painting Artists	CHRIS EVANS
	FRANK ORDAZ
Matte Photography	NEIL KREPELA
Matte Photography Assistant	CRAIG BARRON
Effects Editorial Supervisor	CONRAD BUFF
Effects Editor	HOWARD STEIN
General Manager, ILM	TOM SMITH
Production Coordinators	WARREN FRANKLIN
	LAURIE VERMONT
Animation Supervisor	SAMUEL COMSTOCK
Animators	PEGGY TONKONOGY
	GARRY WALLER
	TERRY WINDELL
	JACK MONGOVAN
Still Photographer	TERRY CHOSTNER
Still Lab Technicians	ROBERTO McGRATH
	KERRY NORDQUIST
Supervising Stage Technician	T.E. MOEHNKE
Stage Technicians	DAVID CHILDERS
	HAROLD COLE
	DICK DOVA
	BOBBY FINLEY III
	PATRICK FITZSIMMONS
	EDWARD HIRSH
	JOHN McCLEOD
	THAINE MORRIS
	PETER STOLZ
Production Accountant	LAURA KAYSEN
Equipment Maintenance	WADE CHILDRESS
	MICHAEL SMITH
Electronic Systems Design	JERRY JEFFRESS
Model Electronics	GARY LEO
Model Electronics	MARTY BRENNEIS
Optical Printer Engineering	GENE WHITMAN
	JOHN ELLIS

CAST

Mary	DEE WALLACE
Elliott	HENRY THOMAS
Keys	PETER COYOTE
Michael	ROBERT MACNAUGHTON
Gertie	DREW BARRYMORE
Greg	K.C. MARTEL
Steve	SEAN FRYE
Tyler	TOM HOWELL
Pretty Girl	ERIKA ELENIAK
Schoolboy	DAVID O'DELL
Science Teacher	RICHARD SWINGLER
Policeman	FRANK TOTH
Ultra Sound Man	ROBERT BARTON
Van Man	MICHAEL DARRELL
Stunts	GLENN RANDALL
	RICHARD BUTLER
	BENNIE DOBBINS
	TED GROSSMAN
	KEITH HARVEY
	FRED LERNER
	BOBBY PORTER
	FELIX SILLA
	CHUCK WATERS
	ALLAN WYATT
Medical Unit	DAVID BERKSON, M.D.
	DAVID CARLBERG, Ph.D.
	MILT KOGAN, M.D.
	ALEXANDER LAMPONE, M.D.
	RONDA MAKOFF, M.D.
	ROBERT MURPHY, M.D.
	RICHARD PESAVENTO, M.D.
	TOM SHERRY, M.D.
	SUSAN CAMERON
	WILL FOWLER, JR.
	BARBARA HARTNETT
	DI ANN LAMPONE
	MARY STEIN
	MITCHELL SUSKIN

"WILLIE" composed by Jenifer Smith
Performed by Jenifer Smith, Peter Meisner, Joe Scrima, Bob Parr

Credits

"PAPA OOM MOW MOW" Published by Beechwood Music
Performed by The Persuasions Courtesy of Elektra Records

"ACCIDENTS WILL HAPPEN" Composed by Elvis Costello
Courtesy of Plangent Visions Music Inc., © 1978

"PEOPLE WHO DIE" Composed and Performed by Jim Carroll
Courtesy of Earl McGrath Music

SESAME STREET segments
Courtesy of Children's Television Workshop

Excerpts from "PETER PAN"
Courtesy of Hospital for Sick Children London, England

Soundtrack available on MCA Records \ UMG Soundtracks

Read the Simon & Schuster Books

The Producers wish to thank the following for their contributions

AMERICAN HI-LIFT
BECKMAN INSTRUMENTS, INC.
DYNATECH LABORATORIES, INC.
EVERYTHING BICYCLES
FIELDTEC, INC.
GOULD, INC.
HERSHEY CHOCOLATE COMPANY
ILC DOVER
IVAC CORP.
THE NORTH FACE
PERKIN-ELMER, INC.
PIKER INTERNATIONAL
QUANTEL BUSINESS COMPUTERS
STANFORD LINEAR ACCELERATOR CENTER
TEXAS INSTRUMENTS INCORPORATED

Respirator Helmets courtesy of
RACAL AIRSTREAM INC., Rockville, Maryland

Lenses and Panaflex cameras by PANAVISION®

Recorded in DOLBY STEREO

Copyright © MCMLXXXII by UNIVERSAL CITY STUDIOS, INC. All Rights Reserved

Photographed at LAIRD INTERNATIONAL STUDIOS, Culver City, California

This motion picture is protected under laws of the United States and other countries. Unauthorized duplication, distribution or exhibition may result in civil liability and criminal prosecution.

20TH ANNIVERSARY EDITION

Executive in Charge of Post Production	MARTIN COHEN
Supervising Sound Editors	CHARLES L. CAMPBELL
	RICHARD LEGRAND JR.
Re-Recording Mixers	ANDY KOYAMA
	JONATHAN WALES
	RICK KLINE
	SHAWN MURPHY
Visual Effects Supervisor	BILL GEORGE
Animation Supervisor	COLIN BRADY
Director of Photography	ALLEN DAVIAU
Color Timer	ROBERT RARING
Post Production	ERICA FRAUMAN
	SVEN E.M. FAHLGREN
Post Production Associate	JEFFREY CAVA
Editorial Assistants	PATRICK CRANE
	DANA E. GLAUBERMAN
	ALEX GARCIA
Sound Editors	NORVAL CRUTCHER III
	GARY S. GERLICH
Dialogue/ADR Editor	BOB MCNABB
Sound Assistant	SAMUEL WEBB
ADR Mixer	TROY PORTER
ADR Recordist	LAVERNE DEWBERRY
Foley Artists	JOHN ROESCH
	ALYSON MOORE
Foley Mixer	MARY JO LANG
Foley Recordist	CAROLYN TAPP
Music Editor	KEN WANNBERG
Research Consultant	LAURENT BOUZEREAU

SPECIAL VISUAL EFFECTS AND ANIMATION by
INDUSTRIAL LIGHT & MAGIC
A Division of Lucas Digital Ltd.
Marin County, California

ILM Visual Effects Producer	SANDRA L. SCOTT
CG Supervisor	PATRICK T. MYERS
Compositing Supervisor	JEFF DORAN
Digital Color Timing Supervisor	KENNETH SMITH
Add'l. VFX Supervision	TIM ALEXANDER
Sequence Producer	JEFF OLSON
Directors of Photography	PATRICK SWEENEY
	MARTY ROSENBERG
Animators	RUDI BLOSS
	ANDREW DOUCETTE

Credits

Animators	MIGUEL FUERTES
	WAYNE GILBERT
	SHAWN KELLY
	GREGORY KYLE
	KEVIN MARTEL
	CHRISTOPHER MINOS
	GLEN MCINTOSH
	MAGALI RIGAUDIAS
	TRISH SCHUTZ-KRAUSE
	DAVID SIDLEY
	SHARONNE SOLK
	JAN VAN BUYTEN
	JAMY WHELESS
Development CG Artists	JEROEN LAPRE
	RYAN COOK
Computer Graphics Artists	VINCE DE QUATTRO
	RYAN GALLOWAY
	MICHAEL HALSTED
	ANDREW HARDAWAY
	CHRISTINA HILLS
	SAMSON KAO
	RUSSELL KOONCE
	JENNIFER MCKNEW
	PATRICK NEARY,
	JENNIFER NONA
	MARY PAYNE
	KIMBERLY ROSS
	DAMIAN STEEL
	ERIC VOEGELS
	ANDY WANG
Lead Digital Compositor	BARBARA BRENNAN
Digital Compositors	JULIE ADRIANSON
	AL BAILEY
	STELLA BOGH
	JAY COOPER
	BILL GILMAN
	JIM HAGEDORN
	SEAN MACKENZIE
	GREG MALONEY
	TIA MARSHALL
	MARCEL MARTINEZ
	PATRICK TUBACH
Digital Modeler	STEPHEN APLIN
Lead Viewpaint Artist	JEAN BOLTE
Viewpaint Artist	DEREK GILLINGHAM
Creature Developer	LENNY LEE
Lead Sabre CG Artist	CAITLIN CONTENT
Sabre CG Artists	MARK CASEY
	CATHERINE TATE
Rebel Unit Artist	BILLY BROOKS
Digital Matte Artist	RONN BROWN
3D Matchmove Lead	DANI MORROW
3D Matchmovers	JODIE MAIER
	DAVID MANOS MORRIS
	DAVID WASHBURN
	JOHN WHISNANT
Lead Digital Paint Artist	MIKE VAN EPS
Digital Paint/Rotoscope Artists	TRANG BACH
	JOANNE HAFNER
	ELSA RODRIGUEZ
	DAVID SULLIVAN
	ERIN WEST
Model Makers	MARK BUCK
	JON FOREMAN
1st Assistant Camera	RICHARD MCKAY
	ROBERT HILL
Stage Technicians	DENNIS BECKER
	JOSEPH FULMER
	MICHAEL OLAGUE
Greensman	GEOFFREY LAKE
Video Assist	CLARK HIGGINS
VFX Prod. Coordinators	CAMILLE EDEN
	LISA TODD
VFX Production Assistants	MEI-MING CASINO
	KINGSTON COLE
Visual Effects Editors	DAVID TANAKA
	GREG HYMAN
VFX Assistant Editor	LARS JENSVOLD
Scanning Operator	MIKE ELLIS
Negative Lineup	JAMES LIM
Digital Plate Restoration	MARIA GOODALE
	MICHELE GRAY
	SAM STEWART
	ALAN TRAVIS
Technical Support	NATALEE DJOKOVIC
	DHYANA BRUMMEL
Visual Effects Coordinator	MARK RUSSELL
Additional Voices	JUNE CHRISTOPHER
	ERIN DONOVAN
	ART KIMBRO

Additional Voices . . . . .LUISA LESCHIN
JONATHAN NICHOLS
CLAY THOMAS SAVAGE
Bike Flight Doubles . . . . .BENJAMIN DUNN
ERIC STIEF
JOHN DENTONI, III
LUKE BAILEY
RYAN CARNEY

Negative Cutter . . . . .GARY BURRITT
End Titles . . . . .PACIFIC TITLE

SOUNDTRACK ON MCA RECORDS/UMG SOUNDTRACKS

Color by Technicolor KODAK Motion Picture Film

COPYRIGHT © 2002 UNIVERSAL STUDIOS
All Rights Reserved.

Country of First Publication: United States of America. Universal Studios is the author of this motion picture for purposes of the Berne Convention and all national laws giving effect thereto.

The characters and events depicted in this photoplay are fictitious. Any similarity to actual persons, living or dead, is purely coincidental.

This motion picture is protected under the laws of the United States and other countries. Unauthorized duplication, distribution or exhibition may result in civil liability and criminal prosecution.

Acknowledgments

The publisher and the editors wish to thank:

Steven Spielberg, Kathleen Kennedy, and the cast and crew of *E.T.: The Extra-Terrestrial* interviewed in this book.

And:
Colleen A. Benn
Cindy Chang
Martin Cohen
Shannon Diffner
Eddie Egan
Bette Einbinder
Elizabeth Gelfand
Brad Globe
Industrial Light + Magic
Stephen Kenneally
Marvin Levy
Kristie Macosko
Kay McCauley
Randy Nellis
David O'Connor
Susan Ray
Barbara Ritchie
Jeff Sakson
Kristin Stark
Universal Studios

Permissions

Page 24: Photograph of Albert Einstein by Oren Jack Turner, Princeton, NJ. © 1947. Courtesy of the Library of Congress. Photograph of Ernest Hemingway courtesy of the John Fitzgerald Kennedy Library's Ernest Hemingway Photograph Collection. Photograph of Carl Sandburg by *New York World-Telegram & Sun* staff photographer Al Ravenna. © 1955. Courtesy of the Library of Congress.

Page 167: *Time* magazine © 1982. Reprinted by permission of Time, Inc.

About the Filmmakers

STEVEN SPIELBERG has directed, produced, or executive-produced seven of the 25 top-grossing films of all time (worldwide), including *Jurassic Park* and *E.T. the Extra-Terrestrial*. In addition, he directed and produced the multiple award-winning motion pictures *Schindler's List* and *Saving Private Ryan*. Spielberg has also been recognized with Academy Award® nominations for Best Director for *E.T. the Extra-Terrestrial*, *Raiders of the Lost Ark*, and *Close Encounters of the Third Kind*.

Producer KATHLEEN KENNEDY has a record of achievement that makes her one of the most successful executives in the film industry today. Among her credits are three of the highest grossing films in motion picture history: *E.T. the Extra-Terrestrial*, *Jurassic Park*, and *The Sixth Sense*, which she produced with Steven Spielberg, Gerald R. Molen, and Frank Marshall, respectively.

MELISSA MATHISON also wrote screenplays of *Kundun*, *The Indian in the Cupboard*, and *The Black Stallion*. For *E.T.*, Mathison won nominations for Best Screenplay from the Academy of Motion Picture Arts and Sciences, the British Academy of Film & Television Arts, and the Golden Globes. Mathison won a Writers Guild of America Screen Award for *E.T.* in the category of Best Drama Written Directly for the Screen.

About the Bookmakers

Interviewer LAURENT BOUZEREAU has written, directed, and produced over 60 documentaries on "the making of" some of America's top classic movies, in collaboration with some of the most acclaimed filmmakers, including Steven Spielberg, Brian De Palma, George Lucas, Martin Scorsese, Clint Eastwood, Mel Brooks, Lawrence Kasdan, and Peter Bogdanovich. He is also the author of six popular books on American cinema.

Editor LINDA SUNSHINE and designer TIMOTHY SHANER have collaborated on many book projects, including the Newmarket Press editions of *Saving Private Ryan: The Men, The Mission, The Movie*; *Crouching Tiger, Hidden Dragon*; *Cabaret: The Illustrated Book and Lyrics*; *Stuart Little: The Art, the Artists, and the Story Behind the Amazing Movie*; and *Titus: The Illustrated Screenplay*.